Paliochora on Kythera: Survey and Interpretation

Studies in medieval and post-medieval settlements

Gillian Ince
Andrew Ballantyne

BAR International Series 1704
2007

Published in 2019 by
BAR Publishing, Oxford

BAR International Series 1704

Paliochora on Kythera: Survey and Interpretation

ISBN 9781407301488 paperback
ISBN 9781407331850 e-book

DOI https://doi.org/10.30861/9781407301488

A catalogue record for this book is available from the British Library

This book is available at www.barpublishing.com

BAR Publishing is the trading name of British Archaeological Reports (Oxford) Ltd.
British Archaeological Reports was first incorporated in 1974 to publish the BAR
Series, International and British. In 1992 Hadrian Books Ltd became part of the BAR
group. This volume was originally published by Archaeopress in conjunction with
British Archaeological Reports (Oxford) Ltd / Hadrian Books Ltd, the Series principal
publisher, in 2007. This present volume is published by BAR Publishing, 2019.

BAR
PUBLISHING

BAR titles are available from:

BAR Publishing
122 Banbury Rd, Oxford, OX2 7BP, UK
EMAIL info@barpublishing.com
PHONE +44 (0)1865 310431
FAX +44 (0)1865 316916
www.barpublishing.com

Contents

Acknowledgements

We would like to thank the Leventis Foundation, Newcastle University, London University and the British School at Athens for funding the fieldwork for this project. The Central Archaelogical Committee waived the need for a permit for the fieldwork and the First Byzantine Ephoreia have been helpful throughout. In particular we would like to thank Mr Vardas and Adonis, the archaeological guard.

In the field we would like to thank Kate Leeming and Simon Adcock. They helped Pamela Armstrong with the pottery study and assisted Prof Andrew Ballantyne in measuring some of the villages on Kythera. The pottery was collected for us by Robert Arnott, John Lenz and Tim Whitmarsh. Dr Richard Jones conducted the resistivity survey. The pottery collection and study and the resistivity survey were overseen by Dr Gill Ince. The honorary surveyor of the British School at Athens, the late David Smyth drew the topographical plans assisted by Dr Gill Ince and Theo Koukoulis. Mr Theo Koukoulis also helped Prof Andrew Ballantyne whilst he took measurements of Church 1 Agia Barbara and House group A, B and C. Dr Gill Ince worked with Prof Andrew Ballantyne on all the other drawings for the settlement.

We are especially grateful to Mr Theo Koukoulis, the Mayor of Kythera, for the accommodation he organised on the island. He is working on a definitive and exhaustive study of the churches at Paliochora, and we hope that his schedule will allow him to publish it in the not-too-distant future. The coverage of the churches in the present volume presents an outline for their interpretation and will be entirely complementary to his work.

Eftychia Bathrellou has been invaluable in helping with Greek translations so has Dr Mary Siani-Davies with Greek and Medieval Italian. In Greece our friends Margie Tokatlidi and her family – Mary and Elftheria and Costa Ardounis- and Dr Theodoros Xenos and Virginaia Fouta-Panayotopoulou, Athina and George Leontsini, and Jane and Tony Eggleston have supported us throughout. Visits to the island would have been less pleasurable without the company of people we met there, including Cheryl and Deiter Wolfe, John Stathatos and Pat Kaufman.

In our wider intellectual enviroment, we enjoyed stimulating academic exchanges with many people in developing the ideas presented here, and we would like to particularly to thank Prof Charalambos Bouras, Prof Chryssa Maltezou, Panayotis Tournikiotis, Dionysios Zivas, Teresa Pentzopoulou-Valalas and Haris and Alexander Kalligas.

This project was strongly supported by the late Prof R. M Cook, by Dr Elizabeth Waywell and Dame Prof Averil Cameron and Dr Jacqueline Coule-Bleakley. Prof Michael Angold read the text for us before publication.

Finally the Ince family helped in the field and anywhere else they could – Tom, Joyce, Susan, Louise, Rachael and Arleen.

List of Figures

Plates

Plate 16: above) Plain glazed jug below) pithoi

Plate 17: reconstructrion of Paliochora, general view across gorge, looking south

Plate 18: reconstruction of Paliochora, general view from the approach to the settlement, looking north.

Abbreviations

BCH	*Bulletin de Correspondence Hellénique*
BSA	*Annual of the British School at Athens*
BZ	*Byzantinische Zeitschrift*
Εὑρετήριο Βυζαντινῶν Τοιχογραφιῶν	Chatzidakis Manolis and Ioanna Bitha, *Εὑρετήριο Βυζαντινῶν Τοιχογραφιῶν Κυθήρων,*(Athens, 1997).
DOP	Dumbarton Oaks Papers
DXAE	*Δελτίον τῆς Χριστιανικῆς Ἀρχαιολογικῆς Ἑταιρείας*
Hesp	*Hesperia: Journal of the American School of Classical Studies,* Athens.
A Social History	Leontsinis, George N, *The Island of Kythera a Social History (1700-1863)* (Athens, 1987).
'Historical geography'	Maltezou, Chryssa, 'A contribution to the historical geography of the island of Kythera during the Venetian occupation', *Charanis Studies: Essays in Honor of Peter Charanis* (Rutgers University Press, 1980) pp. 151–75; reprinted in Βενετικὴ Παρουσία στὰ Κύθηρα, (Athens, 1991).
Documents	Anon., 'L'antique memoire dell'isola di Cerigo', in *Documents Inédits relatifs à l'histoire de la Grèce au Moyen Age,* ed. C. Sathas, 6 vols, Vol. VI (Athens and Paris 1884).

Chapter One

Introduction

Medieval urban settlements in the eastern Mediterranean have not been, at least until recently, a fashionable area to study. There are reasons for this. In the past foreign scholars who came to the eastern Mediterranean to excavate came to find the remains not of Medieval but of classical Greece, the Hellenistic or Roman worlds or the earlier Minoan or Mycenaean civilisations. Any interest there was in the medieval focused on ecclesiastical monuments of the Byzantine period – churches and monasteries – and their decoration. The buildings of Medieval settlements are less attractive and they do not have the formal planning of a Roman forum.[1] Literary sources for the Medieval eastern Mediterranean are less abundant than for the west in the same period, and they often are of little help in understanding urban settlements except for the 'queen of cities' herself – Constantinople.[2]

There is a marked difference in the Medieval city of the Middle Byzantine period (800-1204) and that of the later periods in central and southern Greece. The Middle Byzantine Empire was often on a war footing in the Balkans and Anatolia, but this was not the case in central and southern Greece (the Middle Byzantine themes of Hellas and Peloponnesos) where the region had been peaceful until the events of the Fourth Crusade. The establishment of the Frankish principality of the Morea, the Venetian takeover of Modon (Methone), Coron (Korone), Negroponte (Euboea), Cyprus and the Cycladic and Ionian islands changed this dynamic. Defence became a primary consideration at settlements. On the islands this was exacerbated by the activity of pirates, especially after the

fifteenth century when Moslem corsairs took to the High Seas and Christian population might well find itself in the slave markets of North African.[3]

As a result of these events settlements migrated up hills to naturally defended sites which were enhanced with fortifications. In the Peloponnese we see a generation of settlements which often began life as castles sometimes initially instigated by the Franks – as at Mistras, Geraki, Mouchli.[4] The exception was Monemvasia, in so far as it was already by the Middle Byzantine period situated on a defensible rock. This was due to the disruption in the area in a so-called "Dark Age" (seventh and eighth centuries) after the fall of the Roman Empire and the consequent need for security. The result of the change in the choice of location for many settlements meant a change in the nature of their urban landscape. Not only did fortifications become an issue in the region for the first time since the Dark Age, but the precipitous sites also significantly affected the configuration of the domestic architecture. Houses where the rooms were grouped around a courtyard became rare, while two-storey houses built into the sides of slopes became commonplace.[5]

The settlement at Paliochora belongs to the generation of late settlements where their sites were chosen for defensive reasons. Paliochora is the modern toponym for Agios Demetrios. The Venetians called it the castle of San Dimitri, but now on Kythera it is called Paliochora and we have used the modern toponym of Paliochora throughout this volume. Similarly the Venetians called the island Cerigo, but Kythera is more commonly used nowadays. The settlement at Paliochora has not had subsequent habitation, nor has anything but the churches been used since the mid-sixteenth century. The settlement in effect ended following an attack by Kheir ed-Din Barbarossa in 1537.[6] When we surveyed the settlement it was in a remarkably good state

---

[1] Honourable exceptions to this general trend were the reports of the American School of Classical Studies at Athens for Corinth and Athens in Hesperia and R.L. Scranton, *Corinth XVI. The Medieval Architecture* (Princeton, 1957); C.H. Morgan, *Corinth XI. The Byzantine Pott*ery (Cambridge, Mass., 1942).
[2] For a summary of the situation see Ch. Bouras, 'City and village: urban design and architecture', JÖB 31/1 (1981), pp. 611–53; and more recently 'Aspects of the Byzantine city' in *The Economic History of Byzantium: From the Seventh Through the Fifteenth Century*, ed. Angeliki E. Laiou, (Dumbarton Oaks, 2002), pp. 497-528.

[3] See Chapter Two.
[4] See Chapter Five.
[5] See Chapter Four.
[6] See Chapter Two.

of preservation: twenty-two churches; seventy houses and two defensive circuits. The settlement therefore lent itself to a survey where the site could be reconstructed and the buildings and their layout understood without the need for excavation. This has been done by creating two topographical plans of the whole settlement and a series of plans, elevations and reconstructions that accurately record the buildings. We have also collected and studied the pottery found at Paliochora, which is also published in this volume. The settlement at Paliochora is fascinating because of the socio-economic structure evident in the remains of the buildings and which make it unique for its period. The vast majority of the inhabitants were serfs and this is made very clear from the domestic architecture. The majority of the houses are little better than hovels or stables for animals. They existed solely for the purpose of sleep and no other activities, not even cooking were conducted here. The term 'paroikos' was used by the Bishop of Monemvasia in 1540 when he warned his flock not to settle on Kythera because of the appauling conditions in which the peasants lived.[7] We have used the term 'serfs' throughout the text to convey the condition of the peasants. This term is western rather than Byzantine but it serves to highlight the condition in which the peasants lived. There were two groups of elite houses which indicates two extended families who were responsible for building the large number of churches at Paliochora. They were part of the beginning of a tradition on Kythera where families expressed their status and wealth in church building and decoration; a tradition which continued into the twentieth century.

We have drawn a plan of Kastrisianika. There are two other villages – Aroniadika and Aloizianika – close to Kastrisianika. All three villages formed part of the district of 'Kastrisianika' in the censuses for Kythera. They were contemporary with one another, but only Kastrisianika lent itself to be drawn because the houses were deserted at that time. This is a sixteenth-century foundation and is comparable with other settlements on the Aegean islands at that time: the houses form a fortified orthogonal settlement built by the Italian Maritime States, usually Venice, to protect the populations from pirate raids. Here we see Kythera becoming more fully a part of the sixteenth-century Aegean world. This type of orthogonal settlement can be found on Antiparos and Kimolos. They protected the peasant population from captivity and enslavement by corsairs. Unlike the hovels at Paliochora the settlement at Kastrisianika represents the two-storey dwellings of a free peasantry where the lower storey is used to store agricultural produce and the upper storey is living quarters. The Venetians also refortified their ports at this time.

We were fortunate at the time of our survey because Kythera had not been the focus of modern tourism and the island had been semi-deserted because of twentieth-century population migrations to America, Australia and Piraeus. Consequently, Paliochora had been left to itself and a few mountain goats and so had most of the Venetian remains on Kythera. Since we drew the settlement at Kastrisianika many of the ruins have been demolished and rebuilt making it difficult now to see the orthogonal plan and layout. The island has become popular with those in search of peace, quiet and property away from the hubs of modern tourism. This is also true of the last settlement we drew at Katsoulianika, which appears to have been founded in the eighteenth century. This last was in a semi-ruinous condition when we drew some of the houses. Our initial interest in Katsoulianika was that these houses demonstrated the traditional methods of roof construction which helped us to understand the roofs at Paliochora. It has however turned into a small but interesting case-study of the changing shape of the settlements in the last two centuries. The Venetian character of the settlement at Mylopotamos has been preserved and the settlement drawn up by the First Byzantine Ephoreia. The Venetian settlement at the Chora has also retained its Venetian character and has been studied as have the fortified Venetian villas in the southern part of the island.[8]

The large number of churches on the island has long been remarked upon and is at least partly attributed to the fact the Kythera never fell to the

---

[7] Maltezou, 'Historical geography', p.155.

[8] See Chapter Seven.

Turks. The churches have been surveyed and efforts to preserve them and their wall-paintings instigated by the Ephoreia.[9] Some of the churches and their wall-paintings have been elaborately catalogued by Chatzidakis and Bitha.[10] The survival of the Venetian archives in the Kastron at the Chora has proved a fascinating source of information from the sixteenth-century onwards and Prof. Chryssa Maltezou has brought these to the attention of the international community in a series of erudite articles.[11] The later history encompassing British rule of the island has been the subject of the published doctoral dissertation of Prof G. Leontsini.[12] These studies have made it possible to marry the history of Kythera to the physical remains on the island and bring these centuries to life.

Much earlier Kythera had been inhabited in the Bronze Age and this is the subject of a study centred on the Minoan colony of Kastri.[13] The Kytheran Island Project has over the past several years included a large section of the island in a diachronic survey which uses the intensive fieldwalking techniques and material recovery practices used in the Aegean for over twenty-five years.[14] A similar survey has been instigated by an Australian team in the area around Paliochora (The Australian Kythera-Paliochora Archaeological Survey).

Kythera lies at the edge of the Eurasian tectonic plate where it slides over the African tectonic plate sinking into the Ionian Deep. Kythera is part of the Hellenic arc which is in turn part of the Alpine-Himalayan range. The central plateau of Kythera was a shallow sea a million years ago; and the island is also about 2.5 km further south than it was at that time. The Hellenic arc

is subject to regular earthquakes, which result in uplift and geographical shift. The largest earthquake in the twentieth century was in 1903 and affected Mitata, causing some loss of life. The earthquake in 2006 again affected the Mitata area. Kythera has an area of 284km[2] and is one of the largest Greek islands. The centre of the island is a large plateau, which has deep gorges amongst these Kato Ligadi where Paliochora is located. The eastern side of the island has harbours at Agia Pelagia, Avlemonas, Diakofti and at Kapsali, but the western side of the island is windy because of the prevailing westerly winds and there are no suitable harbours. The most fertile area of the island is between Kastri and Mitata, but generally the island is scrubby and barren.

The unity and diversity of the Mediterranean world is associated with the monumental sweep of Fernand Braudel's vision – *The Mediterranean and the Mediterranean World in the Age of Philip II*.[15] Since then it has formed a focus for another profound and fascinating study – *The Corrupting Sea: A Study of Mediterranean History*.[16] The basic concept underpinning the study is the position of the Mediterranean sea as the stage upon which the Mediterranean islands must be understood and that the land surrounding the sea is the margin or fringe. The second related issue is that sea communications were the easiest means of transport and that these were dictated by a combination of climate, current and technology.[17]

The prevailing winds that blow across the Mediterranean, winter and summer, blow between northwest and northeast; the exception to this is the Sirocco. Apart from the current flowing between Sicily and Libya, the general direction in the Mediterranean is dictated by inflow from the Atlantic at the Straits of Gibraltar and moves in an anticlockwise direction. The winds and currents are therefore working against each other. The south shores of the Mediterranean have the additional hazards of reefs, sandbanks and a lack of deep harbourage.

[9] P.L. Lazarides, *AD* 20 (1965),pp. 84-5, 190, 191, 196, 199. P.L. Vokotopoulos, Η Βυζαντνη τέχνη στά Επτάνσα, *Kerkyriaka Chronika* 15 (1970), pp. 148–80.

[10] Chatzidakis-Bitha, Εὑρετήριο Βυζαντινῶν Τοιχογραφιῶν.

[11] These are conveniently published in a volume, Βενετικὴ Παρουσία στὰ Κύθηρα, (Athens, 1991).

[12] Leontsinis, *A Social History*.

[13] G.L. Huxley, 'The History and topography of ancient Kythera', in *Kythera. Excavations and Studies conducted by the University of Pennsylvania and the British School at Athens*, eds. J.N. Coldstream and G.L. Huxley (Pennsylvania, 1972) pp. 33–40.

[14] C. Broodbank, Kythera Survey. Preliminary report on the 1998 season,' *BSA* 94 (1999), pp. 191–214.

[15] Fernand Braudel, *The Mediterranean and the Mediterranean World in the Age of Philip II*, Transl. Sian Reynolds, 2 vols. (London, 1972).

[16] Peregrine Horden and Nicholas Purcell, *The Corrupting Sea: A Study of Mediterranean History*, (Oxford, 2000).

[17] Horden and Purcell, *The Corrupting Sea*, p. 133.

The technology of ships themselves made it difficult for them to sail at 90 degrees to the wind, even in moderate winds, and therefore voyages from east to west were easier and safer if the chain of islands and coastline was hugged on the northern side of the sea. Typically east-west journeys may leave Alexandria for Beirut or Tyre, then on to the Lycian coast or the south coast of Cyprus, from there to Rhodes and then on to Karpathos and the southern coast of Crete before heading to the Ionian sea. The north-south prevailing winds were more favourable with a greater choice of route, but the major ports of Bonifacio, Malta, Naxos and Rhodes were used.[18]

In the Middle Ages Kythera stood at a major meeting point for trade routes coming down through the Aegean from the Black Sea and from Syria. Nowadays the Corinthian canal has changed this route and ships no longer have to round the southern tip of the Peloponnese, but in the Middle Ages this was not the case. Initially Venice valued the ports of Methone (Modon) and Korone (Koron) on the Peloponnese.[19] It had traded from these ports for centuries before the Fourth Crusade, but after their loss to the Turks in 1540, Kythera took over their strategic role for Venice as their safe harbour at the southern tip of the Peloponnese.

---

[18] Horden and Purcell, *The Corrupting Sea*, pp. 137–8.

[19] The Venetians often had their own names for ports and islands in Greece and Methone and Korone were called Modon and Koron.

Chapter Two

History

A bishop of Kythera appears in the Notitiae of the late-ninth century and it is is the ninth century that the wall paintings in the cave-chapel dedicated to Agia Sophia are dated.[1] However, the Notitiae of this period could be unreliable and it seems unlikely that a bishop lived on an island which was described as deserted until the mid-tenth century. Arab successes on the Aegean sea and their conquest of Crete in the seventh century impacted on Kythera which was uninhabited from then on because of its close proximity to Arab dominated Crete, and remained so until the hardy holy man Theodoros came to the island in the mid-tenth century. Theodoros arrived on Kythera by way of Monemvasia. The Life of Theodoros tells us that the island had been used for seasonal hunting and as temporary harbourage for Saracen pirates. In fact Theodoros had to wait for a ship from Monmevasia to visit Kythera to hitch a lift to the island. Theodoros' companion Anthony found life on Kythera too hard and returned to Monemvasia when the opportunity arose through another ship from Monemvasia visiting Kythera. Theodoros stayed on, but like the biblical prodigal son had to resort to eating carob-beans. Theodoros' dead body was found by sailors from Monemvasia when they visited the island, near the church of Sergios and Bacchos, now the site of the monastery dedicated to Theodoros.[2]

Theodoros' death came at about the same time as the recapture of Crete from the Arabs. An event which made the Aegean safer for the Byzantines and Kythera safe to re-inhabit. This success was attributed to another mid-tenth century holy man – Loukas.[3] We know that Kythera was initially controlled by a member of a family from Sparta – George Pachos. But the island was handed over by this family to the Eudaimoniannis family of Monemvasia. This family together with the Mamonas, Sofianos and Chamaretos were the four archontic families who controlled Monemvasia. These four families controlled the fleets of Monmevasia which were the settlement's life-blood. The Spartan ruler of Kythera retired to Mitata and the Eudaimoniannis family established a tower at Potamos.[4]

We do not know exactly when Paliochora was founded but it may have been established in the late-twelfth century. Locally, the establishment of the settlement is associated with the Eudaimoniannis family and they handed control of Kythera to the Venier in 1238[5] Late twelfth-century pottery has been found in the inner enceinte at Paliochora which may confirm the Eudaimoniannis connection. In the late twelfth-century there was a bishop of Kythera which confirms the island was established in the Byzantine hierarchy and this is further evidenced by a group of twelfth-century churches including some interesting cross-in-square plan churches at Agios Petros and Agios Andreas.[6]

---

[1] J. Darrouzès, *Notitiae Episcopatuum Constantinopolitanae, Géographie ecclesiastique de l'empire byzantin* 1, (Paris, 1981). List 3, p. 244.850 lists a bishop of Kythera in the ninth century who was a suffragan of Corinth. List 9, p. 302.379 and List 13, 361.445 also list a bishop for the island which is again a suffragan of Corinth. These list seem to date to the late-twelfth century. Kythera finally appears in list 21, p. 421.118 which seems to date to the Tourkokratia and by then the bishop is a suffragan of Monemvasia. For the cave-chapel of Agia Sophia see Chatzidakis-Bitha, Ευρετήριο Βυζαντινών Τοιχογραφιών, pp. 292-97.

[2] N. A Oikonomides, Ὁ Βίος τοῦ Ἁγίου Θεοδώρου Κυθήρων', '*Proceedings of the Third Panonian Congress*, (Athens, 1967), lines 149-53, 186-213.

[3] Demetriou Z. Sophianou, Ὅσιος Λουκᾶς. Ὁ βίος του,(Athens, 1993), 60.

[4] L'antique memoire dell'isola di Cerigo', in C. Sathas, *Documents*, pp.301-2 and Haris A. Kalligas, *Byzantine Monemvasia. The Sources*, (Monemvasia, 1990), pp.72-85.

[5] Chryssa Maltezou, 'Le familglie degli Eudaimoniannis e Venier a cerigo dal XII al XIV secolo. Problemi di cronologia e prosopografia', *Rivista di studi Bizantini e slavi 2 (1982) – Miscellanea Agostino Pertusi. T. 2 Bologna 198*, pp. 206-212.

6 Chatzidakis-Bitha, Ευρετήριο Βυζαντινών Τοιχογραφιών, pp. 58-71, 274-285.

The events of the Fourth Crusade in 1204 were to have a marked influence on the history of Kythera. Central and southern Greece had benefitted from a period of peace in the Middle Byzantine period and one consequence was that the region was not heavily militarized like other regions of the Byzantine Empire. The exception to this was the city-port of Monemvasia whose fleets, like other fleets of the time, were capable of naval engagement.[7] In the partiton of the Byzantine Empire following the Fourth Crusade, the French knights and Venetians carved up the Empire between them and this included mainland and island Greece.[8] But Monemvasia held out against the invaders. For a while the Eudaimoniannis held on to Kythera. Clearly the archontic families of Monemvasia were divided in their loyalties, some supporting the Latin invaders and others the Byzantine Empire.[9]

Events in Crete resulted in the island changing hands. The Doge of Venice, Enrico Dandolo, bought Crete for Venice during the division of the Byzantine Empire following the Fourth Crusade. However there were Genoese already living on Crete and it took until 1209 to dislodge them.[10] The noble Venetian family, the Venier were substantial landwoners on Crete, but so too were the Eudaimoniannis of Monemmvasia. In 1238 there was a marriage alliance between the two families and Kythera passed to Marco Venier as part of the dowry when he married the daughter of Nicholas Eudaimoniannis.[11]

The island was back in Byzantine hands in the last quarter of the thirteenth century, as was Constantinople in 1261. It had been thought that this was due to the efforts of Licarios who handed Kythera back to the Eudaimoniannis, but this seems unlikely as Licarios' activities were focused in the central Aegean. In 1278 we have a very famous Venetian document which has the decisions of the judges who made a list of the damages committed by Byzantine pirates operating from Kythera - although one man's pirate was another's patriot. The Byzantine pirate leader was Paul Sebastos: a man trusted by the Byzantine Emperor and entrusted with the administration of Kythera. In 1301 we hear of four Venetians from Crete ransoming a Michael Notaras Sebastos for 6000 hyperpyra. Maltezou has argued convincingly that Michael Notaras Sebastos was Paul Sebastos' son. In 1275 people from Monemvasia with a Notaras as their leader, in line with broader Byzantine policy in the south-eastern Aegean, attacked Kythera and got rid of the Venier which was probably not difficult as the Venier lived on Crete not Kythera. After the treaty of 1302 the Notaras lost power and the Venier took control again.[12]

The Venier were absentee landlords. In the fourteenth century the Kassimatis family arrived from Crete as one of the families acting as agents for the Venier on Kythera. The first to arrive on the island in 1316 was Leon Kassimatis.[13] A year earlier the Venier had asked the Venetian Republic to take control of the island from them because it was uneconomic due to the expense of its maintenance. The Venetians declined but allowed the Venier to import grain to Kythera from Crete.[14] Shortages of food and in particular grain are a constant problem in the centuries of Venetian rule of Kythera.

---

[7] In Spring 1149 a naval battle was fought off the coast of Monemvasia and the King of France was almost taken prisoner *Ioannis Cinnami Epitome*, ed Meineke (Bonn, 1836), III, pp. 87-7, 98-100; and in 1185 ships from Monemvasia were taking an active part in the defence of Thessaloniki against the Normans, Kalligas, *Byzantine Monemvasia*, p. 69.

[8] There is a vast literature covering these events. For good general texts on the period see Peter Lock, *The Franks in the Aegean 1204-1500*, (New York, 1995); Donald. M Nichol, *Byzantium and Venice A Study in Diplomatic and Cultural Relations* (Cambridge, 1988); *The Last Centuries of Byzantium 1261-1453*, (Cambridge, 1993); A Bon, *Le Morée Franque*, (Paris, 1969); Geoffrey Villehardouin, *Le Conquête de Constantinople*, ed. E. Faral, 2 vols. (Paris, 1938-9).

[9] Kalligas, *Monemvasia*, pp. 81-100..

[10] Lock, *The Franks in the Aegean 1204-1500*, pp 142-3.

[11] Chryssa Maltezou, Ἡ Πελοπόννησος τὴν ἐποχὴ τῶν Παλαιολόγων (Μονεμβασία, 20-23 Ἰουλίου).(1989), p.5; 'Le famiglie degli Eudaimonoiannis e Venier a Cerigo dal XII al XIV secolo. Problemi di cronologia e prosopografia', *Revista di Studi Byzantini e Slavi* 2 (1982), p. 208-9.

[12] Chryssa Maltezou, Ἡ Μονεμβασία καὶ Κύθηρα', pp.6-7; 'Le famiglie degli Eudaimonoiannis e Venier a Cerigo dal XII al XIV secolo. Problemi di cronologia e prosopografia', p.213. The connections of the Notaras family beyond Monemvasia and Kythera and with Genoa and Venice is explored by Klaus-Peter Matschke, ' The Notaras family and its Italian connections', *DOP* 49 (1995), pp. 59-72.

[13] Leontsinis, *A Social history*, pp.36-7.

[14] Leontsinis, *A Social history*, p.51.

In 1363 the Venier took part in a revolt on Crete against Venetian rule there. They lost control of Kythera as a result. The administration of the island fell to a Castellano — a Venetian resident of Crete who was a member of the Maggior Consiglio of Venice; his annual stipend of 500 perperi was paid from the Cretan treasury. Appeals against Kytheran Castellano were made to the Cretan administration. Venier fortunes improved again and by 1393 they were given back thirteen of the twenty-four carati into which the whole island had been divided.[15]

Between the thirteenth and sixteenth centuries many of the population of Kythera were serfs.[16] This remained the case in the half, or a little more, of the island returned to the Venier by the Venetian Republic at the end of the fourteenth-century. The *Chronicle of Cheilas* tells us that the land around the monastery of Osios Theodoros belonged to the Venier.[17] Venetian documents penned in the aftermath of Barbarossa's attack on the island in 1537 make clear that the land around Paliochora belonged to the Venier.[18] At the end of the sixteenth century two social classes were formed on Kythera – the *cittadini* and the *popolani*. The *cittadini* made up the elite on Kythera and from its members came the local council. In the eighteenth century this group lived in the Chora – the Kastron or Bourgo – near to the Venetian authorities. The *popolani* tended to be focused at either Potamos or Livadi.[19] These divisions may well reflect the division of land between the Venier and the Venetian Republic at the end of the fourteenth century and the fact that greater social diversity developed in the area controlled by Venice than in the feudal land held by the Venier until the mid-sixteenth century, but also in the main port at Chora/Kapsali in the southern part of Kythera.

The *Chronicle of Cheilas,* which was written in the mid-fifteenth century gives us some interesting information about the socio-economic climate on Kythera at that time. The chronicle concerns the monastery of Osios Theodoros and is a polemic against the Notaras family and their appropriation of the land around the monastery which belonged to the Venier.[20] The fact that the Notaras could do this shows how tenuous the Venier grip of their holdings on the island now was. It also shows us the desperation to grab any land for cultivation. We also hear of the Kaloutzis family for the first time. The first of the Kaloutzis came to the island as builders to help at the monastery, which was in need of some repairs. As Maltezou tells us, it is at this time that we see artisans – builders and painters – arriving and forming a new class on the island.[21] The census of 1470, a decade after the *Chronicle* was written tells us that there were as few as 500 people on the island.[22]

The fall of Constantinople to the Ottoman Turks in 1453 not only changed the political landscape, but within a very short time it changed the seascape: the ensuing century saw large naval engagements between the Christian west and Moslem east and a huge increase in piracy, in particular by Moslem pirates. The Italian maritime states' possessions in the Aegean and the Knights Hospitallers of Rhodes were early targets of Ottoman aggression. Lesbos fell to the Turks in 1461 and Rhodes was under siege in 1480 – on this occasion unsuccessfully. A Venetian-Turkish war was conducted between 1499-1503. The first battle, the Battle of Zonchio was fought off Cape Zonchio in the Ionian Sea, over four days in August 1499.[23]

Piracy in the Mediterranean has a long and distinguished pedigree stretching back to instances in the Homeric epics. In 100BC we hear of Mark Anthony's grandfather (also of the

---

[15] Chryssa Maltezou, 'Historical geography', p.151.

[16] The status of the peasants is made clear in 1547 when Maffeo Baffo wrote that many peasants would not settle on the island because of the exploitation by the local notables. In 1540 the Bishop of Monemvsia warned Monemvasiots not to settle on Kythera for fear their children would become paroikoi. Sathas, *Documents*, 6, 292; Maltezou, 'Historical geography', p. 155.

[17] Charles Hopf, *Chroniques Grèco-Romanes inedited ou peu connues Cheilas Chronicon Monasterii S. Theodori in Cythera Insula siti,* (Berlin, 1873), pp. 346-58.

[18] See Chapter Five and notes 16 and 17 above.

[19] Maltezou, ' Historical geography', p.156.'

[20] Hopf, *Chroniques Grèco-Romanes inedited ou peu connues Chilas Chronicon Monasterii S. Theodori in Cythera Insula siti,* pp. 346-358.

[21] Chryssa Maltezou, Τὸ Χρονικὸ τοῦ Χειλᾶ. Κοινωνικὰ καὶ ἰδεολογικὰ προβλήματα τὸν 15ο αἰῶνα, Σύμμεικτα 8 (1989), pp.17-18.

[22] Maltezou, 'Historical geography', p.157.

[23] Frederic C Lane, *Venice. A Maritime Republic* (Baltimore, 1973), p. 61 and 63.

[23] Lane, *Venice: A Maritme Republic,* p. 63.

same name) trying to sort out Cilician pirates.[24] Arabs on the sea were a problem for the region between the late seventh and the tenth centuries when evidence suggests they were also attacking coastal settlements. Later Longobard pirates are a problem and remained so up to and probably after the Fourth Crusade.[25] The breakdown of political control following the Fourth Crusade no doubt made the High Seas even more dangerous. It seems that in the thirteenth century pirates were using Kythera as a base for their activities.[26] At least in the eyes of the Spanish, a distinction seems to have been drawn between the deeds of pirates and those of privateers or corsairs: the former were acts of piracy in the Atlantic by the French or English, while the latter and more ancient tradition of robbery was covered by familiar customs, agreements, negotiations and a network of intermediaries.[27] Although piracy has always existed on the Mediterranean, trouble on the high seas increased first after the events of the Fourth Crusade in 1204 and the break-up of the Byzantine Empire, and again as a result of the fall of Constantinople to the Turks in 1453. In the late fifteenth and sixteenth centuries the corsairs fall into two broad camps – Christian or Moslem. During the first part of the sixteenth century it is Moslem corsairs who are on the increase. Warfare on the Christian side was complicated by rivalries.

The rise of the Barbary Coast corsairs is associated with the name of Barbarossa. There were two well-known Barbarossa brothers. They were born on Lesbos to an Albanian-born convert to Islam who produced four sons all of whom became sailors and corsairs. One of the brothers was killed off Crete. In 1502-3, Kheir ed-Din, the youngest brother and Isaak (another brother) appeared off Djerba in North Africa. The Barbarossa brothers lived off the population spreading terror through their plundering and killing sprees. It was the campaigns in North Africa, rather than their raiding at sea which

earned the Barbarossas their reputation as great warriors, cruel and courageous. Piracy did continue and in 1504 they seized two Papal galleys and a Spanish ship. In 1518 Aroudj Barbarossa was killed by the Spanish. But by then the Barbarossas controlled Algiers and Tlemcen.[28]

Aroudj's younger brother, Kheir-ed-Din is the more famous of the two brothers and better-known as a pirate. He and his corsair captains attacked Sicily and the coast of Italy in 1519 with twenty-five galleys and then cruised off Provence between Toulon and Heyes. They took Collo in Africa in 1521 and pushed as far inland as Constantine and seized Bone in 1522. In 1529 the formidable Spanish fort of Peñon on the islands approaching Algiers fell to Barbarossa; it had held out for fourteen years but eventually succumbed to a devastating artillery bombardment. Barbarossa executed the fort's governor.[29]

In 1528, the Genoese Andreas Doria, who had been captain-general of the French navy of Francis I, switched sides to Charles V of Spain who were in conflict then with the French. Doria attacked Cherchell on the Barbary coast in 1531. He then turned his attention to the Dalmatian and Albanian coasts as well as Modon (Methone) and Coron (Korone). In 1530 Suleiman signed a treaty with Charles V to gather his forces to deal with the threat from Persia. Kheir-ed-Din was sent with a strong fleet to subjugate rebellion on Syria; by now he was accepted as an Ottoman statesman with his own palace at Aya Sofia in Istanbul.[30]

As Lieutenant-general of the Ottoman navy Barbarossa oversaw the building of a new Turkish fleet better than any before - heavily armed galleys with three decks and their hulls protected by sheets of lead. Barbarossa set sail in 1534 with forty of these galleys. He attacked Fondi in Italy where twenty-thousand janissaries landed near Terracina where they desecrated churches and the Colonna tomb carrying off women and children. However the Spanish were victorious at Tunis and were able to keep Moulay Hassan on the throne as an ally.

[24] Naphtali Lewis and Meyer Reinhold, *Roman Civiilsation Source Book I*, (Columbia New York, 1951), p.325.

[25] S.Lambros, Μιχαῆλ Ακομιάτου τοῦ Χωνιάτου σωζόμενα, 2 vols. (Athens, 1879-80), 2 vols. (Athens, 1879-80), I, 146-7, 315; II 42-3, 84, 125, 129, 98-100.

[26] See above.

[27] Fernand Braudel, *The Mediterranean and the Mediterranean World at the Age of Philip II*, (New York, 1973), transl. Sian Reynolds, Vol. II, pp. 866-9.

[28] Heers, *The Barbary Corsairs*, pp. 62-6

[29] Heers, *The Barbary Corsairs*, pp.67-8.

[30] Heers, *The Barbary Corsairs*, p.70.

Barbarossa, was initially thought to be dead, but he had escaped the battle there and took the offensive in 1535 when he bombarded Mahon on Menorca selling the inhabitants as slaves in Algiers.

In 1537, commanding the large Ottoman fleet, Barbarossa captured a number of Ionian and Aegean Islands belonging to the Republic of Venice – Syros, Ios, Paros, Tinos, Karpathos, Keos and Naxos: he annexed the Duchy of Naxos to the Ottoman Empire. He then besieged the fort at Corfu.[31] He attacked Kythera in the Autumn of 1537.[32] Barbarossa then went on to ravage the Spanish-held Calabrian coast. Pope Paul III assembled a "Holy League" to confront Barbarossa: the Papacy, Spain, Genoa, Venice and the Knights of Malta. The battle was fought in the Gulf of Arta near Preveza. The Holy League had 162 galleys and 140 barques whilst Barbarossa had 122 galleys and galliots. The key to the Turkish victory appears to have been landing troops at Actium on the Gulf of Arta near Preveza: the fortress at Actium was able to support Barbarossa's fleet with artillery fire from there, whilst the League's fleet had to keep away from the coast as a result. The battle also demonstrated Turkish superiority in galley warfare. In 1539 Barbarossa returned and captured almost all the remaining Christian outposts in the Ionian and Aegean seas.[33] In October 1540 the Turks took control of most of the Venetian possessions in the Morea, Dalmatian coast and islands of the Ionian and Aegean and east Adriatic seas, possessions that included Monmevasia but not Kythera or Crete.[34]

In 1546 Barbarossa succumbed to a fever in Istanbul and died. The great age of the Barbary corsairs was between the Battle of Preveza in 1538 and the Third Battle of Lepanto in 1571; and particularly in the years after the battle of Djerba in 1560. There were few major naval engagements – the battle of Djerba in 1560 and the Siege of Malta in 1565 – but much of the naval activity was in the hands of the corsairs. Until 1580 the Moslem corsairs were on the ascendancy, but thereafter Moslem and Christian corsairs increased at about the same rate as the great armadas were no longer used. By 1600 the Algerian corsairs had changed tactics and sailed out into the Atlantic.[35]

---

[31] Heers, *The Barbary Corsairs*, p.71.

[32] Sathas, *Documents*, p. 60.

[33] John Francis Guilmartin, *Gunpowder and Galleys: Changing Technology and Mediterranean Warfare in the 16th Century*, (London, 2003), pp.57-72; Heers, *The Barbary Corsairs*, pp.70-2.

[34] Venice left the Holy League in 1540. Braudel makes it clear that Andrea Doria was responsible for the defeat. See Fernand Braudel, *The Mediterranean andt the Mediterranean World at the Age of Philip* II, Vol. II, p. 905.

[35] Fernand Braudel, *The Mediterranean and the Mediterranean World in the Age of Philip II*, (London, 1973), transl. Sian Reynolds, Vol.II pp. 872-3.

Chapter Three

Churches[1]

Single-cell barrel-vaulted churches

There are twenty-two churches at Paliochora. They are better built and better preserved than the other buildings and as result are one of the settlement's most striking features. Local tradition has exaggerated their number and suggests that there may have been one for each day of the year. Another tradition states that each family had its own church, and this may not be too far off the mark as we shall see. Attaching dedications to these churches is more difficult: we know that Church 1 was dedicated to Agia Barbara (Figures 14 and 15), Church 4 to Kyra tou Forou (Figures 11 and 12, Plate 2) and Church 7 to Agios Antonios (Figures 22, 23). Church 22 has been identified as dedicated to the Archangel Michael, and Church 16 is dedicated to Agios Demetrios.[2] This church is at the highest point of the settlement and is probably the earliest of the churches. The wall-paintings are unhelpful in assigning its dedication, but Paliochora was called Agios Demetrios and so it is not unreasonable to assume that the church at the settlement's highest point is dedicated to the saint who gives his name to the settlement - a military saint for a defensive site.

The churches at Paliochora mostly belong to the single-cell barrel-vaulted type, with or without nartheces. There are two exceptions: Church 1, Agia Barbara (Figures 14 and 15) has a cross in-square plan, and Church 5 was intended to be either a three-aisled basilica or perhaps, or else to have developed as a cross-in-square plan (Figure 16). It appears that most of the barrel-vaulted churches were covered with a symmetrical sloping slate or tile-covered roof, its ridge running along the church's axis. Only Kyra tou Forou (Church 4, Figures 11 and 12, Plate 2) still has this type of roof intact. This type of roof can be found covering the large

number of single-cell barrel-vaulted churches at Paliochora on Aegina.[3] At least twelve of the twenty-two churches were built with blind arcades along one or both walls (Figures 19, 20, 21 and Plate 4). Some may have decayed to the point that they can no longer be identified. These blind arcades stand on solid pilasters except in Church 15 (Figures 20 and 21) where they are supported by corbels made of *poros*, the local sandstone that was used for relatively fine decorative work. Blind arcades are found in other medieval and post-medieval churches on Kythera,[4] and are a regular feature in the Greek world – for example at Laconia, Crete,[5] Rhodes,[6] and Cyprus.[7] At Geraki two of the published churches have blind arcades – Agios Ioannis Chrystostomos and Agios Nikolaos;[8] and in the Mani at Agios Nikolaos (second half of the fourteenth century) and Agios Vasileios (late-thirteenth century).[9] However it is in Epidauros Limera, in the south-eastern Laconia that blind arcades occur most frequently. It seems that barrel-vaulted churches with blind arcades are a common feature of the churches of

---

[1] G.E Ince, Th. Koukoulis and A.N Ballantyne, 'Paliochora: Survey of a Byzantine City on the island of Kythera. Second Report', *BSA* 84 (1989), pp. 407–16.

[2] Chatzidakis-Bitha, Εὑρετήριο Βυζαντινῶν Τοιχογραφιῶν, pp. 97–101.

[3] N.K. Moutsopoulos, Παλιόχωρα τῆς Αἰγίνης, (Athens, 1962) pp. 59–87.

[4] Hagios Georgios of the Calucci family; Hagios Ioannis of Drapenesis; Hagios Ioannis Prodromos; Panagia Mesoporitissa; Panagia Kyra; Anagrgyroi at Paleopolis; Hagios Andreas at Perlegianika; Hagios Plykarpos at Phoenikies; Hagios Theodoros at Spastiras; Hagios Demetrios at Vourgo; the church of Soter at Milopotamos; and Hagia Kyriake sta Sanidia, P.L. Lazarides, *AD* 20 (1965) pp. 84–5, 190, 191, 196, 199, P.L. Vokotopoulos, 'Ἡ βυζαντινὴ τέχνη στὰ Ἑπτάνησα', *Kerkyriaka Chronika* 15, (1970), p. 170.

[5] K. Lassdithiotakis, Κυριαρχοῦντες τύποι χριστιανικῶν ναῶν ἀπὸ τὸν αἰῶνα καὶ ἐντεῦθεν. Δυτικὴ Κρήτη, *KrChron* IE-IΣT, (1963), p.177; and K. Gallas, K. Wessel, M. Borboudakis, *Byzantinisches Kreta* (1983) pp. 216, 227, 241, 310, 393, 440.

[6] A.K. Orlandos, Βυζαντινὰ καὶ μεταβυζαντινὰ μνημεῖα τῆς Ρόδου', *Archeion Byz. Mnem. ΣT,*(1948), pp. 63, 66.

[7] G. Soteriou, Βυζαντινὰ μνημεῖα τῆς Κύπρου, (Athens, 1935), pl. 41.

[8] N.K. Moutsopoulos, G. Demetrokalis, Γεράκι. Οἱ ἐκκλησίες τοῦ οἰκισμοῦ, Thessalonica (1981) pp. 5, 50.

[9] N.B. Drandakis, 'Ἔρευναι εἰς τὴν Μάνην' *PAE* (1977) p. 226.

the Mani and Epidauros Limera.[10] The number of arches in these blind arcades ranges from one to five along each wall, although the usual number is two to three.[11] Millet attributed the occurrence of blind arcades in church architecture to eastern influence and Vokotopoulos and Demetrokalis have followed his proposition.[12]

Paliochora's churches also used strainer arches to support barrel-vaults. Churches 12 (Figure 24) and 21 (Figure 28) have intact roofs and the roof had strainer arches carried on corbels of thick schist plaque. Strainer arches may also have been used to support the vault of Church 13 (Figure 33), although the state of the remains makes this difficult to say for certain. Strainer arches are a feature of church building elsewhere on Kythera at Agios Andreas at Perligianika and Agios Polykarpos at Phoenikies as well as in the Mani and around Epidauros Limera in Laconia.[13] One church, Church 3 (Figure 13, Plate 3) was built with acoustic urns embedded in its walls.[14] The effectiveness of these urns, which were supposed to enhance acoustics in the building, is doubtful. They also occur in churches in Palochora in Aegina.[15]

The churches are all built of rough-hewn local stone and a coarse lime mortar. Blocks of poros stone were also used in church construction in the barrel-vaults of the churches (Church 21 and 22, Figures 28-30) in the blind arcades, doors and the templon screens (Churches 1, 7). For the most part the churches are simple small units as the site afforded little opportunity for anything more elaborate; where we do see larger constructions (Churches 1 and 5) they are beyond the confines and defence of the kastron wall.

There is no evidence that an architect was involved in these small-scale ventures but rather a master builder. The connections between Paliochora's churches and church building in the Mani and Epidauros Limera, both close-by on the mainland of the Peloponnese, probably means that builders for this area were used to building churches on Kythera. This connection is evident across the island of Kythera and in one instance we have evidence of a builder settling on the island – the settling of the Kaloutzis on Kythera in the fifteenth century, initially to help with repairs at the katholikon to Osios Theodoros.[16] A similar, though less self-evident connection can be seen in the church wall-paintings on the island and those on the Mani.

Churches with their apse in their flank

Several churches at Paliochora have their apses displaced to the flanking wall, and sometimes it can be accounted for by the difficult site. An unconventional layout was used in order to bring the apse into an east-facing position (Churches 10 and 15, Figures 20 and 31). However there are two others, on the precipitous north-facing slopes in the east of the settlement that cannot be explained in this way (Churches 13 and 14, Figures 33 and 34). There are comparable churches at Paliochora in Aegina, and Moutsopoulos recognized them as a type. He believed they were deliberately built in this way, and certainly here there is no clear advantage in the adoption of this configuration, and if it can

[10] N.B. Drandakis, N. Gioles, E. Dori, S. Kalopissi, V. Kepetzi, Ch. Konstaninidi, M. Panagiotidi, 'Ἔρευναι εἰς τὴν Ἐπίδαυρον Λιμηράν', PAE (1982) pp. 350, 402, 403, 408–9, 416, 417–8, 425, 430, 434–5, 440, 453, 459. Most of the churches can be dated by wall-paintings to the period between the late-thirteenth century and the first-quarter of the fifteenth century, see N.B. Drandakis, S. Kalopissi, M. Panagiotidi, 'Ἔρευναι εἰς τὴν Ἐπίδαυρον Λιμηράν', PAE (1983) pp. 214, 240, 244, 251, 254.

[11] N.B. Drandakis, N. Gioles, E. Dori, S. Kalopissi, V. Kepetzi, Ch. Konstaninidi, M. Panagiotidi, 'Ἔρευναι εἰς τὴν Ἐπίδαυρον Λιμηράν', PAE (1982) pp. 391–2, n.7.

[12] G. Millet, L'Ecole Greque dans l'architecture Byzantine, (Paris, 1916) pp. 45-6; Moutsopoulos, Demetrokalis, Γεράκι. (Thessalonica, 1981), 3.

[13] N.B. Drandakis, S. Kalopissi, M. Panagiotidi 'Ἔρευναι εἰς τὴν Μάνην',' PAE (1979) pp. 189, 193, 207. These churches are dated to the late Byzantine period. N.B. Drandakis, N. Gioles, Ch. Konstaninidi, 'Ἔρευναι εἰς τὴν Λακωνικὴν Μάνην', PAE (1981) pp. 254–68. This church, Hagios Mamas, is dated to the late thirteenth century. Drandakis, Gioles, Dori, Kalopissi, Kepetzi, Konstaninidi, Panagiotidi, 'Ἔρευναι εἰς τὴν Ἐπίδαυρον Λιμηράν', PAE (1982) pp. 386–7, 450. These churches are dated by their wall-paintings to the late thirteenth century.

[14] Vitruvius, The Ten Books on Architecture, transl. by Morris Hicky Morgan (New York, 1960) pp. 143–5.

[15] Moutsopoulos, Παλιόχωρα, pp. 178–80.

[16] Chryssa Maltezou, 'Τὸ Χρονικὸ τοῦ Χειλᾶ. Κοινωνικὰ καὶ ἰδεολογικὰ προβλήματα τὸν 15ο αἰώνα,' Σύμμεικτα 8, (1989), pp.17–18.

be explained as an act of deliberate will then that seems to be the best explanation going.[17]

Twin churches

Twin churches, two churches built side by side to one another, are common enough in Greece in the later Middle Ages. They can be found on Kimolos and Melos and at Paliochora on Aegina.[18] They are also found on Kythera – Agios Nikolaos at Kapsali, Agios Nikolaos at Potamos, Agia Kyriaki at Gournia.[19] They have been associated with the two different rites – the Latin and Eastern – one church for each rite. This configuration may explain at least one of the phases in the building of Churches 16 and 17 (Figures 17-23). These two churches were built side by side, Church 16 followed by Church 17 and they shared a common narthex.[20]

The cross-in-square plan church (Figures 14 and 15)

We do not know the origin of the Byzantine cross-in-square plan church, but the first example of the type is thought to be the Nea Ekklesia built by Basil I in about 800. The full cross-in-square plan carries a central dome on pillars or piers; however it was preceded by an earlier transitional phase where the dome was carried on walls. Throughout the Middle and Late Byzantine periods the cross-in-square plan is the favoured design for high-status monuments.

The tenth-century Panagia Panaxiotissa at Gavrolimini has a developed cross-in-square plan but still has some of the archaic features of the Church of the Panagia at Skripou - short stretches of wall and a semi-circular apse.[21] The

earliest example we have of a fully developed cross-in-square plan in Hellas and Peloponnesos is the church of the Theotokos-Panagia at the Monastery of the holy Luke near Stiris. It was built by the *Strategos*, Krinites between 946-55 and originally dedicated to Agia Barbara.[22] The church has four barrel-vaulted cross-arms, cross-vaulted corner bays, three apses opening off bays, and a narthex. A Constantinopolitan influence is seen in the apses, which project into three sides of a polygon; the windows are bipartite or tripartite, divided by slight mullions and the four inside supports are slender columns rather than walls.[23]

Church building, and in particular the development of the cross-in-square plan, reaches its apogee in Middle Byzantine Hellas and Peloponnesos during the course of the eleventh and twelfth centuries, and one specific group of churches stands out for presenting a subtle development in the cross-in-square plan. They are generally classified as octagon-domed or Greek-cross-octagon, and the earliest example of this type is the Katholikon at the holy Luke near Stiris (first-quarter of the eleventh century). Here the basic plan is a cross-in-square with an octagon-dome carried on squinches over the domed central square, which is nearly equal to the span of the square. The nave is bordered on all sides by subsidiary cross-vaulted spaces

---

[17] Moutsopoulos, Παλιόχωρα, pp. 93–102, 213.

[18] Moutsopoulos, Παλιόχωρα, pp. 103–38.

[19] Chatzidakis-Bitha, Εύρετήριο Βυζαντινών Τοιχογραφιών, pp. 251, 239–45, 214.

[20] These churches are discussed in greater detail in Chapter Five.

[21] Orlandos, ABME, I (1935), pp. 121–24; N. Gioles, Βυζαντινή Ναοδομία (600-1204), (Athens, 1987), p. 115. Demetriou. Z. Sophianou, Όσιος Λουκᾶς. Ό βίος του (Athens, 1993), 202; S.H. Barnsley and R.W. Schultz, The Monastery of St. Luke of Stiris in Phocis and the Dependent Monastery of St. Nikolas in the Fields near Skripou in Boeotia, (London, 1901) p. 15.

[22] Sophianou, Όσιος Λουκᾶς. Ό βίος του, 202; S.H. Barnsley and R.W. Schultz, The Monastery of St. Luke of Stiris in Phocis and the Dependent Monastery of St. Nikolas in the Fields near Skripou in Boeotia, (London, 1901) p. 15.

[23] Krautheimer, Early Christian and Byzantine Architecture, p. 408; Gioles, Βυζαντινή Ναοδομία, pp. 126–7; Lyn Rodley, Byzantine Art and Architecture. An Introduction, (Cambridge, 1994), pp. 204–5; S.H. Barnsley and R.W Schultz, The Monastery of St. Luke of Stiris in Phocis and the Dependent Monastery of St. Nikolas in the Fields near Skripou in Boeotia, (London, 1901), pp. 17-21. The Katholikon at the holy Luke has extensive galleries. Barnsley and Schultz pointed out in their work that the "gynaikeion", or women's gallery is a usual feature in Byzantine churches of this type, but it is not often found in those belonging to monasteries. The galleries constitute the main difference between the Katholikon at the holy Luke and the Katholikon at Daphni. They suggest that because Osios Loukas was famous the monastery inevitably attracted a large number of male and female pilgrims, p. 21.

which support a gallery.[24] There are a number of associated churches: Panagia Lykodemou, Athens (second-quarter of the eleventh century)[25] and Christianou at Tryphylia in the Peloponnese (1070),[26] which have galleries like the Katholikon at the holy Luke; and the Katholikon at Daphni, Attica (fourth-quarter of the eleventh century)[27] and Agia Sophia at Monemvasia (twelfth century),[28] which do not have galleries.

Mistras, on the Peloponnese, is one of the most important centres of Paleologan architecture. One of the most interesting churches at Mistras is the Theotokos Hodegetria (c.1310) dubbed the 'Mistras type.' Here we have a domed cross-in-square plan overlying a galleried basilica. It is reminiscent of Justinian's Agia Irene in Constantinople. However the basilica is at ground-floor level with columns on either side of the nave, whilst the masonry piers on which the dome rests have their footing on the gallery floor.[29]

Agia Barbara at Paliochora has been dated to the tenth century and also to the fifteenth century and it is not difficult to see why this has happened (Figures 14-15).[30] The church cannot be independently dated from either literary sources or wall-paintings. As a cross-in-square plan it has some archaic features such as the dome being carried on heavy walls, and as a result it it tempting to date the church early in the evolution of this building-type. The tenth century is the period when Osios Theodoros arrived on Kythera, but we do not have a secure date for the original foundation of his monastery

at Logothetianika and its cross-in-square plan katholikon.

It is really the study of the development of the settlement which gives us the key to the chronology of Agia Barbara along with the building of the churches elsewhere on the island. If Agia Barbara was built in the tenth century, then we must explain its remote location at some distance from the settlement pattern of that time which seems to have focused on Potamos and nearby Logothetianika associated with Osios Theodoros. We cannot explain away Agia Barbara's existence by suggesting that it was the site of veneration which is the only other customary explanation for such a remote location. If Agia Barbara had been built in the tenth century then it could have been built on the high-point of the crag itself, a far more spectacular location than its current site because at that time there was no other building on the crag where Paliochora now stands.

Agia Barbara's location only makes sense if it was one of the last buildings constructed at Paliochora when all other suitable building sites had already been used. It stands not only outside the kastron wall but also beyond an aborted Venetian defensive wall. This suggests that it was built before the piratical activities of Barbarossa had become a serious issue in the Aegean Islands. In a relative chronology of the site, Agia Barbara should date after Agios Antonios and Churches 2 and 3, but before the Barbarossa attack in 1537.

That Agia Barbara is an earlier cross-in-square plan type does not make less plausible a fifteenth or early sixteenth century date. The dome carried on solid walls rather than pillars, the main characteristic of the early type, is less exacting for the builders of the church. And it was master builders who built the churches at Paliochora and elsewhere on Kythera. We are not dealing here with a major centre which would attract fine architects or craftsmen preoccupied with pushing the limits of their arts. A similar argument is easily proposed to explain the so-called 'Kytheran type' of church and Agios Nikon not far from Paliochora is a good

[24] Cyril Mango, *Byzantine Architecture*, (Milan, 1978), p. 118; Richard Krautheimer, *Early Christian and Byzantine Architecture*, (Middlesex, 1981), p. 408; Gioles, Βυζαντινή Ναοδομία p. 129; Orlandos, *ABME* I (1935), pp. 35–52.

[25] G. Millet, *L'école grecque dans l'architecture byzantine* (Paris, 1916), p. 72, note 1; A.H. Megaw, 'The chronology of some Middle Byzantine Churches', *BSA* 32 (1931-32), pp. 95-96, 129.

[26] Millet, *L'école grecque*, pp. 117-18; Mango, *Byzantine Architecture*, p. 127; E Stikas, *L'église byzantine de Christianou*, (Paris, 1951).

[27] E.G. Stikas, 'Καθολικὸν τῆς Μονῆς Δαφνίου', *DXAE* 4/3 (1962-63), p. 21; Megaw, 'The chronology', pp. 93–4, 129; Gioles, Βυζαντινή Ναοδομία, pp. 129–30.

[28] E.G. Stikas, Ὁ Ναὸς τῆς Ἁγίας Σοφίας Μονεμβασιᾶς', *Laconian Studies* 8 (1986), pp. 271–376; H A Kalligas, 'The Church of Hagia Sophia at Monemvasia', *DXAE* 4/9 (1977-79), pp. 217–21.

[29] Mango, *Byzantine Architecture*, p. 159; Rodley, *Byzantine Art and Architecture*, p. 289.

[30] P.L. Lazarides, *AD* 20 (1965), p.170.

example of this.[31] Here the church is basically the dome and gives the impression of the arms of the cross have been truncated or cut off into stumps—a body with under-developed limbs. In a tradition as conservative as Greek orthodoxy it is difficult to imagine how this came about except perhaps as the result of a mistake by a master builder. The church has the hallmarks of an early Christian martyrium and has been likened to them.[32] But this church and the others like it on Kythera leave us with the impression of a builder who has not mastered the conception of the cross-in-square plan rather than a leap of creative imagination. This was an era when relations across the Byzantine world had become fractured due to political fragmentation, and perhaps even conformity in the conservative orthodox tradition of building may have become stretched in remote outposts like Kythera. Therefore Agia Barbara belongs more plausibly to the late fifteenth or early sixteenth century.

---

[31] Chatzidakis-Bitha, Ευρετήριο Βυζαντινών Τοιχογραφιών, pp. 258–65.
[32] P.L. Lazarides, AD 20 (1965), p.177.

Chapter Four

Houses[1]

One basic house type in the Mediterranean world had remained in many respects the same from Antiquity to Medieval times. The basic configuration is a group of rooms - either single or multiple storied - arranged around a courtyard. In Classical architecture this manifested itself as the Greek peristyle or Roman atrium house.[2] The basic type is eminently well suited to Mediterranean lifestyle and the ability to be out of doors for a significant period of any year.[3] Christian modesty changed the decoration and the use of space; by the Middle Byzantine period icons were located in wall niches and the wealth of an occupant was denoted by silk tapestries and hangings rather than the wall and floor mosaics of the Roman era.

The move of settlements to precipitous sites for defensive reasons made the courtyard style house difficult if not impossible in many instances. The two-storied domestic architecture of this time, without a courtyard configuration, is evident in a number of settlements—Monemvasia, Mistras, Geraki and Pergamon to name but a few.[4] Churches were

given priority by the planners in the Middle Ages, and were situated on the naturally flatter outcrops of rock at these sites. It was difficult to create a platform for building, because of the precipitous bedrock at these sites. It would have been hazardous and laborious to cut back the bedrock to make a level platform, and it was not attempted. Houses were built around the bedrock and this often resulted in the lower storey of houses having an awkwardly angular shape with bedrock protruding into the lower storey.[5] This is evidently what must have been the configuration of the three houses in the northern section of the site at Paliochora (Figures 45–7). Here the bedrock protruded into the houses, making lower-storey space restricted. Lower storeys in this era and beyond can be barrel-vaulted to aid circulation and keep the space cool. Generally it is thought that the lower storey was used for storing agricultural produce and/or animals. The upper storey was used as living quarters. How living quarters were arranged is difficult to tell but probably most of the space was multi-functional and could have been divided by curtains when subdivision was required.[6]

Single-cell house unit

The houses at Paliochora are a basic rectangular unit – most are single-storey (Figures 38 and 39). The width of the house unit seems to have been limited by the useable part of an olive tree trunk. This is evident in the better-preserved houses in the south-eastern section of the site beyond the kastron wall. Here because of the flatter terrain the houses follow a more regular shape (Figure 38, Plates 7 and 8). House H has long walls of 9.75m and 9.35m, the two shorter

---

[1] A good survey of many Middle and Late Byzantine houses is given by Ch. Bouras, 'Houses in Byzantium', *DXAE* 11 (1982-83), pp. 1-26; Eleftherios Sigalos, *Housing in Medieval and Post-Medieval Greece*, BAR (Oxford, 2004). For the early work at Paliochora see G.E. Ince, Th. Koukoulis, D. Smyth, 'Paliochora: Survey of a Byzantine City on the island of Kythera. Preliminary Report', *BSA* 82 (1987), pp. 95–106.
[2] *Vitruvius, The Ten Books on Architecture*, transl. Morris Hicky Morgan (New York, 1960), pp. 170–82, 185–9.
[3] For some examples of Middle Byzantine houses grouped around a courtyard see k. setton, 'The archaeology of Medieval Athens', *Essays in Medieval life and thought presented in honour of Austen Patterson* (New York, 1955) pp. 241-42; R.L. Scranton, *CorinthXVI. The Medieval Architecture*, (Princeton, 1957), Plan VI; at Thebes, *AD* 23B (1968), pp. 208–10.
[4] For a summary of the evidence for Byzantine houses see Ch. Bouras, 'Houses in Byzantium' *DXAE* 11 (1982) pp. 1–26. A.G. and H.A. Kalligas, Monemvasia, in *Greek Traditional Architecture*, ed. D. Philippides (Athens, 1986) pp. 9–39. There are some in stances of the courtyard configuration at the Upper town in Monemvasia, pp. 15–17. For Mistras see A.K. Orlandos, Τὰ παλάτια καὶ τὰ σπίτια τοῦ Μυστρᾶ, Archeion Byz. Mnem 3 (1937), Archeion Byz. Mnem 3 (1937). P. Simatou and R.

Christodoulopoulou, 'Παρατηρήσεις στὸν μεσαιωνικὸ οἰκισμὸ τοῦ Γερακίου', *DXAE* 15 (1989-90) pp. 67–88. W. Radt, *Die byzantinische Wohnstadt von Pergamon. Wohnungbaum Alterum 3* (Berlin, 1978) pp. 199–223; K Rheidt, 'Byzantinishe Wohnhauser des 11 bis 14 jahrhunderts in Pergamon', *DOP* 44 (1990) pp.195–204.
[5] This is evident at Mistras see Orlandos, Τὰ παλάτια καὶ τὰ σπίτια τοῦ Μυστρᾶ pp. 55–6; Sigalos, *Housing in Medieval and Post-Medieval Greece*, p. 208.
[6] See Chapter Seven.

15

walls measuring 4.20m and 4.35m. The entrance to the house is marked by a 1.33m gap in the east wall. The walls of the houses in this section of the site stand to a considerable height; the south wall stands at a height of 4.2m and the east wall 3.9m (Figure 39). In this group of houses there are rounded beam sockets of about 0.3m, which must have held up the roof. It is likely that the roofs were constructed in the same way as those of later traditional buildings that survive intact or partially decayed.[7] The main beams were substantial, but they were not planed straight. They were allowed to follow the grain of the wood, sometimes including some branching. The beams were strong for their depth. Smaller branches were then placed to span between the beams. This then supported a thick layer of beaten earth, which may have been slightly pitched towards the external walls for drainage. The roof may then have been topped with schist plaque or limestone plaques. There is a further parapet of about 0.5m above the level of the beams which probably corresponds to the thickness of the roof. It is also possible that the roof may have been slightly sloped and the parapet used to drain water to a downpipe for collection and storage.[8] These single-cell house units do not have windows, so the only source of light and ventilation was the door which was probably a simple affair battened closed with a wooden beam.[9]

Variations on the rectangular house-shape are the result of the terrain at Paliochora and some very odd shapes were created where the terrain made it impossible to create the "ideal" rectangle (Figures 3 and 4). At the northern section of Paliochora the houses are of a very irregular shape and built on any available outcrop of rock. For example House F measures 7.3m and 7.7m for its two long walls and 2.6 and 2.27m for its shorter walls. However most of the south-western corner of the house is taken up with bedrock which protrudes into the house and also forms part of the west wall (Figure 36).

The majority of the population on Kythera, before the sixteenth century, were serfs and this is reflected in the domestic architecture of Paliochora. The single-storey dwellings at Paliochora are miserable affairs. Here the serfs slept but did little else, the rest of their lives being spent in the fields. There are no windows and no fireplaces in these houses and it is difficult to tell whether any cooking was done there. It may be that there was some kind of soup kitchen principle operating at Paliochora which would well account for the fact that storage vessels are found more commonly in the inner enceinte.[10] There were constant food shortages on the island.[11] There are few amphorae or pithoi found at these hovels.[12]

The very particular character of the social structure at Paliochora is further emphasized when we compare the basic house units at Paliochora with those excavated or surveyed elsewhere for the same period. At Geraki there is one house (House 25) that is single-storey, with a rectangular shape.[13] Most of the houses at Mouchli which have a single rectangular unit have a second floor. But there is some suggestion that these houses belonged to the wealthier class and the lower classes lived in even smaller single-storey structures built of rough stones joined with mud.[14] It is much easier to find comparisons elsewhere for the Paliochora house groups A, B and C and K, L and M.

The principal building material used to construct the houses is local rough-hewn limestone of various sizes. The masonry is held together with a coarse hard white/grey mortar, which sometimes has inclusions.

Two-storey houses (Figures 40-47 and Plates 8 -10)

The group of houses A, B and C are the best-preserved at Paliochora (Figures 40–44 and Plate 8). House A has two storeys: the east wall is 10.53m long and 4.45m high; the west wall is

---

[7] See the discussion of the houses at Katsoulianika in Chapter Eight.

[8] See below.

[9] The nearest published examples we have of these single-cell house units are the houses at Mouchli. M. Moutsopoulos, Βυζαντινὰ σπίτια στὸ Μουχλὶ Ἀρκαδίας', Βυζαντινὰ 13.1 (1985), pp.321-53.

[10] See Chapter Five.

[11] Leontsini, A Social History, pp. 214-17.

[12] See Chapter Five.

[13] Sigalos, Housing in Medieval and Post-Medieval Greece, p. 206.

[14] Sigalos, Housing in Medieval and Post-Medieval Greece, p. 208.

7.9m long and 4.75m high; the short south wall is 2.9m long and 3.8m high; the north wall has fallen into the ravine. Large beam sockets are visible along the walls and were the supports for the first floor. There are two entrances to the house, both on the west wall, one on the upper floor and the other on the lower floor. The lower storey door is about 1.3m wide, the doors are not directly above each other but the upper storey door is further south along the wall.

There are a number of niches and windows in this house. Along the east wall there are two niches in the lower storey and three in the upper storey. These niches are about 1m high by about 0.4m wide and 0.3m deep, give or take a centimetre, they are fairly uniform. This house had three windows in the upper storey and two in the lower storey. Another feature in the lower section of the east wall is a vertical slot 1.44m high and 0.9m wide. No other house at Paliochora has such a feature. It is difficult to determine its use, but perhaps it housed the end of a timber partition, or was covered over to make a downpipe for the rain-water (if it were being collected inside the house). Whatever its use it is suggestive of a more refined kind of house here, an impression confirmed by its fireplace. This is the only surviving house to have a built-in fireplace. It is in the southwest corner of the lower storey, is funnel-shaped, about 1.2m high and 0.9m wide at the base and the flue is visible in the west wall. Its size and shape is not dissimilar to the fireplaces in traditional Greek architecture of the more recent past.[15] We should note that fireplaces are often the most solidly built part of a house, and their absence from the other houses cannot be accounted for simply by the buildings' decay. It is more likely the serf-like status of the occupants that gives us the best clue as to why this basic house-feature is o generally absent.

Houses B and C are less well preserved than is House A. The crag is steeper and these two houses are now filled with rubble from fallen walls. It is clear that the lower storey of House C sloped because of the steep terrain. Two-storey houses are a feature of the group of houses in the eastern section of the site (Houses J, K and L). Here too niches were built into the walls (Figures 44–7 and Plates 8-10).

Two-storeyed dwellings are a feature of other settlements of this era. At Longanikos, one excavated house had a long rectangular shape but this was subdivided on the lower storey by an arched doorway and the second storey of the house was topped with a pitched roof. It is also believed that a tower was added to the building.[16] The units of houses at Geraki also show similarities with Paliochora. House 8 at Geraki has a single space and has two storeys but with a double-pitched roof rather than the flat roofs we find at Paliochora. But House 14 has two communicating rooms in linear arrangement rather than the one room we find at Paliochora and at Geraki there are also a number of L-shaped two-storey houses.[17]

The contents of a middle class Byzantine house of the Middle and Late Byzantine periods has been discussed by Prof Oikonomides. The source of his information is detailed wills deposited at monasteries. His study excluded the peasant dwellings at one extreme (these account for the vast majority of the houses at Paliochora) and the palaces of the rich at the other extreme. The houses he discusses are close to the two groups of three houses, most two-storeyed which we have just described above. The most common items to occur are sleeping equipment: rugs used instead of mattresses or pallets, blankets of wool and animal furs and pillows. Occasionally there are curtains or canopies suspended from the ceiling to create privacy. However beds are rare and seem to be the preserve of the rich.[18] Tables and chairs are equally rare. It seems that the answer to this conundrum can be found in the arrangement of the houses. Oikonomides suggests that the arrangement at houses mirrored that found at the better-documented monasteries, three walls of the living space had wooden benches set against them and these were used instead of chairs or stools. Food could be placed at the side, or tables (trellis tables) could be erected between the benches when they were needed. These wooden benches placed around the walls could double up as beds, as an alternative to laying

[15] See Chapter Seven.

[16] Sigalos, *Housing in Medieval and Post-Medieval Greece*, p. 199.
[17] Sigalos, *Housing in Medieval and Post-Medieval Greece*, pp. 205–6.
[18] Nicholas Oikonomides, 'The contents of the Byzantine house from the eleventh to the fifteenth century', *DOP* 45 (1991), pp. 209. (205-14)

mattresses or rugs on the floor.[19] Kitchen ware and serving equipment is commonly mentioned: cauldrons, kettles, frying pans, saucepans and grills all usually made of copper. Pitchers and bottles and large storage jars are common enough, but cups, individual plates, knives, forks and spoons are not common: it seems that household food was eaten from a common bowl with the fingers and liquids drunk from a common jar.[20] These were far from being the poorest households, bathing equipment is frequently found amongst the itineraries and this includes bowls for washing, separate bowls for washing the feet and linen and cotton towels.[21]

These two groups of houses (Houses A, B and C and K, L and M) clearly are home to the elite of the settlement, who were probably the agents of the Venier. A number of pithoi and amphora for storing produce have been found at the group of houses in the north-eastern section as has fineware pottery; this further confirms the status of the owners.[22] No doubt the quality of life was much the same in the houses in the northern section of the site (Houses K, L and M), but here much has fallen into the gorge below (Figures 45-47).[23] As there are two such groups of houses it is tempting to speculate that there were two family groups controlling Paliochora at this time. This would fit well the extended family socio-economic unit so characteristic of the Mediterranean world and which was certainly a feature of this period of history.

The living arrangements of an extended family are evident throughout the Middle Ages. At Geraki there are four buildings which are closely associated with each other but clearly do not interconnect. At Paliochora each of the two two-storey groups of houses could clearly house an extended family. In the fourteenth century from the will of Theodore Karavas (1314) we learn that he owned six houses sharing a courtyard with a property belonging to a nephew, and another two houses shared a courtyard with a nephew and a husband of his god-daughter.[24] Eustathios Boilas, in his will, expected his two daughters and their husbands to continue living in his house opposite his church.[25] This may have been the type of arrangement we see in the upper town at Monemvasia. Here the buildings are not dense and what we can discern from amongst the ruins are that the dwellings are organized into groups within which one house dominated and they were shut in some sort of enclosure.[26]

The domestic architecture at Paliochora reflects the serf-status of many of the settlement's inhabitants. Here the settlement is unusual and this is why the Bishop of Monemvasia warned those leaving Monemvasia in the sixteenth century not to settle on Kythera.[27] The report of Maffeo Baffo makes clear the social structure on Kythera. The Venier rented out their land to the local notables, and in their turn, in order to pay the Venier and make a profit themselves, they exploited the peasants.[28] It was probably for this reason that the settlement was abandoned in the mid-sixteenth century: because most of the houses were unsuitable for free-peasant dwellings in the sixteenth century. Two elite groups of houses at the settlement stand out but we can find parallels for them elsewhere. It is tempting to speculate that these two groups of houses, like many of the churches at Paliochora, were built by peripatetic builders from the Peloponnese who probably knew the houses at Longanikos and Geraki.

---

[19] Oikonomides, 'The contents of the Byzantine house', pp. 211–13.
[20] Oikonomides, 'The contents of the Byzantine house', pp. 211–12; and these utensils can be found in representations of th Last Supper from the thirteenth and fourteenth centuries where bowls and jugs could be shared by three or four people, Joanita Vroom, *After Antiquity. Ceramics and Society in the Aegean from the seventh to the twentieth century AC* (Leide, 2003), p. 321.
[21] Oikonomides, 'The contents of the Byzantine house', p. 210.
[22] See Chapter Five.
[23] See Chapter Five.

[24] P. Magdalino, ' The Byzantine aristocratic oikos', ed. M. Angold, *The Byzantine Aristrocracy XI–XIII Centuries*, BAR International Series 221, (Oxford, 1984), pp. 99-100; *Actes de Chilander* I, Actes grecs (Actes de l'Athos V) Vizantijssil Vremennik 17 (1910), Suppl. I.pp. 59–64.
[25] P. Lemerle, *Cinq Études*, pp. 15–63.
[26] Kalligas, 'Monemvasia', pp. 15–17.
[27] See Chapter Two.
[28] The status of the peasants is made clear in 1547 when Maffeo Baffo stated that many peasants would not settle on the island because of the exploitation by the local notables. In 1540 the Bishop of Monemvsia warned Monemvasiots not to settle on Kythera for fear their children would become paroikoi. Sathas, Documents, 6, 292; Maltezou, 'Historical geography', p. 155.

Chapter Five

The development of the settlement at Paliochora

The events of the Fourth Crusade resulted in a new generation of settlements developing on mainland and island Greece. The political fragmentation of the Byzantine Empire led to insecurity and the need to protect settlements. But in the Peloponnese and island Greece the conquering French knights and Venetians of the Fourth Crusade needed to control and subjugate a large indigenous population. A generation of French castles stand testimony to this on the Peloponnese—Mistras began life this way.[1]

In the thirteenth century settlements such as Mouchli and Geraki came into being. These settlements were not located on the fertile plains of the Peloponnese but used hills and mountains to aid their defence. Geraki was part of the Frankish building campaign and was built in 1250 by Guy de Nivelet, along with Maina, Leuktro and Mistras. It is located on the road from Mistras to Monemvasia. The settlement is spread over two hilltops. There are eight churches on the northern hilltop and three distinct areas apart from the actual fortified area. Few traces of the fortifications now exist. Mouchli was built at the end of the thirteenth century and dominates the Achladokambos valley. It was destroyed in 1458-60. The settlement has three fortification walls dividing it into three areas. We have very little idea of what Venetian architecture in the Aegean was like before the sixteenth-century when much was rebuilt and fortified to counter the Ottoman threat.

The Inner enceinte (Figures 1, 2, 48–51 and Plates 10–1, 17 and 18)

The boundary of the inner enceinte of the settlement is determined by the crag, except in one section. Here the crag offers no natural protection and so a wall was constructed in this area which is also the only landward approach to Paliochora (Figures 1 and 2). There were at least three phases in the construction of the wall. The lower section of the wall stood to a height of about 5m above the internal ground level, and

9m above the ground outside. It was crenellated and had a stone buttress or walkway behind it; this section of the wall is the most substantial and thickest (Figure 50) and takes advantage of a steep change in ground level. At a later stage the wall was heightened by about 2m and ended in new crenellations but here the wall is thin and not very substantial. Later again, a third and final stage was built, this highest point of the wall is thinner still, filling in the older crenellations and presumably establishing new even less substantial ones finishing at a height of at least 12m. The kastron wall is constructed of the same material as the other buildings at Paliochora: rough hewn limestones bonded with a coarse and hardwearing mortar, liberally used (Figures 48–51).

The surviving remains of the wall show that there was some kind of bastion at the end of it that would have overlooked the point of entry abd been the focus for defensive action. It was the principal guard post, and in order to reach the settlement any aggressors would have had to come very close to it, making them vulnerable to defensive measures. This is precisely the part of the wall that was blown away by explosive charge, not only giving access to the settlement, but also eliminating its main defensive point. The surviving remains of the wall will support this interpretation, as the sturdily constructed parts of the defence survive except at this point. The loss of the higher flimsier parts of the wall can be put down to occasional earthquake activity over the centuries. If the crenellations were ever to be useful, they must have been backed up by timber walkways (passerelles) either bracketed from the wall or supported on some kind of scaffolding. While such an arrangement might have been adequate before the advent of gunpowder, it seems, except for the bastion by the point of entry, to have come to be little more substantial than a stage set. The most significant aspect of even this section of the defence was the steep change in the natural ground level, reinforced by the bastion that was blown away.

---

[1] See Chapter Two.

The inner enceinte is not built-up and has substantial open space. This was confirmed by a resistivity survey immediately behind the kastron wall. This at first seems remarkable because of the extremes to which the builders at the settlement had to go to build churches and houses on the inhospitable outcrops of rock whilst areas of relatively flat land were left as open space. The only logical explanation for this is that Paliochora was initially established to provide a stockade where the peasants could retrench in times of danger. It was not established to cope with siege-warfare. It was framed to cope with pirate raids and the target of these raids was the peasant population of the island who could be sold into slavery. The inner enceinte was established in the late-twelfth century.[2] Thereafter we have no idea at what times the height of the kastron wall was increased, but we can get some idea from the fact that most building activity occurred at Paliochora in the fifteenth and sixteenth centuries. The kastron wall pre-dates Barbarossa's attack and was not subsequently rebuilt.

Agios Demetrios (Church 16, Figures 17, 21, 22 and 23) is the first church in a group of what seems to be five churches. Agios Demetrios (Church 16) is a single-cell barrel-vaulted church with blind arcades along its walls. The fact that the earliest wall-paintings date to the fourteenth century is tantalising for historical and socio-economic reasons. We know that socially most of the inhabitants were serfs, but we do not know how the island was organized before the early fourteenth century when the Kassimatis family arrived (1316) as agents for the Venier.[3]

In later centuries when we have documentary evidence, it is clear that prominent families built and owned a number of churches on the island. The land register of the Calucci family list the churches owned by them. We know the estates on the island that were owned by churches, which in turn belonged to families like the Stai, Mormori and Calucci, and that the estates of the leading families were dominated by the owners' private church.[4] Most of these families were

well-established by the time a *libro d'oro* was established on Kythera in 1572–3. One of them, the Kassimatis, arrived on Kythera in the early fourteenth century to act as agents for the absentee Venier,[5] who no doubt had other agents here. But the Venetian grip on Kythera, whether by the Venier or the Republic itself, was tenuous before the sixteenth century, and this would easily have allowed the development of a local oligarchy who stepped out of the shadows into documented history in the sixteenth century.[6] At Paliochora we see the beginnings of this social structure and the tradition of prominent families building numerous churches. The twenty-two churches at Paliochora are not the product of twenty-two families—and it is remembered on Kythera that the churches of Paliochora had been built by families—but subsequent generations of a much more limited group of families. This is the reason why there are only two groups of elite houses at Paliochora and not more.[7]

A second church (Church 17, Figures 17 and 23) was built alongside Agios Demetrios (Church 16) with similar build, size and proportions. Further buildings were added but the chronological sequence is unclear. A third church (Church 15, Figures 18–21, Plates 3 and 4) was built at right angles to Agios Demetrios (Church 16) and Church 17. Again its size and proportions are similar to the other two churches – single-cell and barrel-vaulted with blind arcades. However in the case of Church 15 (Figures 18–21 and 23) its orientation made an east-facing apse impossible in the long axis of the church and so the apse was placed in the flanking wall. At some time thereafter all three churches had a second storey added above their barrel-vaults. In the case of Agios Demetrios (Church 16) and Church 17 a narthex and stairs seem to have been added at the entrances to the two churches which would have also allowed access to the upper floors of the churches.

It has been suggested that houses were built on top of the churches at Paliochora,[8] but most Greek people find the idea implausible because it seems impious. An alternative explanation is

[2] See Chapter Two and Chapter Six.
[3] See Chapter Two, p.4.
[4] Leontsini, *A Social History*, pp. 71, 73, 83, 200.

[5] Sathas, *Documents*, 6, 304-5.
[6] See also Chapters Three and Four.
[7] See Chapter Three.
[8] This suggestion was made by T.G. Koukoulis.

that this area above the barrel-vault could have been used to store the amphorae which held grain and supplies to feed the serfs.[9] However if we look further afield for precedents the only buildings to be found above churches are other churches, the most plausible explanation is that a second church was built above the first. However there is nothing in the surviving walls that acts as a conclusive confirmation. The crag poses a great many restrictions for building and there may have come a point when there was no further land available for church building inside the protection of the inner enceinte. At Church 19 we have an instance where a church was built on top of a house (Figures 26 and 27). This ultimately proved to be unsatisfactory because the builders used timber beams to support the masonry of one of the church walls. Eventually the church and house collapsed because of the weight, presumably after the settlement was abandoned and the beams rotted away. There is no surviving timber at the settlement, only traces of where it once was. The arrangement—a church above a house—demonstrates the pressure on building space. However it is the social structure at the settlement that really answers the reasons behind the church-building programme. There were probably only two families controlling Paliochora as agents of the Venier.[10] The church building programme is their creation. Churches were owned by families on Kythera, and building one church on top of another required permission from the owner of the original church. Because of restricted building space one church was built on top of another instead of at the side of another church, as we find elsewhere on the island.[11] Remarkably there were four churches in the group of Agios Demetrios at Pourko[12] which seems to lend weight to theses groups being the creation of families. It may also exhibit competitiveness between families in much the same way as new floors added to the towers of the Mani were manifestations of social status there.

Another church on Kythera posed a problem of interpretation for Lazarides and Bouras, forty or more years ago. At the monastery of Soteiros an external stone staircase led to a door in the barrel-vault of the church (now blocked). Lazarides and Bouras found this difficult to explain and suggested perhaps a "woman's gallery". The church is small for such a configuration and elsewhere these galleries are accessed internally and not externally.[13]

There was another church in the inner enceinte below this group and nearer to the kastron wall (Church 11, Figures 24, 25, Plate 5). All that survives of it are two small sections of wall which must have stood either side of the door (Figures 19 and 20). There were glazed bowls embedded into the walls but the glaze has now gone (Figure 25 and Plate 5). Behind these two sections of wall lies a heap of rubble of what must once have been the walls of the church itself. It is unusual to find a church so badly damaged at Paliochora because as the churches were sturdily constructed they have tended to survive the vicissitudes of time better. Here, at Church 11, it is possible that the building saw violence. This church is not far away from the door in the kastron wall blown up by Barbarossa to gain access to the inner enceinte. It may be that due to its position it was caught up in the conflict when the Kastron wall was breached.

Church 12 is not far away from Church 11 and there is a tradition that Church 12 was dedicated to the Panagia.[14] It has a roof but no door and much of the wall near the door has gone. It is perched precariously on the very edge of the inner enceinte with a sheer and precipitous drop directly below. Building the wall must have been challenging for the builders as it is on the edge of the sheer drop. Like most of the other churches at Paliochora it is a single-cell barrel-vaulted building. Its location on the edge of the inner enceinte again is a testimony to a policy of leaving space behind the kastron wall to accommodate and protect the population for short periods of time. A small tower-like building abuts the long wall of Church 12 and peaks above the barrel-vault of the church. The only other building in the inner enceinte is a

---

[9] See Chapter Five.
[10] There are only two groups of elite houses at Paliochora. See Chapter Three.
[11] Bitha-Chatzidakis, Εὑρετήριο Βυζαντινῶν Τοιχογραφιῶν, pp. 240, 251.
[12] Bitha-Chatzidakis, Εὑρετήριο Βυζαντινῶν Τοιχογραφιῶν, pp. 162-183.

[13] P.L. Lazarides, AD 20 (1965), p.177.
[14] This information came from some of the older residents on Kythera.

puzzling right-angle of two short stretches of wall. These walls are higher than the average single-storey dwelling at the settlement.

The inner enceinte yielded evidence of a large number of amphorae and pithoi.[15] This is evidence that produce was stored here. The majority of the inhabitants of Paliochora were serfs.[16] There is virtually no evidence of storage vessels in most of the houses, which suggests that food must have been stored and controlled in the inner enceinte. There is no evidence of a cistern, or indeed any water supply at the settlement. Water must have been obtained somewhere and we can only assume that there was a spring close by. It is clear, though, that the inner enceinte was not designed for, nor capable of withstanding, any form of siege warfare. It was established to deal with raids where the population and livestock could huddle behind the walls for a short period of time. Much of the space behind the kastron wall was left open for this purpose, which was obviously of prime importance, as the land here would have otherwise have been seen as a much better place to build than some of the awkward and precarious sites that were eventually developed.[17]

Down the slopes – Buildings (Figures 3, 4 and 5 Plates 17 and 18)

In its original conception Paliochora may well have been little more than the zone of safety within the inner enceinte, which was to be used in times of danger perhaps with a church to confirm the place as a sanctuary of sorts. This changed in the ensuing centuries because of continued political instability. The crag is precipitous, but despite this buildings were erected down three sections of the crag on the northern and northwest sides (Figures 3 and 4). There was no attempt to carve out platforms from the rock and anyway this would have been very labour intensive; buildings were modified and changed to suit the terrain.

One section of the northern slope is the gentlest of the three areas developed for building. Immediately below the open zone behind the kastron wall, two small barrel-vaulted churches (Churches 21 and 22) (Figures 28–30 and Plate 6) were built in a style and with a plan similar to those we find in the inner enceinte (Churches, 15, 16, 17 and 12) (Figures 17-23). One other platform of rock is also used to build a church in this area at Churches 9 and 10 (Figures 31 and 32). Here it was impossible to build an east-facing apse in the short end wall of the church, as would have been normal, and so it was built in the long flanking wall (a solution we have already seen at Church 15, Figures 19-21 and 23). In this case, though, the decision was revised at a later date. An apse was blocked up, and the church seems to have been used in a more conventional arrangement, even though the alignment would not have been ideal. Unusually, at the lower reaches of this area some prominent building platforms are not used for the construction of churches, but to build a group of three houses, two of which are two-storeyed (Figures 40–44, Plate 8)). Any other horizontal outcrops from the crag in this area were used to build the small hovel-like dwellings that populate the site (see below).

The north-eastern slope of Paliochora is steeper in a section a little further north than that just described. The horizontal outcrops of rock would have been too small and awkwardly shaped for church-building and so houses were built on them. They are misshapes and distortions of the basic orthogonal plan that reflect the shape of the bedrock (Figure 5).

Only two other areas (Churches 13 and 14) (Figures 33 and 34) have been used for church buildings, but only the apse survives of Church 14 to identify it as a church (Figure 34). This section of the site is by far the most precipitous and the buildings, including the churches, at this side are the least well preserved of any part of Paliochora. Closer to the line of the inner enceinte is a group of three two-storeyed houses, most of the walls of which now lie in the gorge below, but enough has survived to show that this is a second group of two-storey dwellings similar to those on the northern slope. The abundance of niches in the surviving walls as well as the fact that it is clear they had two-

---

[15] See Chapter Five.
[16] See Chapter Three.
[17] A resistivity survey was conducted for us by Dr R. E. Jones, Director of the Fitch Laboratory at the British School at Athens, of the area immediately behind the kastron wall. As we expected no evidence of buildings was found.

storeys justifies the comparison and sets them apart from the single-storey dwellings.

Dating this area of the settlements is not straightforward. There is only one church we can date. Church 21 (Figure 28) has wall paintings dating to the first half of the fifteenth-century according to Chatzidakis-Bitha; however Lazarides and Vokotopoulos date these paintings earlier to the fourteenth and fifteenth centuries.[18] Fineware pottery has been found in houses A and B: Italian imports dating to the late fifteenth or early sixteenth centuries.[19] This pottery may not date the houses and may well indicate the period when Italian imports found their way to the island or the settlement. Literary sources tell us that the thirteenth century was a period when the island changed hands four times –to the Venier from the Eudaimoniannis in 1238, back to the Byzantines and the Notaras family in 1275, and then again back to the Venier in 1302. This climate is hardly conducive to the development of the settlement. We know the Kassimatis family arrived on Kythera in 1316 and they acted as agents for the Venier. It is likely that the fourteenth and fifteenth centuries saw the development of this area of Paliochora and more particularly the fifteenth-century. After the fall of Constantinople to the Ottoman Turks, the high seas became dangerous as we see the beginning of the Christian-Turkish wars that marked the history of the Aegean islands during the next century. It may be that this area of the settlement was developed in the late-fifteenth century as part of increased Venetian activity and the need to protect the population from the beginnings of the Moslem corsair threat.

Outside the kastron wall[20]

Paliochora is reached across a neck of land which is the only approach to the settlement, as a result it is the area most vulnerable to attack, but it is also the flattest land at Paliochora, and the best suited to building. Ultimately this land was indeed exploited for building, and the buildings outside the confines of the kastron wall have amongst them some of the most interesting buildings at Paliochora. The group of buildings nearest the kastron wall is reminiscent of church group 15, 16 (Agios Demetrios) and 17 (Figures 17-23). The first building of this group is Church 6 which is another single-cell barrel-vaulted church with blind arcades (Figures 6-10). At some stage a narthex may have been added to the entrance and a second-storey was added above the church which like the arrangement at churches 15, 16 (Agios Demetrios) and 17 was most likely to have another church (Figures 17-23). There is another two-storey building abutting the outer wall of church 6, the upper floor of which was reached by an external staircase. Church 7 (Agios Antonios) was built last and does not have two storeys (Figures 6-10). We know it was built after Church 6 because the apse of Church 6 protrudes into the narthex of Church 7 (Agios Antonios). The latter is one of the best-preserved churches at Paliochora. Its wall-paintings date to the fifteenth and sixteenth

---

[18] M. Chatzidakis, I. Bitha, Εὑρετήριο Βυζαντινῶν Τοιχογραφιῶν, (Athens, 1997) p.107.

[19] See Chapter 5.

[20] A ruined windmill stands close to Paliochora, above the church of Agia Barbara (Church 1). T.G. Koukoulis makes the claim that this windmill was contemporary with the settlement. (T.G. Koukoulis 'A Late Byzantine windmill at Kythera', *Philolakon. Studies in Honour of Hector Catling* (London, 1992), pp. 157–63). We do not agree. The principal reasons for making this assertion are 1) that the windmill is close to the settlement and 2) that pottery shards date to the thirteenth and fourteenth centuries. However the pottery sherds found near to the windmill has been found frequently elsewhere at Paliochora (see Chapter Six). It probably belongs to the fifteenth and sixteenth centuries and is conclusively linked neither to the windmill, nor with the time-frame of the Late Byzantine Empire (Constantinople fell to the Ottoman Turks in 1453). Such a date for a windmill would make it highly unusual. It would be one of the earliest in Greece, and a remarkable building indeed. On the other hand, the land here was in use at other times. It was under cultivation in the nineteenth century, when the ground was terraced. The other windmills on the island belong to the nineteenth and twentieth centuries, and the construction of the building is not obviously different from them. In the absence of a stronger argument to the contrary, therefore, we suggest that a nineteenth-century date is more plausible.

centuries.[21] The roof of the church is intact and covered in fired tiles that carry low-key patterns—simple marks (a diagonal cross, a wavy line) made by the fingers of the people who shaped the clay. The small bell-tower and pointed-arched door are reminiscent of the arrangement at the katholikon of the monastery to Osios Theodoros near Logothetianika. It also has RMR Ware pottery embedded in the external wall of the church.[22]

Beyond this group of buildings there is a large unfinished church, Church 5 (Figure 16). Its extant walls stand at a uniform height and clearly the building was halted at an early stage of construction. The remains point indistinguishably to either a three-aisled basilica or a cross-in-square plan, as the internal subdivisions of the structure were never made. Nearby there is another small church, Kyra tou Forou (Church 4, Figures 11 and 12). It is a simple building with an intact tiled roof over the barrel-vault, but the tiles seem to be more modern than those of Church 7 (Agios Antonios) and were probably put there in the nineteenth century as a conservation measure, as the church is well maintained and is the only one at Paliochora that remains in use. Adjoining it is the small section of the aborted Venetian defensive wall—presumably begun after Barbarossa's attack, but before the decision to abandon Paliochora (Figure 12). Beyond these buildings are three further churches – Churches 1, 2 and 3 (Figure 13). Churches 2 and 3 are again the familiar single-cell barrel-vaulted church with blind arcades. But beyond them is Church 1 (Agia Barbara) – a cross-in-square plan church (Figure 14 and 15). In the part of this area to the south of Churches 6 and 7 there is a scatter of single-cell houses, larger and more regular than the misshapes we see down the slopes of Paliochora. They are not densely packed. The dating of this area is linked to the abandonment of the settlement.[23]

The destruction and abandonment of Paliochora[24]

At the time that Barbarossa attacked Kythera there were only three settlements on the island—Paliochora, the Chora and Mylopotamos. We know that the Chora—Kastron and Bourgo—were refortified in 1502.[25] Mylopotamos was smaller than Paliochora. Barbarossa probably attacked Paliochora because it had the largest population and was not well defended. His corsairs would have had to walk inland for about 8km to do this. Their interest was in the peasants, whom they could sell as slaves. It is doubtful that there was much of anything else worth selling at Paliochora, even in the churches. We are told that the settlement was ruined, but clearly enough survived for rebuilding to be considered. The Venetians did indeed collect money to rebuild the fortifications at Paliochora.[26] The Venetian authorities recommended a new defensive wall as the only means of securing the settlement against future attack.[27] In fact a second defensive wall was begun and the small section that was built stands adjoining the Kyra tou Forou (Church 4, Figure 12). It was abandoned early in its construction and stands to a uniform height. It shows the beginnings of a characteristic Venetian *glacis* and is built in the style of Venetian defences at

---

[21] Bitha-Chatzidakis, *Ευρετήριο Βυζαντινών Τοιχογραφιών*, pp.88-95.

[22] See Chapter Six.

[23] See Chapter Four.

[24] The only dissenting voice to the abandonment of Paliochora in the sixteenth century is G.D.R. Sanders, 'Two kastra on Melos and their relationship in the Archipelago', in eds. Peter Lock and G.D.R. Sanders, *The Archaeology of Medieval Greece* (Oxford, 1996) pp. 147–78. Here Sanders argues that Paliochora was not abandoned and may have continued in use into the seventeenth century. As evidence Sanders quotes two passages in Italian—Sathas, *Documents*, VI, 54, 60. Although, as we have shown in this chapter, the new defensive wall was begun it was abandoned at an early stage in its construction. The Italian documents make clear that the new defences are essential if Paliochora is to continue as a settlement. Prof Chryssa Maltezou is an exacting scholar and has assessed and quoted all of the Italian see Maltezou, 'Historical geography'. It is clear that the refortification of Paliochora was abandoned and with it the settlement. Sanders had evidently not visited Paliochora before he wrote the article, otherwise he would have seen that the fortifications were not in fact rebuilt. He is also unaware of the three fortified villages in the centre of Kythera, comparable to villages elsewhere in the Aegean, which were built to house the peasants after Barbarossa's attack. These villages are discussed in the next chapter.

[25] See Chapter 7.

[26] Sathas, *Documents*, VI, 54.

[27] Sathas, *Documents*, VI, 292.

the Chora, Mylopotamos and elsewhere in the Aegean world. Church 5 had a similar fate and was abandoned early in its construction when its walls too stood at a uniform height.

The Venetian authorities decided to abolish serfdom as part of a policy to attract new settlers to the depopulated Kythera after 1545 and the Venier seem to have acquiesced.[28] They had never taken much interest in Kythera, and it would not have furthered their to have Paliochora refortified, since it was no longer peopled by their serfs. The domestic architecture of Paliochora was not as well suited to a free peasantry as was that at Mylopotamos, and Paliochora was not located near to the most fertile land on the island, which is in the centre between Paliochora and Mylopotamos.[29] Here in the mid-sixteenth century three small fortified settlements were built (see Chapter Seven). They are comparable to settlements of this era found elsewhere in the Aegean.

Paliochora's status as a settlement[30]

The status of Paliochora like other settlements of its generation is difficult to establish. Is it a town, village or city? Initially it was thought to have city status and it is remembered in local tradition as the 'city of the Eudaimoniannis'.

The large number of churches at Paliochora is responsible for this assumed status.

Generally nowadays urban status is determined on functional grounds. Urban settlements perform functions over and above those performed by a village in terms of politics, administration and economy. In a pre-industrial context an urban settlement is often the home of an elite who control the politics and the administration of the settlement and its hinterland. The elite also make up the main market for luxury products, which may be imported or, if the market is large enough, may be produced locally.

There are four principal factors that act as a pre-urban nucleus for settlements: 1) agriculture or irrigation, 2) trade—either local or long-distance, 3) a religious or sanctuary-site, and 4) defence. Generally, the agriculture or irrigation is seen as the principal generator in the so-called 'hydraulic cultures', such as those at the beginning of urban development in the Fertile Crescent and in particular Mesopotamia.[31] Local trade can result in an urban centre acting as a focus for redistribution for its hinterland even in a barter economy. Long-distance trade is associated with Pirenne's thesis for medieval trade in the Mediterranean.[32] It accounts for many trading stations set up in Scandanavia in the Middle Ages. It is also associated with Venetian trading in this era across the Levant. Many of the settlements founded on the Aegean and Ionian islands were acting as part of a chain of ports connecting Venice with its Black Sea and Levantine trade. This is certainly the case with the settlement at Kapsali/Chora on Kythera founded after the Fourth Crusade, but it is clearly not the case with Paliochora. The settlement is too isolated and remote to serve as a trading post. Some settlements begin life as sanctuary-sites, for example in classical Greece where they acted as a unifying force in state-formation.[33] The tenth-century holy man,

---

[28] Leontsini, *A Social History*, p.80.

[29] Sathas, *Documents*, VI, 293.

[30] It has been claimed that Paliochora was a city, and that claim has been questioned by G.D.R Sanders (G.D R Sanders,' Two kastra on Melos and their relationship in the Archipelago', in eds. Peter Lock and G. D. R Sanders, *The Archaeology of Medieval Greece*, (Oxford, 1996), pp. 147-78.). In two reports for Paliochora published in the current project's early stages we referred to paliochora as a'Byzantine city' (G. E Ince, Th. Koukoulis, D. Smyth, 'Paliochora: Survey of a Byzantine City on the island of Kythera. Preliminary Report', *BSA* 82 (1987), pp. 95 – 106; G.E Ince, Th. Koukoulis and A.N Ballantyne, ' Paliochora: Survey of a Byzantine City on the island of Kythera. Second Report', *BSA* 84 (1989), pp. 407-416.). This was at the insistence of T.G Koukoulis whose conviction was based on local tradition, which associated the settlement with the Eudaimoniannis family, and saw Paliochora as 'urban' because of the large number of churches. However we do not agree with Sanders' view that Paliochora was merely a village. There are few villages anywhere which have twenty-two churches. In assigning status to Paliochora and other Aegean settlements, Sanders shows no familiarity with the functional debate about urban settlements. See also Chapter Seven, footnote 1.

---

[31] L. Woolley, 'The urbanisation of society', in eds. J. Hawkes and L. Woolley, *The History of mankind. Vol. 1. Prehistory and the Beginnings of Civilisation* (London, 1963), p. 414.

[32] Henri Pirenne, *The Medieval Cities. Their Origin and the Revival of Trade*, (New Jersey, 1952).

[33] This is the basic thesis of Wheatley, *The Pivot of the Four Quarters. A Preliminary Enquiry into theOrigins and Character of the Ancient Chinese City* (Edinburgh, 1972)

Loukas became a focus for veneration and pilgrimage at Steiras near Delphi in the eleventh century, but this did not happen to Osios Theodoros on Kythera, and in any case his monastery is not located at Paliochora but near Logothetianika.

The pre-urban nucleus of a settlement can begin as a defensive site and across history there are a number of examples of this phenomenon.[34] The cities of classical Greece for the most part have an acropolis for defence. Defence was part of the Norman expansion across Europe in the Middle Ages and the castles in Europe and the Levant stand as testimony to this. Paliochora was clearly developed with defence in mind. There can be no other reason for locating a settlement at this crag. Moreover, Paliochora was founded to cope with a particular type of threat: pirates.

Aegean piracy goes back to ancient times. Kythera, as we have seen, was uninhabited in the ninth and tenth centuries because of Arab pirate raids. In the late-twelfth century, at the time the inner enceinte at Paliochora was established, piratical activity on the Aegean continued. The Metropolitan Archbishop of Athens, Michael Choniates, bemoans the activity of the Longobard pirates[35]; but equally Monemvasia and Venice's fleets were capable of this type of activity. It seems that in the late-twelfth century the Eudaimoniannis family felt that protection was needed on Kythera.

The main expansion of the settlement belongs to the fifteenth and sixteenth centuries and the majority of the population were serfs. One criterion upon which urban settlements are judged is economic diversification. This is not evident at Paliochora. The serfs toiled on the land and did not have any income to buy products, so there was no class of artisans or shopkeepers catering to their needs. The social structure reflected in the buildings suggests that two extended family groups dominated Paliochora. The land around the settlement belonged to the Venier until the mid-sixteenth century and the two dominant families acted as agents for the Venier. In reality they were autonomous as the Venier had little interest in the island. The ease with which the Notaras family seized Venier land near the monastery dedicated to Osios Theodoros is evidence of Venier indifference to events on Kythera.[36] The dominant families at Paliochora spent their money on building the twenty-two churches at the settlement Six. But they also imported Italian fineware pottery. Builders may have settled permanently on Kythera in the fifteenth-century and this is evidenced in the *Chronicle of Cheilas* which tells us that the Kaloutzis family arrived on Kythera to effect repairs to the monastery dedicated to Osios Theodoros at Logothetianika.[37]

It is tempting to characterize Paliochora as an "agro-town". These settlements can occur for a number of reasons when agricultural workers choose to live together because of the need for security, the scarcity of drinking water or because they are working on large estates.[38] In the case of Paliochora the economic dimension that this produces is restricted because the inhabitants are serfs. There was probably a population of about 300-400 people at Paliochora at its peak.[39] Paliochora is neither rural nor urban—perhaps proto-urban is a way to describe it. The social structure and concomitant economics make it more than a village but less than a town. Arguably before the sixteenth century the insecurity on the island meant that dispersed villages did not exist and rural life was therefore underdeveloped and part of the island uncultivated because of this.

The building of Kastrisianika brings about a new settlement dynamic.[40] There are three small fortified units close together (Kastrisianika,

---

A. M Snodgrass, 'Archaeology and the study of the Greek polis', in eds. John Rich and Andrew Wallace-Hadrill, *City and country in the Ancient World*, (London, 1991), p. 17.

[34] Max Weber, *The City*, translated and edited by Don Martindale and Gertrud Neuwirth, (New York, 1958), p. 76.

[35] See Chapter Two, p.5.

[36] See Chapter Six.

[37] See Chapter Two.

[38] Hans Buechler,' Spanish urbanism from a grass-roots perspective', in eds. Michael Kenny and David L. Kertzer, *Urban Life in Mediterranean Europe: Anthropolgical Perspectives* (Illinois, 1983), pp. 135-161; Anton Blok, 'Southern Italian Agro-towns', in *Comparative Studies in Society and History*, Vol. 11, No.2 (Apr, 1969), pp.121-135.

[39] Maltezou, 'Historical geography', p. 157. The population of Kythera was 500 in 1470 and 1850 in 1545.

[40] See Chapter Seven.

Aloizianika and Aroniadika – referred to as the district of Kastrisianika) and their form fits into the settlements which have been studied elsewhere in the Aegean. They represent the fortified villages of a free peasantry and no social stratification is evident here or at Mylopotamos. The houses are the same basic unit repeated throughout. But by this time the island's elite had gone to live in the Chora, joining those already resident there. From the sixteenth century to the present time the Chora has been the administrative capital of the island.

Chapter Six

The Pottery at Paliochora

Nearly nine-hundred pottery sherds were collected at Paliochora and its environs. The collection involved picking up surface pottery; the exception to this is the recording of two bowls immured in the walls of Church 7 (Agios Antonios) and one bowl immured in the wall of Church 11. The pottery falls into three broad categories: glazed fine wares, glazed coarsewares and unglazed coarsewares.

Glazed fine wares

Most of the glazed pottery found during the survey is composed of Italian imports; Monochrome Sgraffito Ware from Italy and Polychrome Sgraffito Ware from Italy, Italian Maiolica and RMR Ware. Most of the fineware pottery dates to the fifteenth and sixteenth centuries. The notable exception to this is the Green and Brown Painted Ware found at the inner enceinte and dating to the late-twelfth century and a piece of Painted Fine Sgraffito Ware of late-twelfth century or early-thirteenth century date. The fineware pottery unsurprisingly is associate with the churches at Paliochora and with house group A, B and C. The peasants who formed the majority of the population at Paliochora had no income to buy fineware pottery. It is also interesting to note the composition of the fineware pottery. The pottery is mainly bowls and jugs and this corresponds with the research by Oikonomides and Vroom about eating habits and pottery use already discussed.[2] Both the bowls and jugs were used communally for eating rather than individually. Just over 18% of the total number of pottery sherds collected at Paliochora were from fineware pottery; and of these, 15% were bowls and just over 3% jugs.

Painted Fine Sgraffito Wares

This pottery consists of designs incised in the interior of the vessel through a white slip. Around the central medallion there are scrolls and tendrils and spirals. There are painted spirals and linear motifs in green and brown.[3] The type has a wide distribution which includes Constantinople, Sparta,[4] Corinth,[5] Eastern Phokis and Thebes.[6] This pottery is usually assigned to the mid and second-half of the twelfth century.

1.Glazed bowl rim d. 22.0(Figure 57 b Plate 14) Fabric. Deep orange-red colour (2.5 Y/R 5/6). White slip with incised decoration and green and brown spirals.

Green and Brown Painted Wares

In this type of pottery the decoration is painted on top of the white slip. Morgan divided the pottery into four groups. The pottery found at Paliochora corresponds to Morgan's Group III with solid areas outlined in brown.[7] The shapes included shallow dishes with everted rims and cups. This type is dated to the late- twelfth century and the beginning of the thirteenth century. Its origins are looked for in central Greece[8] and the Peloponnese, perhaps Sparta[9] or Corinth.[10] It is also found across the

---

[1] Pamela Armstrong drew the pottery, and made the fineware identifications. Unanticipated circumstances arose that meant she missed the second season, but the work was completed by Kate Leeming and Simon Adcock, who assisted during the first season.

[2] See the discussion in Chapter Four.

[3] Joanita Vroom, *Byzantine to Modern Pottery in the Aegean. An Introduction and Field Guide,* (Utrecht, 2005), pp.86-7; *After Antiquity. Ceramics and Society in the Aegean from the 7th to the 20th Century A.C. A Case Study from Boeotia, Central Greece,* (Leiden, 2003), pp. 152-3.

[4] P. Armstrong, 'The Byzantine and Ottoman Pottery', in eds. W. Cavanagh, J. Crouwell, R.W.V. Catling and G. Shipley, *The Laconian Survey II Archaeoligical Data,* (London, 1996) p. 127.

[5] C. H. Morgan, *Corinth XI. The Byzantine Pottery,* (Cambridge, Mass., 1942) p. 141, pls. 46–7.

[6] P. Armstrong, 'Some Byzantine and later settlements in Eastern Phokis', *BSA* 84 (1989) pp. 304, 307.

[7] Morgan, *The Byzantine Pottery,* pp.77–80.

[8] Armstrong, 'Some Byzantine and later settlements in Eastern Phokis', pp. 304, 307.

[9] R.M. Dawkin and J.P. Droop, 'Byzantine pottery from Sparta', *BSA* 17 (1910-11), no. 52

[10] Morgan, *Byzantine Pottery,* p. 72; P. Armstrong, 'The Byzantine and Ottoman Pottery', p. 126.

Mediterranean and on Kythera at Kastri,[11] as well as bowls immured in the walls of churches.[12]

2. Glazed bowl rim (Figure 57, a)
Medium-fine fabric orange-red colour (2.5 YR 7/6).

3. Glazed bowl base (Figure 57, c)
Medium-fine fabric orange-red colour (2.5 YR 7/6).

RMR Ware (Ramina, Manganese, Rossa) (Plate 14)[13]

This pottery orginates in southern Italy probably Apulia and Basilicata. The group includes bowls with a long ring foot, a carinated wall and an everted, bevelled rim; and jugs with flat bases. The interior and rim of the vessel are covered with a white-creamish slip and a transparent lead glaze. Geometric motifs are common on the interior but decoration also includes concentric horizontal bands and stripes in reddish-brown and bluish-grey and green borders. Other designs include cross-hatching, triangles, lozenges, animals and human figures. The pottery has a wide distirbution: central Greece— Arta, Corinth,[14] Patras, Argos, Isthmia, Merbaka; the islands of Rhodes and Melos; central and southern Italy and Sicily;[15] the Adriatic coast; and the Near East e.g. Acre. This type has a date range of the mid-thirteenth century through to the fifteenth century.

4. Bowl base l.2.9, w.0.4 (Figure 58a and Plate 14). Chalky buff coloured clay with a few inclusions (2.5 Y8/3). Creamish slip (10YR 8/3).Concentric horizontal bands of green and blue.

5. Bowl base. Two pieces (Figure 58b and Plate 14). Chalky buff coloured clay with a few inclusions (2.5 Y8/3). Creamish slip (10YR 8/3). Stilt mark on glaze. Decoration of concentric rings in bluish-grey and green paint.

6. Glazed bowl base (Figure 58c)
L 3.6, w 2.8, d.0.4. Chalky buff coloured clay with a few inclusions (2.5 Y8/3). Creamish slip (10YR 8/3). Traces of green borders. Concentric rings in blue.

Monochrome Sgraffito Ware from Italy[16] (Figure 59 Plates 14 and 15)

The origin of the pottery is north Italy, most probably the Veneto region. The pottery has a wide-ranging distribution: Italy, the Aegean area and the Near East. The date range is from the late fifteenth to the early sixteenth century. The vessels are covered with a white slip and glaze on the inside and just under the rim on the outside. There is a dull orange-buff wash on the rest of the exterior. There are two variants in the colour of the glaze: Monochrome Green Sgraffito Ware covered with an olive green to green glaze. This type has been found on Rhodes and at Paphos on Cyprus.[17] Monochrome Yellow Sgraffito Ware which is covered with a bright yellowish brown to dark yellow glaze. The decoration is incised on the interior of the vessels and there are horizontal lines just under the rim and above the base and stylised geometric and vegetal motifs in between. The shapes round lip and convex divergent upper wall. The base is flat with an angular transition and straight divergent lower wall.

7. Bowl rim l.29 (Figure 59a and Plate 14)
Dull orange fabric (7.5 YR 7/4) Green glaze with incised horizontal lines.

[11] J. Herrin, 'Byzantine Kythera', in eds. J.N. Coldstream and G.L. Huxley, *Kythera. Excavations and Studies conducted by the University of Pennsylvania and the British School at Athens*, (Pennsylvania, 1972), p.47.

[12] Vroom, *Byzantine to Modern Pottery in the Aegean*, p. 83; *After Antiquity*, pp. 151, 200–1.

[13] Vroom, *Byzantine to Modern Pottery in the Aegean*, pp. 128–9; *After Antiquity. Ceramics and society in the Aegean*, pp. 167–8.

[14] G.D.R. Sanders, 'An assemblage of Frankish pottery at Corinth', *Hesp.* 56 (1987) pp. 170–2.

[15] H. Patterson and D. Whitehouse 'The Medieval domestic pottery' in eds. F.D. D'Andina and D. Whitehouse, *Excavations at Otranto I. The Finds* (Galatina, 1992) p. 148.

[16] Vroom, Byzantine to Modern Pottery in the Aegean, pp. 140-1; *After Antiquity. Ceramics and society in the Aegean*, p. 170.

[17] M. Michailidon, 'Ceramica veneziana dalla citta medievale di Rodi (1309-1522). Nota preliminare', in S. Gelichi, *La ceramica nel mondo bizantino tra XI e XVe secolo e i suoi rapporti con l'Italia* (Florence, 1993) pp. 333–40; at Paphos in fifteenth and sixteenth century contexts M. L. Wartburg, 'Mittelalterliche keramik aus dem Aphroditeheilrgum im Palaiopaphos' (Grabungsplatz TA) *Archäologische Anzeiger* (1998) no. 64, Fig. 82.

8. Bowl rim l. 2.5 (Figure 59 b and Plate 14)
Dull orange fabric (7.5 YR 7/4)
Green glaze with incised horizontal lines

9. Bowl rim d. 20.0 (Figure 59 c and Plate 14)
Dull orange fabric (7.5 YR 7/4)
Green glaze with incised horizontal lines.

10. Bowl rim l.2.7 (Figure 59d Plate 14)
Dull orange fabric (7.5 YR 7/4)
Green glaze with incised horizontal lines.

11. Bowl rim (Figure 59e and Plate 14)
Dull orange fabric (7.5 YR 7/4)
Green glaze with incised horizontal lines.

Polychrome Sgraffito Ware from Italy[18] (Figure 59 Plates 14 and 15)

The origin of the pottery is north Italy in particular the Veneto region and it is widely distributed throughout the Mediterranean from the Dalmatian Coast, throughout the Aegean to Constantinople/Istanbul, Egypt and the Near East.[19] The interior and exterior of the vessel is covered with a white slip and a transparent lead glaze. On the inside incised and gouged out motifs are enhanced with alternative green and ochre-yellow oxide colours. The decoration can include some elaborate designs: animals, portraits, bands of foliage, flowering stems, a bird or herald surrounded by a geometric band or concentric lines. Dishes and bowls with straight rims and rounded lips or flanged rims, or one-handled trefoil-mouth jugs are common. The handles of the jugs have broad straps and the bases have a ringed foot and are concave underneath. The pottery dates to the late fifteenth and early sixteenth century.

12. Bowl rim l. 2.7 (Figure 59g and Plate 14)
Pale yellow fabric with few inclusions (10 YR 8/3) Pale yellow fabric with few inclusions (10 YR 8/3). Concentric lines in green oxide colour.

13 Bowl rim. L. 2.8, d 26.0. Badly abrazed (Figure 59 h and Plate 14)

Pale yellow fabric with few inclusions (10 YR 8/3). Whitish slip with yellow and green oxide.

14. Glazed bowl rim (Figure 59 g Plate 14)
Pale yellow fabric with few inclusions (10 YR 8/3).

15. Glazed bowl rim (Figure 59 j)
Pale yellow fabric with few inclusions (10 YR 8/3).

Maiolica from Italy[20] (Plate 15)

This type was produced in northern Italy and has a widespread distribution stretching from north-west Europe and the Adriatic coast across the Aegean, including mainland and island Greece and Cyprus. The surface of the pottery is covered with an opaque white tin glaze providing the foundation for blue painted designs, usually a ladder medallion design. The forms are confined to dishes and plates with an everted, flattened rim, hemispherical bowls and one-handled jugs. The jugs have knife-trimmed bases with a flattened underside and trefoil-mouth rims. This type is usually date to the late fifteenth and early-sixteenth century.

16. Jug body sherd l. 2.9 (Plate 15)
Fabric. Whitish colour (2.5 y 8/3)
white tin glaze and blue paint

17. Jug body sherd d. l. 2.
Fabric. Whitish colour (2.5 y 8/3)
White tin glaze and blue paint

18. Jug body sherd d l. 2.
Fabric. Whitish colour (2.5 y 8/3)

19.Bowl body sherd d l. 2.
Fabric. Whitish colour (2.5 y 8/3)

20. Jug body sherd
Fabric. Whitish colour (2.5 y 8/3)

---

[18] Vroom, *Byzantine to Modern Pottery in the Aegean*, pp. 142–3; *After Antiquity. Ceramics and society in the Aegean*, pp. 170–1; T.E. Gregory, 'Local and imported Medieval pottery from Isthmia', in ed. S. Gelichi, *La Ceramica*, pp. 299–302.
[19] T. Wilson, *Ceramic Art of the Italian Renaissance* (London, 1987) pp. 61–9.

[20] Vroom, *Byzantine to Modern Pottery in the Aegean*, pp. 146–7; *After Antiquity*, pp. 172–3; 'Medieval and post-Medieval pottery from a site in Boeotia. A case study example of post-classical archaelogy in Greece,' BSA 93 (1998) pp. 531–34; T. Wilson, *Ceramic Art of the Italian Renaissance*, p. 28; P. Armstrong, 'Byzantine Thebes. Excavations on the Kadmeia', *BSA* 88 (1993) p. 328, no. 327, pl. 36.

Plain glazed jug (Figure 61 Plate 16)

21. Complete profile – rim and body sherds
White greyish colour fabric (7.5 YR 6/2)

Bowls immured in the walls of churches

Glazed bowls were commonly used to decorate the facades of Greek churches in the Middle Byzantine period (eleventh and twelfth centuries). This practice appears to have spread to Italy from Greece.[21] At Paliochora we have two churches where bowls have been immured in the walls of churches. Only two sections of the wall surrounding where the door would once have been now survives at Church 11, but it is evident that there were two bowls immured in the walls. One of the two bowls survives but its decoration has now worn away (Figure 60, Plate 5). At Church 7 (Agios Antonios) there are two surviving bowls in the church walls: one above the window in the apse and another above a window in the eastern long wall of the church. The decoration of the latter has survived and can be identified as 'RMR' Ware (Figure 58d).

Coarseware pottery

Coarseware pottery makes up over 80% of the total pottery sherds collected. The pottery falls into three categories: amphorae, pithoi and cooking pots. Amphorae made up 45% of the total pottery sherds found at Paliochora and pithoi a further 26 % with cooking pots least common of the coarsewares and making up just over 11% of sherds.

A large proportion of the storage vessels were found in the area of the inner enceinte. We know from the survey of the physical remains that the inner enceinte was not built up and can only conclude that this was a deliberate policy to act as a refuge for the population in times of danger. It seems likely that food was stored here. It was unlikely that any storage was a contingency for siege-warfare. What is striking is we did not find widespread evidence of

storage vessels in the houses and can only conclude that this is further proof of the serf-like status of the population who did not own the produce. Thirty amphorae sherds were found in the southeastern section of the settlement. However a large number of coarseware pottery sherds were found in the higher status houses, A, B and C – amphorae, pithoi and cooking pots. A lot of coarseware sherds had been washed down into the gorge.

Amphorae[22]

This was the characteristic earthenware vessel for transporting wine and oil over long distances by land or sea. From the tenth century onwards the traditional shapes of antiquity are abandoned and Byzantine amphora diminish in number and finally disappear to be replaced by other types of container introduced by Italian merchants eg the wooden boutsia.

22. Base and body d. 3.6 (Figure 63)
Fabric medium coarse orange (7.5 YR 8/2)

23. Base and body. d.14.0 (Figure 62 f)
Fabric medium coarse orange (7.5 YR 8/2)

24. Base d. 6.2 (Figure 62 b)
Fabric medium coarse orange (7.5 YR 8/2)

25. Base d. 9.0 (Figure 62 c)
Fabric medium coarse orange (7.5 YR 8/2)

26. Base (Figure 62 d) d.6.2
Fabric medium coarse orange (7.5 YR 8/2)

27. Base d. 7.0 (Figure 62 a)
Fabric medium coarse orange (7.5 YR 8/2)

28. Base d. 9.0 (Figure 62 e)
Fabric medium coarse orange (7.5 YR 8/2)

[21] A.H.S. Megaw, 'Glazed bowls in Byzantine churches', *DXAE* 4 (1964) pp.145–6; and G.D.R. Sanders 'Three Peloponnesian churches and their importance for the chronology of late thirteenth and early fourteenth century pottery in the Eastern Mediterranean', *BCH Suppl. XVIII* (1989) pp. 189–99.

[22] Ch Bakirtzis, Βυζαντίνα Τσουκαλγήα, (Athens, 1989) p. 133, pls. 15–24; for a distinctive type of Laconian amphora manufactured in the twelfth-century see P. Armstrong, 'Lakonian amphorae', in eds. P. Déroche and J.-M. Spieser, *Recherches sur la céramique byzantine (BCH Suppl. 18, 1989)*, pp. 267–76.

Pithoi[23] (Figure 64 and Plate 16)

This was a commonly used vessel for storage in antiquity and the medieval periods. Larger vessels were usually placed in position and left there. The shape seems to have been similar for a long period of time both before and after the medieval era. The pithos is the second most frequently occurring pottery at Paliochora after the amphora and its distribution about the settlement is similar. The greatest concentration is in the area of the inner enceinte and some sort of storage facility may have existed in the inner enceinte for distribution amongst the peasants. A large number of sherds were found in the house group A, B and C – 36 in total. These houses were the elite dwellings at Paliochora.

29. Base and body d.28.0 (Figure 64 b)
Eight sherds
Medium coarse gritty clay, pale creamish orange (7.5YR 8/3)

30. Body d.28.0 (Figure 64 c)
Medium coarse gritty clay, pale creamish orange (7.5YR 8/3)

31. Base and body d.26.0 (Figure 64 a)
Medium coarse gritty clay, pale creamish orange (7.5YR 8/3)

Cooking pots (Figure 65)[24]

Two types of pots can be distinguished by their bases: the flat bottom which rested directly on the embers and the round-bottomed which rested on metal cooking stands or portable braziers. The grooves on the outside of cooking pots were also functional and made the pot easier to handle. There are also two categories of pots distinguished by their handles: - one or two-handled.

At Paliochora the cooking pots were flat bottomed and had two handles.

32.Glazed cooking pot (Figure 65 a)
Estimated diameter 16.0

Medium coarse gritty clay. Plae creamish-orange (7.5 YR 8/3)
33. Unglazed Cooking pot (Figure 65b)
Estimated diamter 10.0 –12.0
Medium coarse gritty clay. Plae creamish-orange (7.5 YR 8/3)

34. Unglazed Cooking pot (Figure 65 c)
D. 10-12.0
Medium coarse gritty clay. Pale creamish-orange (7.5 YR 8/3)

Conclusion

The pottery study at Paliochora confirms what we know historically and architecturally about the social structure and the broad chronology at the settlement. The fifteenth and sixteenth century bias of the fineware pottery corresponds with the period of greatest activity at the settlement when the Venetians were taking an interest in Kythera because of the Ottoman threat. Thie Italian provenance of the pottery again shows that links were with the Italian world. The earliest fineware pottery is however not Italian and reflects the early twelfth century links with the Peloponnese – Sparta and Monemvasia. The social structure and the serf-like status of the peasants is clear from the pottery – very few pottery sherds, even coarsewares, are to be found in the houses except for Houses A, B and C, where we also find fineware pottery. Elsewhere fineware pottery is only found associated with the churches.

---

[23] Bakirtzis, *Βυζαντινά Τσουκαλολάγηνα*, p.135, pls. 30–31.
[24] Bakirtzis, *Βυζαντινά Τσουκαλολάγηνα*, pp. 130–1, pls. 1–10.

Chapter Seven

The settlement of Kastrisianika

Venice's colonies in the Aegean were an accident of the Fourth Crusade and not the result of any direct colonial policy by the Serenissima. They took the opportunity afforded by the Crusade to acquire ports and areas which they had frequented for trade before 1204; whilst some of their nobles prowled the Aegean seizing whatever had not been allotted or already claimed - Dandolo's (Doge of Venice) nephew Marco Sanudo acquired the Duchy of Naxos this way. Throughout the period of Venetian rule, at least until the loss of Crete to the Turks in 1669, Kythera was closely associated with the administration of Crete. Cretan administration was modelled on Venice; but security and the appointment of high officials was decided by the Venetian Senate. A Duke led the colony, appointed by Venice for two years, and was assisted by Consillari. Venetian settlers could be elected to the Senate or the Maggior Consiglio of Candia; although very few Venetians moved to the colonies and they made up less than ten percent of the population.[1] The judicial system followed that of Venice, though special judges could be used to resolve issue involving Greeks or Jews. The highest court on the island was the Duke with two counsellors and their decision could only be overturned by Venice. Byzantine policies in agriculture were maintained and the Venetian aim here was to make the colony self-sufficient.[2]

After 1363 a Castellan-Proveditore was appointed to Kythera for a two years term of office by Venice. These officials were dependent on Crete and were paid from there until 1669.

Settlement Types

The Chora

The capital of Kythera, the Chora like the Anokastro at Melos,[3] Methone and Korone shows characteristics typical of a type of Italian settlement developed in the sixteenth century. In fact there is nothing before the sixteenth century to distinguish a Venetian colony.[4] The hill sites chosen provide natural defences and these are enhanced by gateways. Small streets and two-storey dwellings often with a lower-storey barrel-vault are characteristic. These houses are larger and more elaborate and show a much higher socio-economic status than the peasant villages. Nowadays these sixteenth-century settlements are iconic and provide the backdrop for many of the calendars and postcards of tourist Greece, whilst providing the

---

[1] M. Georgopoulou, *Venice' Maritime Colonies. Architecture and Urbanism*, (Cambridge, 2001), p. 19.

[2] Georgopoulou, *Venice's Maritime Colonies*, p. 44.

[3] G.D.R. Sanders 'Two kastra on Melos and their relationship in the Archipelago', in eds. Peter Lock and Guy Sanders, *The Archaeology of Medieval Greece* (Oxford, 1996) pp. 147–78. Sanders has claimed that there are two kastra on Melos, Anokastro clearly has similarities with Chora and. other Venetian settlements of the fifteenth and sixteenth centuries. However the claims about the second kastro are tenuous. Today there is no physical evidence of the tower he talks about nor the tracks near to it at one of the two kastra. Therefore it is difficult to know when it was built, or what shape the kastro took. The fortified settlements elsewhere on the Aegean have survived, even in a ruinous condition, and Melos is the first example where there is no physical evidence at all today of one of the two kastra. Bernard Randolf travelled in the Aegean at the end of the seventeenth-century and says that Melos had only one town. Arguably the second kastro on Melos may have been regarded as a village by Randolf, but it is strange he does not say so since he tells us about villages on Paros and Amorgos. And he does refer to the fortified settlement on Antiparos as a town. If the evidence of the second kastro on Melos had been removed before 1687 for cultivation this is indeed quick work, especially when he tells us most of the island earned their living from piracy rather than agriculture. Bernard Randolf, *The Present State of the islands of the Archipelago (or Arches): Sea of Constantinople, the Gulf of Smyrna; with the islands of Candia and Rhodes* (Oxford, 1687) pp. 22–4, 32–4. Sanders has used the drawings of the settlements from the publications by Apostolou and Schmidt-Hoepfner, but does not appear familiar with the Greek texts of these publications.

[4] Georgopoulou, *Venice's Maritime Colonies*, p. 24.

space for the bars, restaurants, shops and providing accommodation for modern tourists.

Kythera did not feature significantly with the Venetians until the sixteenth century. There was clearly some sort of settlement at the Chora before the rebuild in 1502/3. There seems to have been no buildings at Kapsali except the harbourage for galleys. At this time the potential of Avlemonas as a small harbour is also exploited. The ports of Modon (Methone) in particular and Coron (Korone) were the main bases for the Venetian fleet at the southern tip of the Peloponnese where the trade routes to Syria and the Black Sea met.[5] In 1502, at the end of the Venetian-Turkish War, the Chora on Kythera was rebuilt on the orders of the Venetian Senate and following a request by the inhabitants. For the first time Venice appointed a Proveditore to Kythera rather than the island falling under the Proveditore of Crete. The date 1503 is carved above the gateway into the kastron at the Chora on Kythera along with the Lion of Venice. The fifteenth and sixteenth century settlement was contained in two areas - the Kastron and the Bourgo.[6] This is typical of many Venetian settlements across the region and was dictated by the type of terrain: Canea, Retimo and Coron (Korone) incorporate fortified rocky hills which resulted in the main civic functions being divided into two areas.[7] We see this at the Chora on Kythera. The Kastron at the Chora is situated on top of a crag. The northern and western sides of the Kastron are the most heavily fortified, the sheer rock protects the castle elsewhere. The main entrance is in the north-west and there is a secondary entrance in the north connecting the Kastron to the Bourgo. The Kastron was divided into two rectangular plots with a rectangular street system. Today only the residence of the Proveditore, the barracks, the gunpowder magazine, government house and four churches survive. The defensive wall around the Bourgos was formed by the outer wall of the houses and churches as well as some sections of specially constructed walls. There was a definite system of streets following the contours of the land; here was located the administration buildings, the important churches, the residences of the notables and the market.[8]

Like so many other Venetian colonies we do not know what the settlement at the Chora looked like before the sixteenth century.[9] However at the Chora we are seeing houses and churches forming part of the defences which gives the impression of a planned build rather than walls thrown up to defend a pre-existing settlement. This may be because the original settlement at the Chora was a defensive plan which in 1502 was extended and strengthened. The Venetian Senate acted on an appeal by the residents to refortify.[10]

The houses in the Chora are characterized by Venetian types found throughout the Aegean and Ionian islands. The mansions of the nobles do not follow a particular type nor are they homogeneous but what sets them apart is size – they are bigger than the other houses – their careful construction and decoration. Many of the other houses at the Chora were built at a later period in the eighteenth and nineteenth centuries.[11]

Agricultural Settlements (Figures 52 and 53)

The marked increase in piratical raids and in slavery in the sixteenth century, particularly after the Battle of Preveza in 1538, meant that the Venetians also had to protect the population of the islands that they controlled beyond those living in the administrative capital. They did this with fortified settlements. The basic concept is simple. The backs of the houses themselves formed the defensive wall which normally formed a square. The rest is then down to the scale and the number of peasants who needed to be protected. The settlements vary in size. At Antiparos the orthogonal settlement comprises of a zone of houses built

[5] Georgopoulou, *Venice's Maritime Colonies*, p.18.

[6] 'Kastron' and 'bourgo' are the words used by the Greeks to describe what the Venetians referred to as the *fortezza* and *bourg*. This is the castle and associated settlement. We have used the terms kastron and bourgo throughout.

[7] Georgopoulou, *Venice's Maritime Colonies*, p.79.

[8] Panos Grigorakis, Eleni Makris, Sofia Migadis, Giorgos Dellas, Litsa Spiliotopoulou, Despoina Charambous, *Greek Traditional Architecture. Kythera*, (Athens, 1984), transl. Philip Ramp, p. 14; Georgopoulou, *Venice's Maritime Empire*, pp. 84–91.

[9] Georgopoulou, *Venice's Maritime Empire*, pp. 59–64.

[10] Chryssa Maltezou, 'Historical geography', p.153.

[11] Grigorakis, Makris, Migadis, Dellas, Spiliotopoulou, Charambous, *Greek Traditional Architecture*, pp. 18–22.

around a central tower (Figure 53a).[12] The settlement at Kimolos is bigger than Antiparos with two rings of houses around a central area which included a large house and a church (Figure 53b).[13] Mesta on Chios is probably the largest extant example. Here there are a series of concentric rings of houses each forming a line of defences with a narrow alleyway between each line; this made it impossible to storm the settlement. The central position at Mesta was occupied by a tower and this is also a feature of the much smaller Kastro on Antiparos. At Sifnos the same principle is followed without the orthagonal plan (Figure 53c).

The antecedents of these settlements are looked for in Norman castles and the subsequent development of fortified settlements in Northern Italy. They embody the idea of a defensive wall and central tower (instead of keep) in at least two instances.[14] However these were villages and not castles. It is also possible to see some of these characteristics in the monasteries of Byzantine Greece.[15] The peasants were living here permanently rather than fleeing to the fortifications in times of danger. Access into these settlements was often by only one gate, thus maximising the defence of the settlement. – for example at Mylopotamos, Kastrisianika and Antiparos.

The houses which formed these settlements are very consistent across the Aegean, no doubt because most were instigated by the Venetians. The houses are two-storeys. The lower storey often had a barrel-vault (kamara) which assisted with air circulation and therefore kept the room cool in the heat of the summer, and could accommodate an olive or grape press. The space was used for the storage of agricultural produce and/or animals. Although wooden half-floors could be constructed and used for

sleeping. The upper floor was accessed by an external stone staircase. This assisted in separating completely the function of the two floors. The upper floor often consisted of two rooms and any windows looked internally into the settlement. Wall niches and a fireplace are common features in this living area. These dwellings saw constant use over many centuries and it is really only the mass exodus of the population from the islands, particularly after Greek independence in the nineteenth century and the economic migrations of the twentieth century. On Kythera these houses can be found at Kastrisianika, Aroniadika, Aloizianika and Mylopotamos (Figure 52 and Plate 12).[16]

The settlements of Kastrisianika and Mylopotamos both demonstrate the characteristics of these defensive settlements across the Aegean. The vast majority of these settlements belong to the fifteenth and sixteenth centuries. The earliest datable settlement of this type is at Antiparos which probably dates to 1440-1446 (Figure 53a). This is also the only settlement where the houses are not two storey: the ground floor is one house and the upper floor a separate house. Here there are eighty houses and a population of about four to five hundred people - probably the whole population of Antiparos was living there in the fifteenth and sixteenth centuries.[17]

Dating of Kastrisianika

Paliochora was not refortified after the Barbarossa attack. The settlement at Kastrisianika is nearest to Paliochora. Mylopotamos was rebuilt in 1565 and because of the similarity of build we should place the settlement of Kastrisianika (and the settlements of Aroniadika and Aloizianika located close to Kastrisianika) at about the same time: they would have accommodated the remnant population from Paliochora and any newcomers settling on the island. Kastrisianika first appears in the census of 1579 but this refers to the whole district.[18] The settlement at Antiparos built in the mid-fifteenth century was built when the peasants there were still serfs and this is reflected in their houses and the central

---

[12] M. Philippa-Apostolou Τὸ Κάστρο τῆς Ἀντιπάρου. Διδακτορικὴ διατριβή, (Athens, 1978) pp. 14-15.

[13] W. Hoepfner and H. Schmidt, 'Κιμωλιακά', Tomos H (Athens, 1978) pp. 23–8; Philippa-Apostolou, Τὸ Κάστρο τῆς Ἀντιπάρου, p. 15; Katerina A. Mathioudaki, 'The Kastro at Kimilos and its origins', M.Arch. Dissertation, University of Bath, 1999/2000, pp.18–40.

[14] Philippa-Apostolou, Τὸ Κάστρο τῆς Ἀντιπάρου, pp. 88–90.

[15] A.K. Orlandos, Μοναστηριακὴ Ἀρχιτεκτονική (Athens, 1958) p. 7.

[16] It was only possible to draw the settlement of Kastrisianika, see Chapter One.

[17] Hoepfner and Schmidt, 'Κιμωλιακά'; Philippa-Apostolou, Τὸ Κάστρο τῆς Ἀντιπάρου p. 15.

[18] See Chapters Three and Four.

tower in the settlement built to accommodate either the local notable or his agent. This reflects a social structure much closer to that of Paliochora.[19] The two-storey houses at Kastrisianika, Aloizianika, Aroniadika and elsewhere indicate a free peasantry who are able to store their produce on the ground floor of their houses. We know the serfs were freed after 1545, as a consequence of the Barbarossa attack and as part of a Venetian policy to attract settlers to the island; in 1540 the Bishop of Monemvasia was warning his flock not to settle on Kythera because of the serfdom.[20]

The settlement of Kimolos also shows an interesting social structure. It was built by a man called John Raphos in 1592 who was also responsible for the building of the church at the centre of the settlement.[21] Raphos' sailors lived in the settlement and they were probably pirates themselves.[22] We learn from Bernard Randolf that the inhabitants of Melos were involved in piracy in the seventeenth century.[23]

Kastrisianika, and the two closely associated settlements of Aroniadika and Aloizianika began as small units although other houses and churches developed around the original orthogonal defence in much the same way as on Antiparos. It is interesting to speculate as to why three separate small settlements were built instead of one larger settlement such as we find on Kimolos or Antiparos. The social structure may again provide the answer. We know that the suffix -ianika on Kythera is added to the surname of the founders of villages; thus Logothetianika was founded by the Logothetis family. The three units at Kastrisianika, Aroniadika and Aloizianika may tell us that three families or extended families settled there as the authorities encourage immigrants after 1545.

---

[19] See Chapters Two and Three.

[20] Maltezou, 'Historical geography', p. 155.

[21] Hoepfner and Schmidt, *Κιμώλακά*, pp. 36–7.

[22] Hoepfner and Schmidt, '*Κιμωλιακά*', pp.32-3.

[23] Bernard Randolf, *The Present State of the islands of the Archipelago (or Arches). Sea of Constantinople, the Gulf of Smyrna; with the islands of Candia and Rhodes*, p. 33.

Chapter Eight

The settlement of Katsoulianika

In the censuses of the eighteenth and nineteenth centuries seventy-four settlements are listed on Kythera, including Katsoulianika, a small settlement on the north of the island. It is not known exactly when it was founded but the two churches of Agios Demetrios at Gouria and Agia Triada are first mentioned in the censuses of 1724 and 1753 respectively.[1] There were 150 inhabitants in the village in 1920, barely half the number that had been there back in 1836, when 282 were recorded. Looking further back the population remained fairly steady: 305 in 1814, 245 in 1788.[2] Katsoulianika is spread on a comparatively flat area of land with a view to the valley of Platani to the north and the village of Logothetianika to the south. The village seems to have developed around two locations and gradually formed a linear settlement along both sides of the main road.

The Houses (Figures 54-56 and Plate 13)

The houses at Katsoulianika have undergone repairs and recently some have been rebuilt, but by and large the village like most of Kythera has remained unaffected by large-scale post-war development. At the time of this study most of the houses had remained unchanged during the course of the twentieth century. The house of Antonakes (Figure 54 and Plate 13), a two-storey house on the main road of the settlement, has the date 1871 carved in a lintel above the door of the upper storey. A single-storey barrel-vaulted house (2m southwest of the church of Agia Triada) has the date 1863 carved into a stone lintel above the main entrance. The two-storey house next to the Patrikainas house has an eighteenth-century date, although not clearly legible, engraved near to the entrance to the lower storey. However these dates may not be the dates of construction, but when renovations were undertaken or a second storey added (Figure 55 and Plate 13).

The houses at Katsoulianika, including the oldest house, have a roughly rectangular plan: the lengths of the buildings vary from 5 to 10m and the widths vary from 2.6 to 3.8m. The L-shaped houses that form the second main group of houses at Katsoulianika, appear to have developed from the rectangular ground-plan with the addition of a room placed perpendicular to the long axis of the existing house. But in at least one instance the house was built at the outset in a L-shape plan, not adapted into it. In this particular case the longer section of the house is narrower than the shorter section; the former is 2.6m wide whereas the latter is 2.9m wide. The everyday activities of cooking, washing and watering the animals were conducted in the yard, which was usually configured as rectangular.

The house of Nicholas Katsoulis, situated south of the church of Agia Triada is regarded by the villagers as the oldest house of Katsoulianika, belonging to the village's founder (Figure 56a). The house consists of a long narrow room (10x3.7m) with a north-south orientation. East of this long room another room was added later. Access to the house is through a door with a segmental arch, situated in the west wall. Externally, the house differs very little from other one-storey houses in the village. However the internal space is dominated by four arches, built parallel to each other at regular intervals.

The earliest houses at Katsoulianika are characterized by a ground floor covered by a barrel-vault; and in many cases the upper storey is smaller than the lower storey, leaving free space at the front to act as an open terrace (Figure 55). The upper storey of a house at Katsoulianika would serve as living quarters, which would be reached an external staircase, built in most cases against the front wall (Figure 55). There seem to have been no internal communications between different floors in any of the domestic buildings.

The most common from of roof at Katsoulianika is flat. The roof rests on beams which run

---

[1] Maltezou, 'Historical geography', pp. 167–8.
[2] Leontsini, *A Social History*, pp. 183–211.

parallel to the short walls of the house. In the cases where beams are used, branches are then placed adjacent to each other and at right angles (more or less) to the beams. Spanish brooms (*poterium spinosum* or *spatium junceum*) were then positioned to fill in any gaps left between the branches. A thick layer of puddled clay was then spread on top and beaten to form a compact mass. The clay can protect the dwelling from even the heaviest rainfall for up to two winters. To combat erosion clay was added at regular intervals. Traditional houses with flat roofs are rare on the island today because most have fallen in, though some have been replaced by concrete. In the case of the house of Nicholas Katsoulis, the arches assume the role of the beams, obviating the need for large timbers, which would have been difficult to find here, and using readily available stone (Figure 56a). In this house there was a layer of large stone slabs beneath the puddled clay, which would have stopped muddy dust from falling into the rooms, and would have helped to give the house good insulation and made it solidly secure. The weight of these slabs would have been too great for wooden beams. Other roof types at Katsoulianika include the pitched roof which is tiled and built with precision. Its construction was dependent upon the availability of straight lengths of sawn timber.

The lower-storey barrel-vaults are usually divided by a thin wall, forming a small room which may have acted as a kitchen. The rest of the vault may have been used as a storeroom. L-shaped houses are usually divided into three rooms, one of which is a kitchen. Almost no windows are to be found in the barrel-vaulted lower storeys and as a result they are climatically very stable—cool in summer, and free from frost in winter. They would be good for storage, but susceptible to damp, and in the absence of a fireplace it is difficult to imagine them being inhabited through the winter. Windows are common in the upper floors, and in the single-storey houses. The most common internal feature is the niche and each house has at least one fireplace. Winepresses, stables and storerooms cater for the agricultural activities of the inhabitants. Infant mortality remained high on Kythera in the nineteenth-century and of the 50 houses built before 1900 only two have lavatories.

Conclusion

Katsoulianika is not created in the same climate of fear that shaped Paliochora, Kastrisianika, Aroniadika, Aloizianika or Mylopotamos—or even the Chora/Kapsali. The arrangement of the houses along the main road forms a linear village, showing that access to the main artery and ease of movement was more important than defence.

There are a great many similarities in the domestic buildings of Katsoulinika, Kastrisianika, Aloizianika, Aroniadika and Mylopotamos. The division of space, and where there were two storeys, the use of the ground floor barrel-vault for storage of agricultural produce or related activities such as pressing grapes or olives. The upper floors are the living quarters and these are often divided into only two rooms. The concept of privacy and bedrooms is a recent one even in western Europe, and it cannot have been a priority here. The building materials used in construction are what are available on the island—limestones, lime mortar, poros stone. It is only with the introduction of industrially produced cement, tiles and bricks in the latter part of the twentieth-century that we see changes. Katsoulianika was, from the outset, open to the world in a way that Kastrisianika and the other defensive villages on Kythera were not. It is in the morphology of the villages that these changes can be read, not in the individual dwellings, which remain much the same from one peasant village to another.

Conclusion

Mediterranean islands, including Kythera, look both inwards and outwards. The remains of the settlement at Paliochora are evidence of the failure of co-existence between the insular and the wider world between the thirteenth and sixteenth centuries on Kythera, when the settlement was in use. And the reasons for that failure can be inferred by placing the evidence in its historical context. Paliochora is, in a sense, a pirate settlement—not because it was inhabited by pirates or benefited from piracy, but because it was created, sustained and destroyed by piracy in the Aegean, especially by the climate of fear engendered by piracy.

Piracy may well have been invented in the Mediterranean, and the idea that some people make their living through piracy has certainly been accepted in these parts through the years stretching back to Antiquity. But the breakdown of the Byzantine Empire and the rise of the Ottoman Empire changed the character of Mediterranean piracy into a form of organized warfare. The economic consequences were felt across the Mediterranean as North-African settlements (such as Algiers) benefitted from the trading of booty to the Italian maritime states whose trade was hurt by it; in the sixteenth century this illegal trade may have accounted for more than legal trade. It was the human cargo – slaves – that had perhaps the most profound effect. There had of course been a long history of slavery in the Mediterranean, but now slavery was used in the physical and psychological war between the Christians and Ottoman Turks.

In the sixteenth century the populations of the Mediterranean islands were constantly threatened by slavery, which for most people remained as a vague generalized fear, drawing them into leading more cautious and protected lives than they otherwise might. For many of the people who lived at Paliochora in 1537 the threat became real, and they were taken away and sold. The threat, however, had been there since its foundation: it was piracy that turned the settlement in on itself, behind a defensive wall, and which – even more fundamentally – had led to the settlement being founded in a difficult place, deliberately hiding itself away from the world. Its links with the outside world were therefore always problematic, and there is no doubt that it suffered economically and socially as a consequence.

Had members of Venice's elite, in particular the landowning Venier family, lived on the island or been directly involved in running it in the thirteenth century, then Paliochora may not have developed into a settlement at all, but have remained a protective fortification for use in times of danger. The oligarchy that controlled the island's interior did not control its relationship with the outside world, and had no wider view of their own or the island's interests. They exploited only its agriculture and as a result Paliochora developed into a hybrid between a village and a town. Clearly the place had few visitors, but even people from elsewhere around the Mediterranean would have found the settlement unusual. The dynamics of Paliochora's political and social structure till the sixteenth century was dominated by this reliance on the exploitation of agriculture by a bonded peasantry.

The village of Kastrisianika was built subsequently by a free peasantry who still feared pirates and protected themselves against that threat. They continue the story begun at Paliochora, looking to the island for agricultural production, but they worked in tandem with the Chora, a Venetian colonial town that faced out to the Mediterranean world and its trade links.

Settlements reflect the politics, society and economy that created them. Three elements shaped the history of Kythera from the Fourth Crusade to the end of the Venetian Republic in 1797. First an Empire built on trade and its need to maintain the flow of goods and money. Second, piracy, which was as constant as the sea itself but whose ebb and flow was controlled by the clash of great empires. And finally, a strange oligarchy that owed its existence to Venetian lack of interest in the island. It was these oligarchs who caused a peasant revolt in the eighteenth century, but their legacy can still be seen today in Kythera's numerous churches.

Index

Bibliography

Primary Sources

Darrouzès, J. *Notitiae Episcopatuum Constantinopolitanae, Géographie ecclesiastique de l'empire byzantin 1* (Paris, 1981).

Faral, E ed.,Villehardouin Geoffrey, *Le Conquête de Constantinople*, ,..2 vols. (Paris, 1938-9).

Hopf, Charles. *Chroniques Gréco-Romanes inedited ou peu connues Cheilas Chronicon Monasterii S. Theodori in Cythera Insula siti* (Berlin, 1873), pp. 346-358.

Lambros, S. Μιχαὴλ Ἀκομιάτου τοῦ Χωνιάτου σωζόμενα, 2 vols. (Athens, 1879-80).

Lemerle, P. *Cinq Études sur le Xie siècle byzantin* (Paris, 1977).

Lewis, Naphtali and Reinhold, Meyer. *Roman Civilisation Source Book I*, (Columbia New York, 1951).

Meineke, A. ed. *Ioannis Cinnami Epitome* (Bonn, 1836), II

Oikonomides, N. A, 'Ο Βίος τοῦ Ἁγίου Θεοδώρου Κυθήρων', *Proceedings of the Third Panionian Congress* (Athens, 1967), lines 149-53, 186-213.

Petit, L. ed. *Actes de Chilander* I, Actes grecs (Actes de l'Athos V) Vizantijssil Vremennik 17 (1910), Suppl. I.

Sophianou, Demetriou. Z. Ὅσιος Λουκᾶς. Ὁ βίος του (Athens, 1993).

Vitruvius, The Ten Books on Architecture, transl. by Morris Hicky Morgan (New York, 1960).

Modern sources

Armstrong,, P.' Some Byzantine and later settlements in Eastern Phokis', *BSA* 84 (1989), pp. 304, 307.

— 'Byzantine Thebes. Excavations on the Kadmeia', *BSA* 88 (1993), p. 328, no. 327, pl. 36.

— 'Lakonian amphorae', in eds. P Déroche and J-M Spieser, *Recherches sur la céramique byzantine (BCH Suppl. 18, 1989)*, pp. 267-76.

— The Byzantine and Ottoman Pottery', in eds. W. Cavanagh, J. Crouwell, R.W.V. Catling and G. Shipley, *The Laconian Survey II Archaeoligical Data* (London, 1996).

Bakirtzis, Ch. Βυζαντινά Τσουκαλολάγηνα, (Athens, 1989), pp. 125-40.

Barnsley, S.H. and Schultz R.W, *The Monastery of St. Luke of Stiris in Phocis and the Dependent Monastery of St. Nikolas in the Fields near Skripou in Boeotia* (London, 1901).

Blok, Anton. 'Southern Italian Agro-towns', in *Comparative Studies in Society and History*, Vol. 11, No.2 (Apr. 1969), pp. 121-135.

Bon, A. *Le Morée Franque*, (Paris, 1969) 2 Volumes.

Buechler, Hans.' Spanish urbanism from a grass-roots perspective', in eds. Michael Kenny and David Kertzer, L. *Urban Life in Mediterranean Europe: Anthropological Perspectives*, (Illinois, 1983) pp. 135-161.

Bouras, Ch. 'Houses in Byzantium',*DXAE* 11 (1982-83)

— 'City and village: urban design and architecture', JÖB 31/1 (1981), pp. 611-53; and more recently

— Aspects of the Byzantine city' in ed. Angeliki E. Laiou, *The Economic History of Byzantium: From the Seventh Through the Fifteenth Century*, (Dumbarton Oaks, 2002), pp. 497-528.

Braudel, Fernand. *The Mediterranean and the Mediterranean World in the Age of Philip II*, transl. Sian Reynolds, 2 vols. (London, 1972).

Broodbank, C. 'Kythera Survey. Preliminary report on the 1998 season,' *BSA* 94 (1999), pp. 191-214.

Dawkin, R. M and Droop, J.P. ' Byzantine pottery from Sparta', *BSA* 17 (1910-11), no. 52

Drandakis, N. B. 'Ἐρευναι εἰς τὴν Μάνην,' *PAE* (1977),p. 226.

Drandakis, N. B., Kalopissi S., Panagiotidi M., 'Ἐρευναι εἰς τὴν Μάνην,' *PAE* (1979),pp. 156-57.

Drandakis, N. B. Gioles N., Konstandinidi, Ch. 'Ἐρευναι εἰς τὴν Λακωνικὴν Μάνην', *PAE* (1981), 254-68.

Drandakis N.B, Gioles N., Dori E, Kalopissi S., Kepetzi, V., Konstaninidi, Ch., Panagiotidi, M., 'Ἐρευναι εἰς τὴν Ἐπίδαυρον Λιμηράν', *PAE* (1982), pp. 349-466.

Drandakis N.B, Kalopissi, S., Panagiotidi, M.,'Ἐρευναι εἰς τὴν Ἐπίδαυρον Λιμηράν', *PAE* (1983), pp. 209-63.

Frantz, A. 'The Middle Byzantine pottery', *Hesp.* 7 (1938), pp. 429-67;

Gallas, K. Wessel K, Borboudakis M, *Byzantinisches Kreta* (1983), 216, 227, 241, 310, 393, 440

Guilmartin, John. Francis. *Gunpowder and Galleys. Changing Technology and Mediterranean in the Warfare in the 16th Century*, (London, 2003).

Georgopoulou, Maria. *Venice' Maritime Colonies. Architecture and Urbanism*, (Cambridge, 2001)

Gioles, N. *Βυζαντινή Ναοδομία (600-1204)*, (Athens, 1987).

Gregory, T. E, ' Local and imported Medieval pottery from Isthmia', in ed. S Gelichi, *La Ceramica nel mondo bizantino tra Xie e XV secolo e I suoi rapporti con l'Italia, (Florence, 1993)*, pp. 283-306.

Grigorakis, Panos, Makris, Eleni., Migadis, Sofia., Dellas, Giorgos., Spiliotopoulou, Litsa., Charambous, Despoina., *Greek Traditional Architecture. Kythera*, (Athens, 1984), transl. by Philip Ramp.

Horden, Peregrine and Purcell, Nicholas, *The Corrupting Sea: A Study of Mediterranean History* (Oxford, 2000).

Huxley, G. L. 'The History and topography of ancient Kythera' in eds. J.N. Coldstream and G.L Huxley, *Kythera. Excavations and Studies conducted by the University of Pennsylvania and the British School at Athens*, (Pennsylvania, 1972), p.33-40.

Ince, G. E , Koukoulis, Th., Smyth, D. 'Paliochora: Survey of a Byzantine City on the island of Kythera. Preliminary Report', *BSA* 82 (1987), pp. 95 – 106.

Ince, G. E, Koukoulis, Th., and Ballantyne, A. N. ' Paliochora: Survey of a Byzantine City on the island of Kythera. Second Report', *BSA* 84 (1989), pp. 407-416.

Kalligas, A. G and H. A, Monemvasia, in eds. D. Philippides, *Greek Traditional Architecture*, (Athens, 1984).

Kalligas Haris A., *Byzantine Monemvasia. The Sources*, (Monemvasia, 1990).

— 'The Church of Hagia Sophia at Monemvasia', *DXAE* 4/9 (1977-79), pp.217-221.

Koukoulis, T.G. ' A Late Byzantine windmill at Kythera', *Philolakon. Studies in Honour of Hector Catling,*(London, 1992), pp. 157-163.

Krautheimer, Richard. *Early Christian and Byzantine Architecture* (Middlesex, 1981).

Heers, Jacques. *The Barbary Corsairs. Warfare in the Mediterranean 1480-1580*, (London, 2003)

Herrin, Judith. 'Byzantine Kythera', in eds. J.N Coldstream and G.L Huxley, Kythera. Excavations and Studies conducted by the University of Pennsylvania and the British School at Athens, (Pennsylvania, 1972), pp. 47-55.

Hoepfner, W and Schmidt, H, *Κιμωλιακά*, Tomos H (Athens, 1978), pp. 3-27.

Lane, Frederic. C, *Venice. A Maritime Republic* (Baltimore, 1973).

Lassdithiotakis, K. *Κυριαρχούντες τύποι χριστιανικῶν ναῶν ἀπὸ τὸν αἰῶνα καὶ ἐντεῦθεν. Δυτικὴ Κρήτη, KrChron* ΙΕ-ΙΣΤ (1963).

Lazarides P.L, *AD* 20 (1965), pp. 84-5, 190, 191, 196, 199.

Lock Peter, *The Franks in the Aegean 1204-1500*, (New York, 1995).

Magdalino P., ' The Byzantine aristocratic oikos', ed. M. Angold, The Byzantine Aristocracy XI -XIII Centuries, *BAR International Series 221* (Oxford, 1984), pp. 99-100

Maltezou, Chryssa. 'Le famiglie degli Eudaimoniannis e Venier a Cerigo dal XII al XIV secolo. Problemi di cronologia e prosopografia', *Rivista di studi Bizantini e slavi 2 (1982) – Miscellanea Agostino Pertusi. T. 2 Bologna 198*, pp. 205-217. Also published in *Βενετικὴ Παρουσία στὰ Κύθηρα*, (Athens, 1991).

— 'Τὸ Χρονικὸ τοῦ Χειλᾶ. Κοινωνικὰ καὶ ἰδεολογικὰ προβλήματα τὸν 15ο αἰῶνα,' *Σύμμεικτα* 8 ,(1989), pp.15-25.

— Μονεμβασία καὶ Κύθηρα. Ἀνακοίνωση στὸ Συμπόσιο Ἱστορίας καὶ Τέχνης μὲ θέμα: Ἡ Πελοπόννησος τὴν ἐποχὴ τῶν Παλαιολόγων (Μονεμβασία, 20-23 Ἰουλίου). (1989), p. 1-9. Also published in *Βενετικὴ Παρουσία στὰ Κύθηρα*, (Athens, 1991).

Mango, Cyril. *Byzantine Architecture,* (Milan, 1978)

Mathioudaki, Katerina. A., 'The Kastro at Kimolos and its origins', Dissertation towards the degree of Master of Architecture at the University of Bath, 1999/2000.

Matschke, Klaus-Peter. 'The Notaras family and its Italian connections', *DOP* 49 (1995), pp. 59-72.

Megaw, A. H, 'The chronology of some Middle Byzantine Churches', *BSA* 32 (1931-32),

— 'Glazed bowls in Byzantine churches', *DXAE* 4 (1964), pp.145-162.

Michailidon, M, 'Ceramica veneziana dalla citta medievale di Rodi (1309-1522). Nota preliminare', in S. Gelichi, *La ceramica nel mondo bizantino tra XI e XVe secolo e i suoi rapporti con l'Italia* (Florence, 1993), pp. 333-340

Millet, G. *L'Ecole Greque dans l'architecture Byzantine*, (Paris, 1916).

Morgan, C., *Corinth XI. The Byzantine Pottery*, (Cambridge, Mass., 1942), p141, pls. 46-7.

Moutsopoulos, N.K. *Παλιόχωρα τῆς Αἰγίνης,* (Athens, 1962), pp.59-87.

— Βυζαντινὰ σπίτια στὸ Μουχλὶ Ἀρκαδίας', *Βυζαντινὰ* 13.1 (1985), pp.321-53.

Moutsopoulos N. K., Demetrokalis , G., *Γεράκι. Οἱ ἐκκλησίες τοῦ οἰκισμοῦ*, Thessalonica (1981).

Nichol Donald. M, *Byzantium and Venice. A Study in Diplomatic and Cultural Relations*
— (Cambridge,1988).
   The Last Centuries of Byzantium 1261-1453, (Cambridge, 1993).
Oikonomides, Nicholas. 'The contents of the Byzantine house from the eleventh to the fifteenth
   century', *DOP* 45 (1991), pp. 209. (205-14)
Orlandos, A.K., *ABME* I (1935), pp. 121-24, p.115.
   Τὰ παλάτια καὶ τὰ σπίτια τοῦ Μυστρᾶ, Archeion Byz. Mnem 3 (1937)
— 'Βυζαντινὰ καὶ μεταβυζαντινὰ μνημεῖα τῆς Ῥόδου', *Archeion Byz. Mnem. ΣΤ*
   (1948).
— *Μοναστηριακὴ Ἀρχιτεκτονική*, (Athens, 1958)
Patterson, H. and Whitehouse, D. 'The Medieval domestic pottery' in eds. F D D'Andina and D
   Whitehouse, *Excavations at Otranto I. The Finds* ,(Galatina, 1992), pp. 87-195.
Philippa-Apostolou, M. Τὸ Κάστρο τῆς Ἀντιπάρου. Διδακτορικὴ διατριβή, (Athens, 1978).
Radt, W. *Die byzantinische Wohnstadt von Pergamon. Wohnungbaum Alterum 3,* (Berlin, 1978), pp. 199-223
Randolf, Bernard, *The Present State of the islands of the Archipelago (or Arches). Sea of*
   Constantinople, the Gulf of Smyrna; with the islands of Candia and Rhodes,
   (Oxford,1687).
Rheidt, K. 'Byzantinishe Wohnhauser des 11 bis 14 jahrhunderts in Pergamon', *DOP* 44 (1990), pp.195-204.
Rodley, Lyn . *Byzantine Art and Architecture. An Introduction,* (Cambridge, 1994).
Sanders, G.D.R. ' Two kastra on Melos and their relationship in the Archipelago', in eds. Peter Lock
   and G D R Sanders, *The Archaeology of Medieval Greece,* (Oxford, 1996),pp. 147-78
— 'An assemblage of Frankish pottery at Corinth', *Hesp* 56 (1987), pp. 170-2.
— 'Three Peloponnesian churches and their importance for the chronology of late
   thirteenth and early fourteenth century pottery in the Eastern Mediterranean', *BCH*
   Suppl. XVIII (1989) pp. 189–99.
Scranton, R. L. *Corinth XVI. The Medieval Architecture,* (Princeton, 1957).
Setton, K. 'The archaeology of Medieval Athens', *Essays in Medieval life and thought presented in*
   honour of Austen Patterson, (New York, 1955), pp. 227-58.
Sigalos, Eleftherios. *Housing in Medieval and Post-Medieval Greece,* BAR (Oxford,2004).
Simatou, P. and Christodoulopoulou R, 'Παρατηρήσεις στὸν μεσαιωνικὸ οἰκισμὸ τοῦ
   Γερακίου',pp. 67-88.
Snodgrass, A. M. 'Archaeology and the study of the Greek polis', in eds. John Rich and Andrew G
   Wallace-Hadrill, *City and country in the Ancient World,* (London, 1991), pp. 1-24.
Soteriou, G. *Βυζαντινὰ μνημεῖα τῆς Κύπρου* (Athens, 1935).
Stikas, E. G. 'Καθολικὸν τῆς Μονῆς Δαφνίου', *'DXAE* 4/3 (1962-63), pp. 1-47.
— Ὁ Ναὸς τῆς Ἁγίας Σοφίας Μονεμβασιᾶς' *Laconian Studies* 8 (1986).
Vokotopoulos, P..L. 'Ἡ βυζαντινὴ τέχνη στὰ Ἑπτάνησα', *Kerkyriaka Chronika* 15 (1970)
Vroom, Joanita. *After Antiquity. Ceramics and Society in the Aegean from the seventh to the twentieth*
   century AC (Leiden, 2003).
— *Byzantine to Modern Pottery in the Aegean. An Introduction and Field Guide,*
   (Utrecht, 2005).
Wartburg, M. L. ' Mittelalterliche keramik aus dem Aphroditeheilgrum im Palaiopaphos
   (Grabungsplatz TA), *Archäologische Anzeiger* (1998), no.64, Fig. 82.
Weber, Max. *The City,* translated and edited by Don Martindale and Gertrud Neuwirth,
   (New York, 1958).
Wheatley,Paul . *The Pivot of the Four Quarters. A Preliminary Enquiry into the Origins of the Ancient*
   Chinese City, (Edinburgh, 1971).
Wilson, T, *Ceramic Art of the Italian Renaissance* (London, 1987).
Woolley, L. 'The urbanisation of society', in eds. J. Hawkes and L. Woolley, *The History of mankind. Vol. 1.*
   Prehistory and the Beginnings of Civilisation (London, 1963), p. 411 - 39.

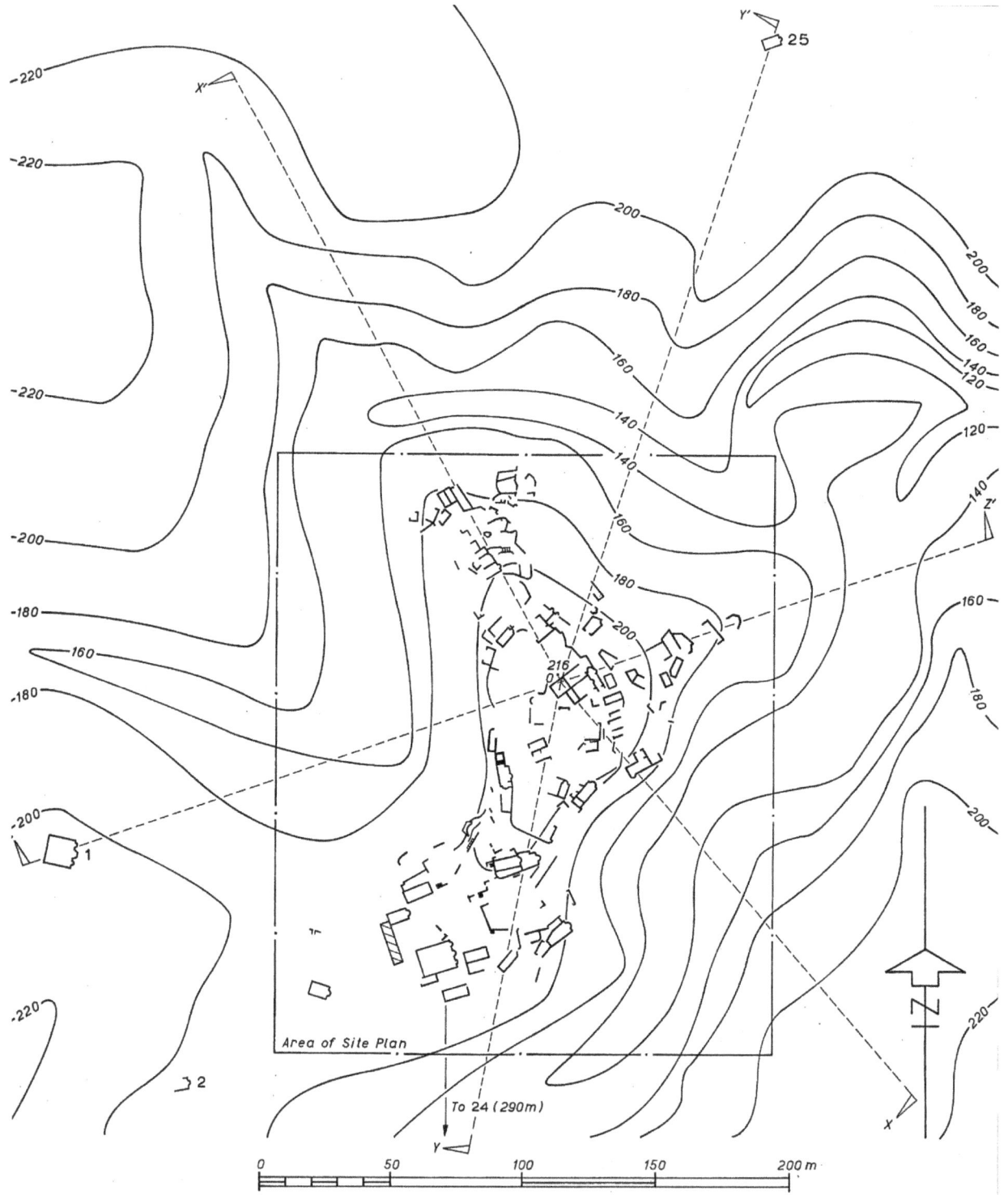

Fig. 1. Topographical plan showing 20m contour and area of site plan

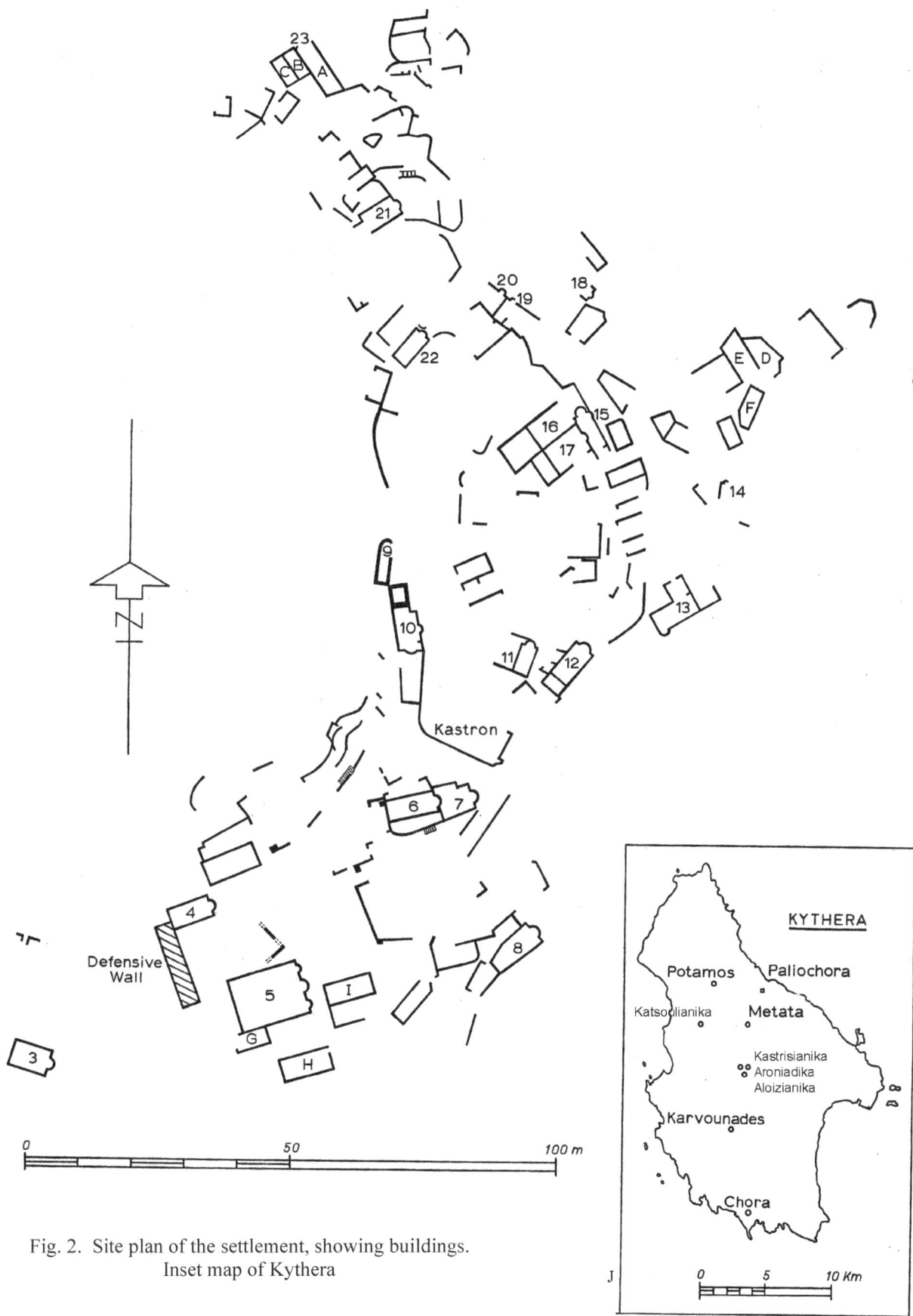

Fig. 2. Site plan of the settlement, showing buildings.
Inset map of Kythera

Church 22

Church 21

House A

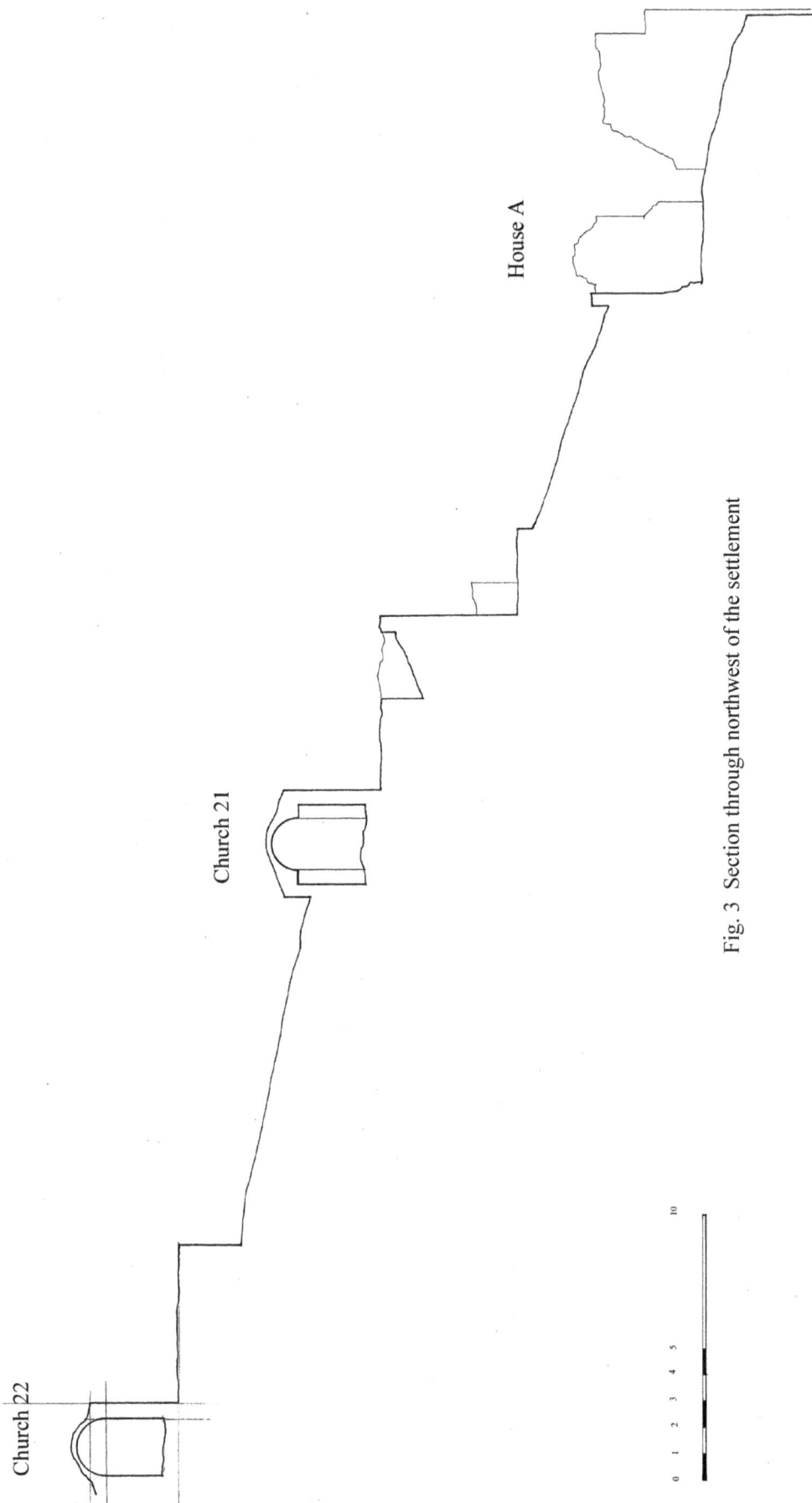

Fig. 3 Section through northwest of the settlement

0 1 2 3 4 5   10

Church 17   Church 15

House E   House F

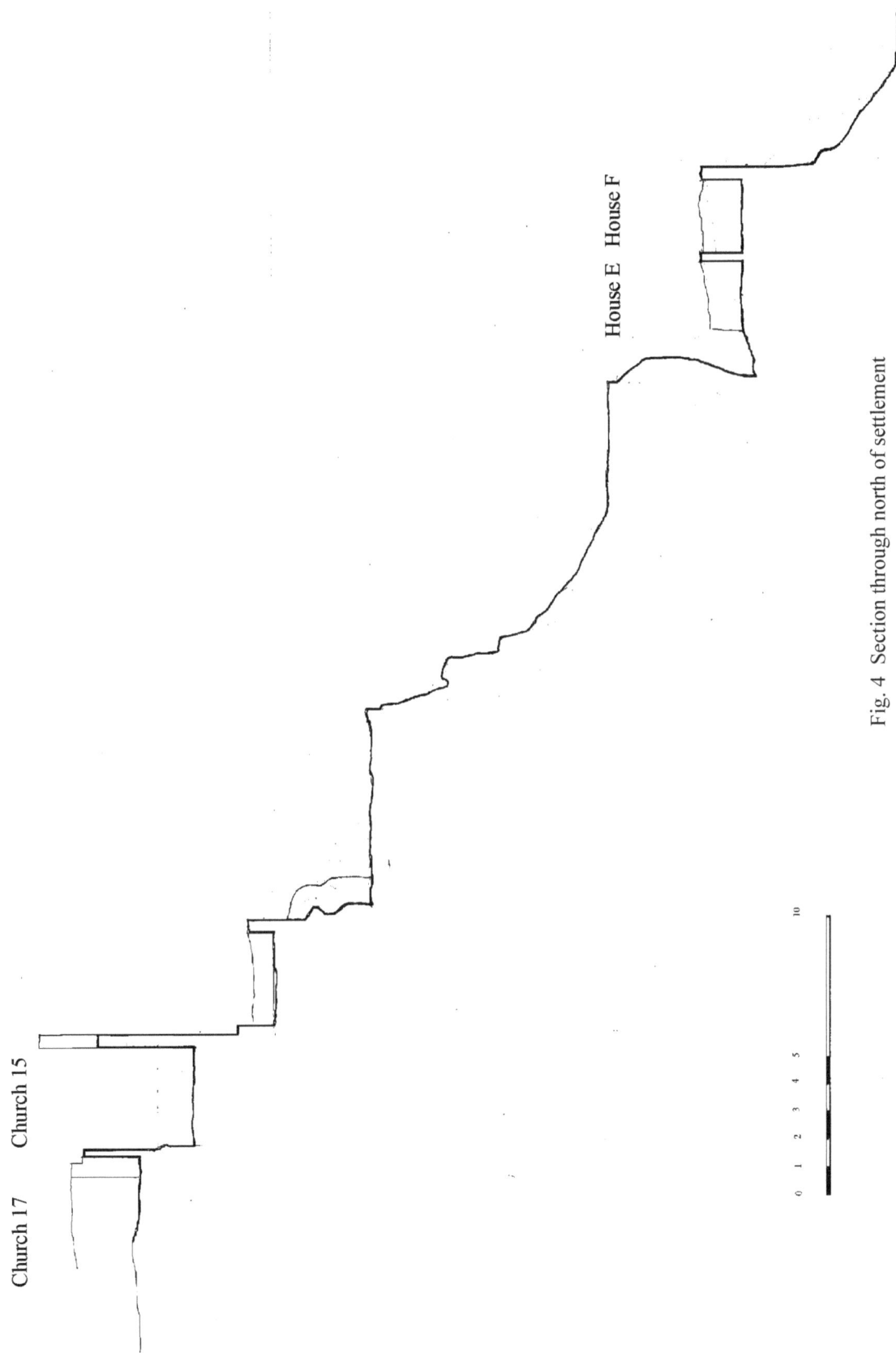

Fig. 4 Section through north of settlement

0 1 2 3 4 5   10

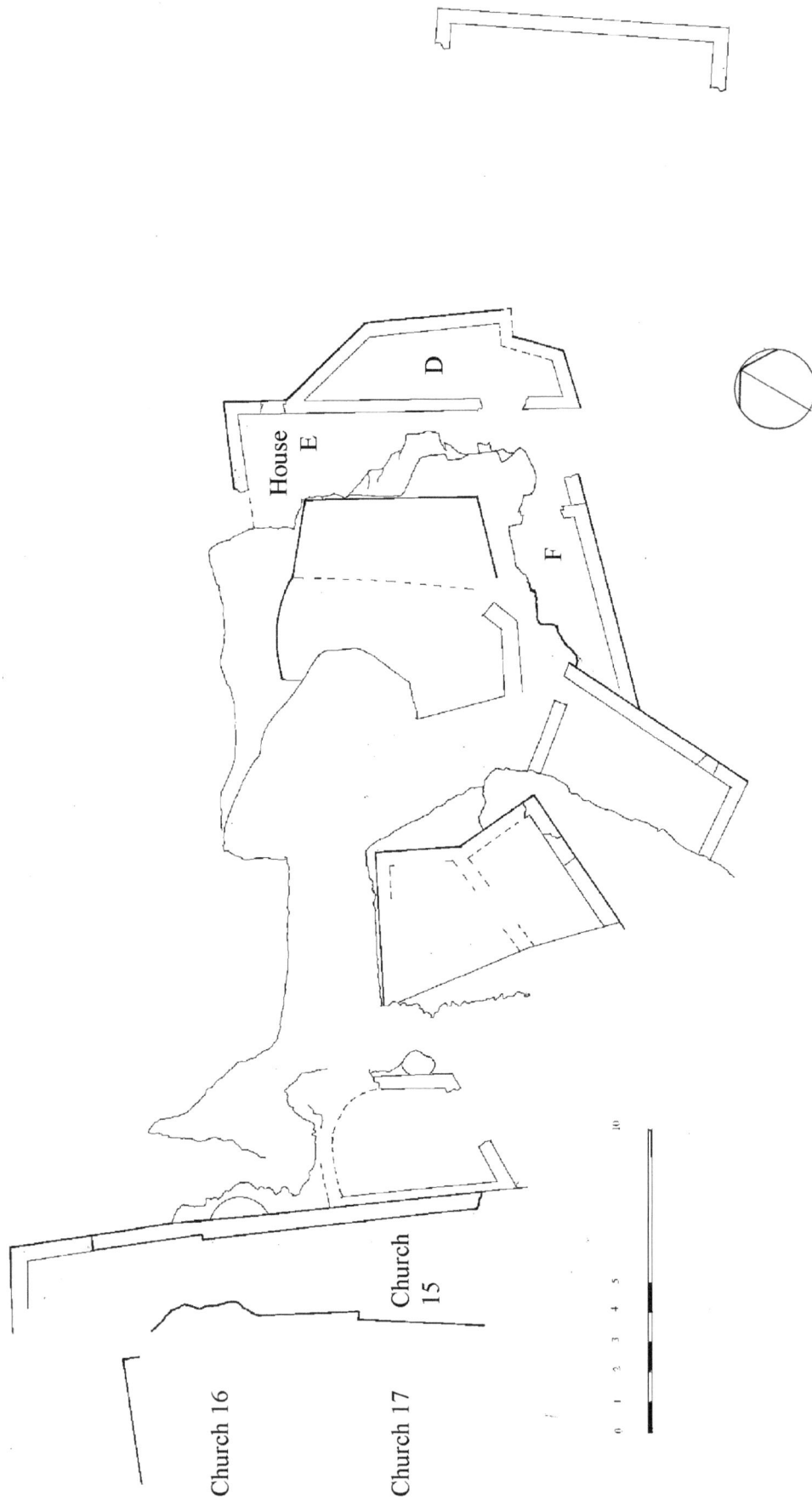

Fig. 5 Plan of churches and dwellings north of settlement (see Figure 4)

Church 7

Church 6

0   1   2   3   4   5   10

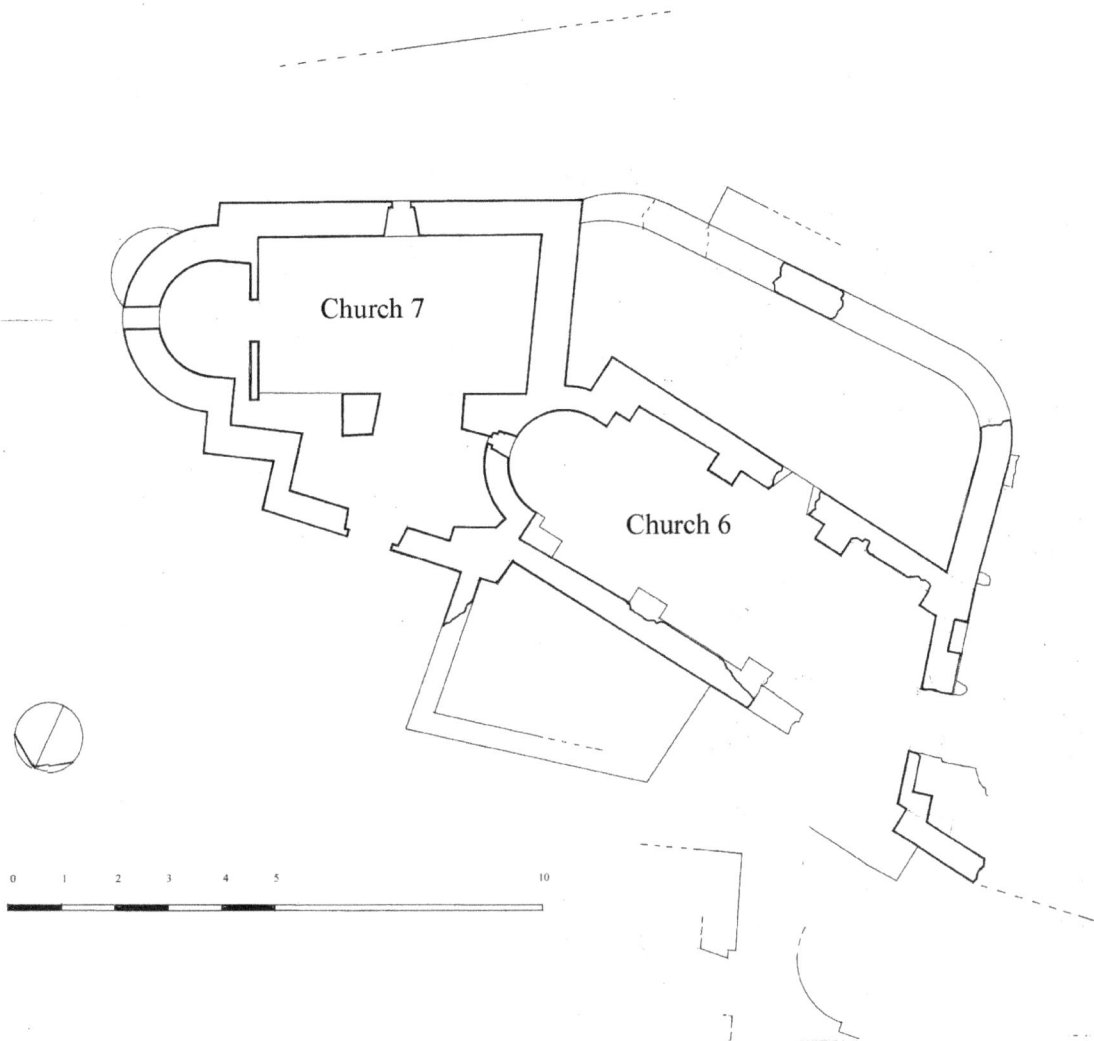

Fig. 6 Section of churches 6 and 7

a

b

0 1 2 3 4 5

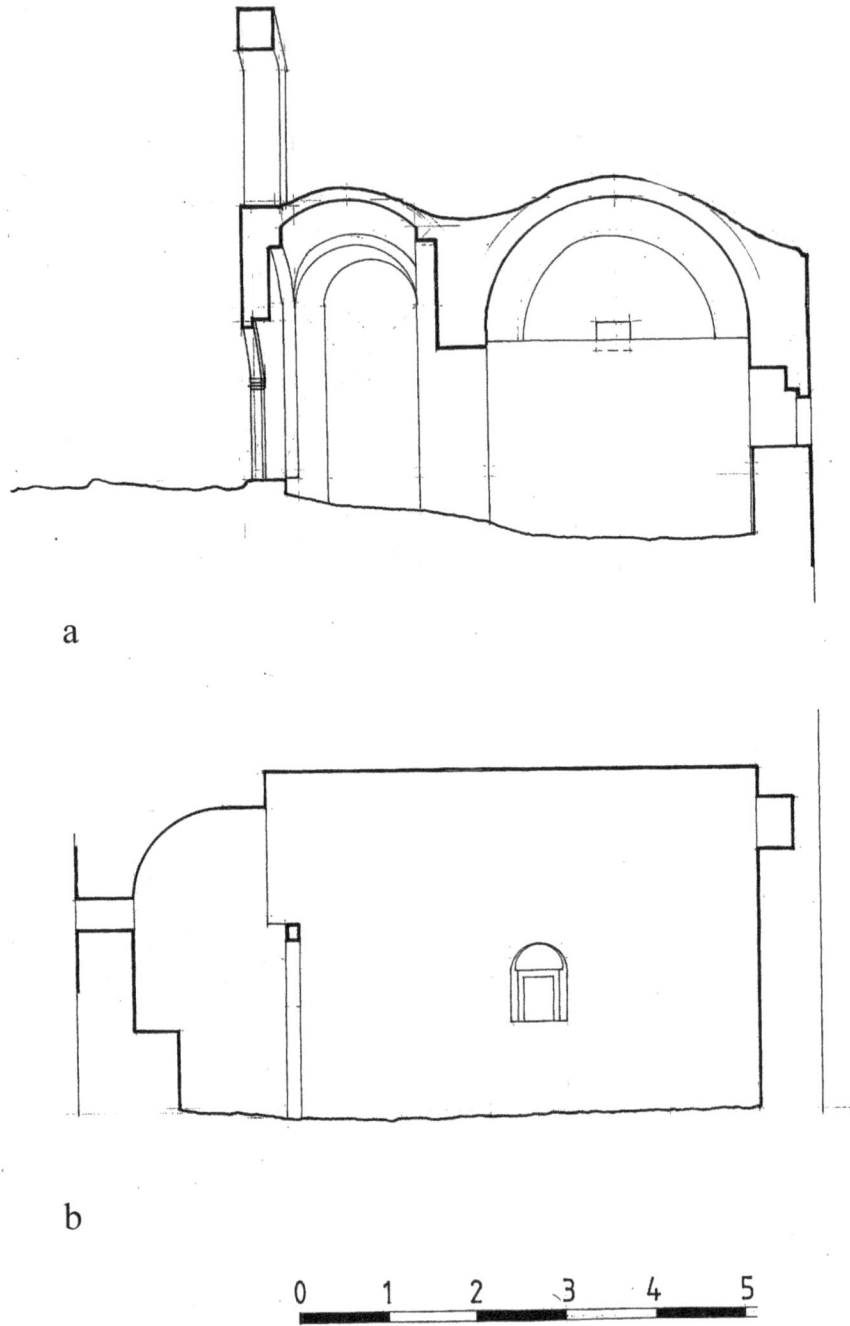

Fig. 7 Sections of church 7 (Agios Antonios) a. looking east; b. looking south

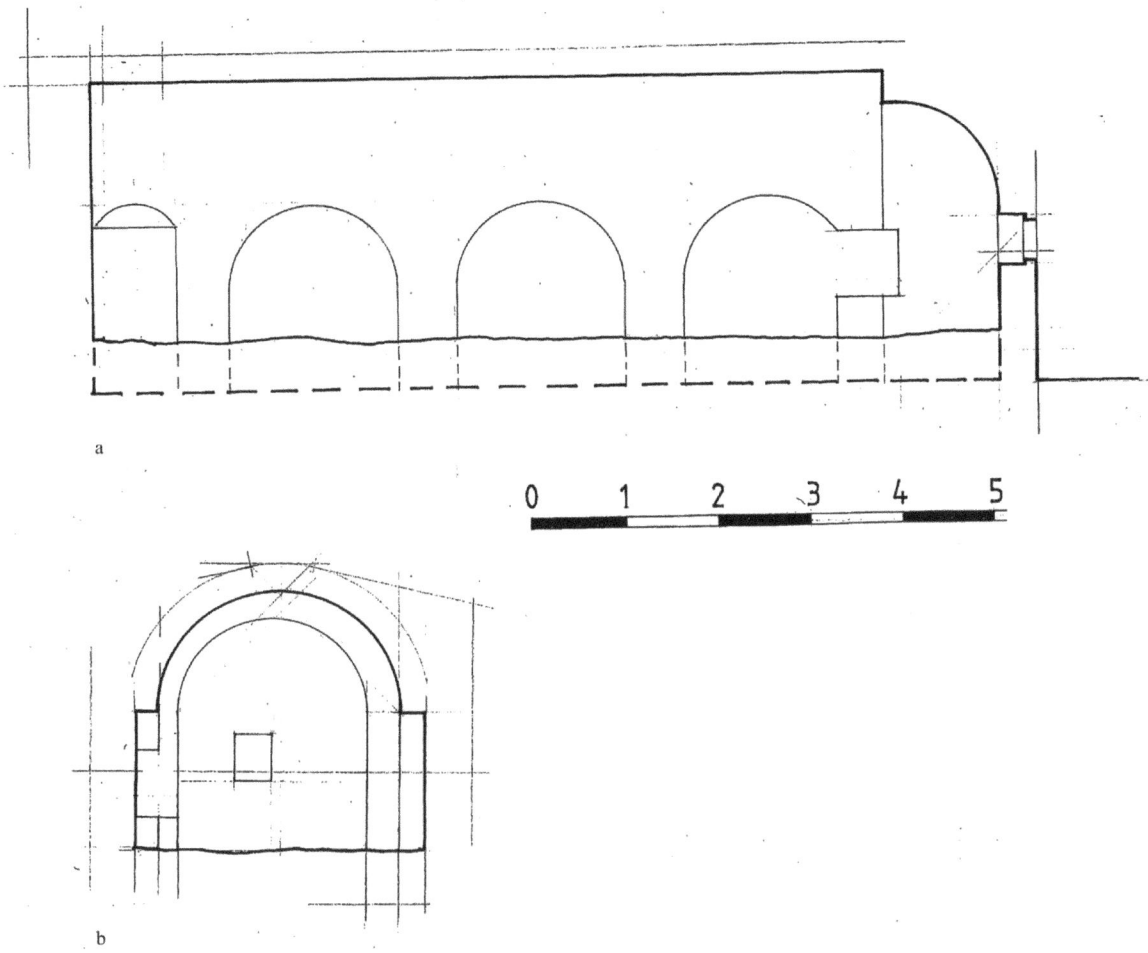

Fig. 8 Section across church 6, a. looking north, survey of east end, reconstruction of west end; b. looking east

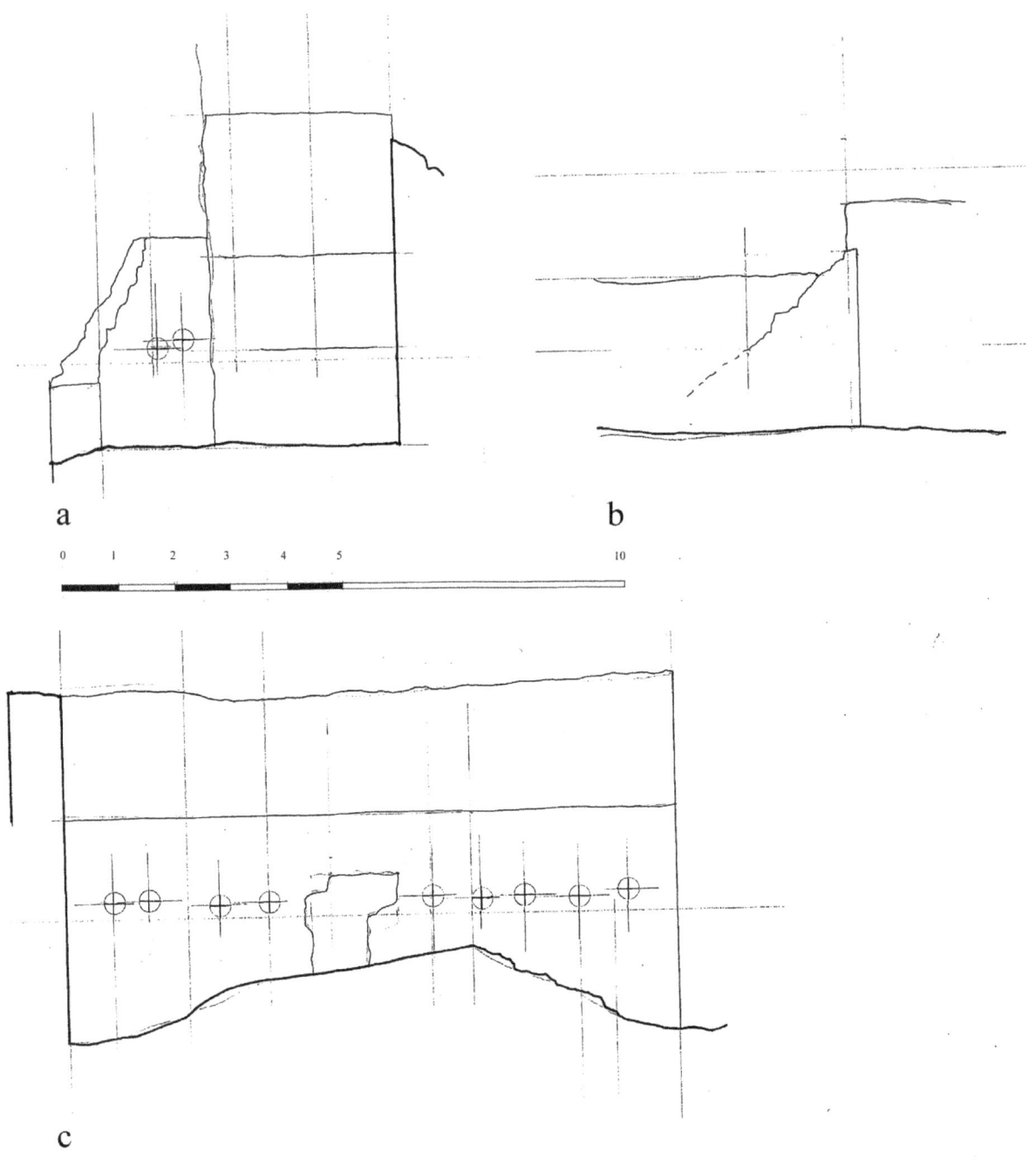

Fig. 9 Building behind church 6, a. cross-section looking west; b. elevation of possible staircase;
c. section looking north, showing location of postholes.

54

Fig. 10 Reconstruction of churches 6 and 7, with adjoining buildings

Church 4

Defensive
wall

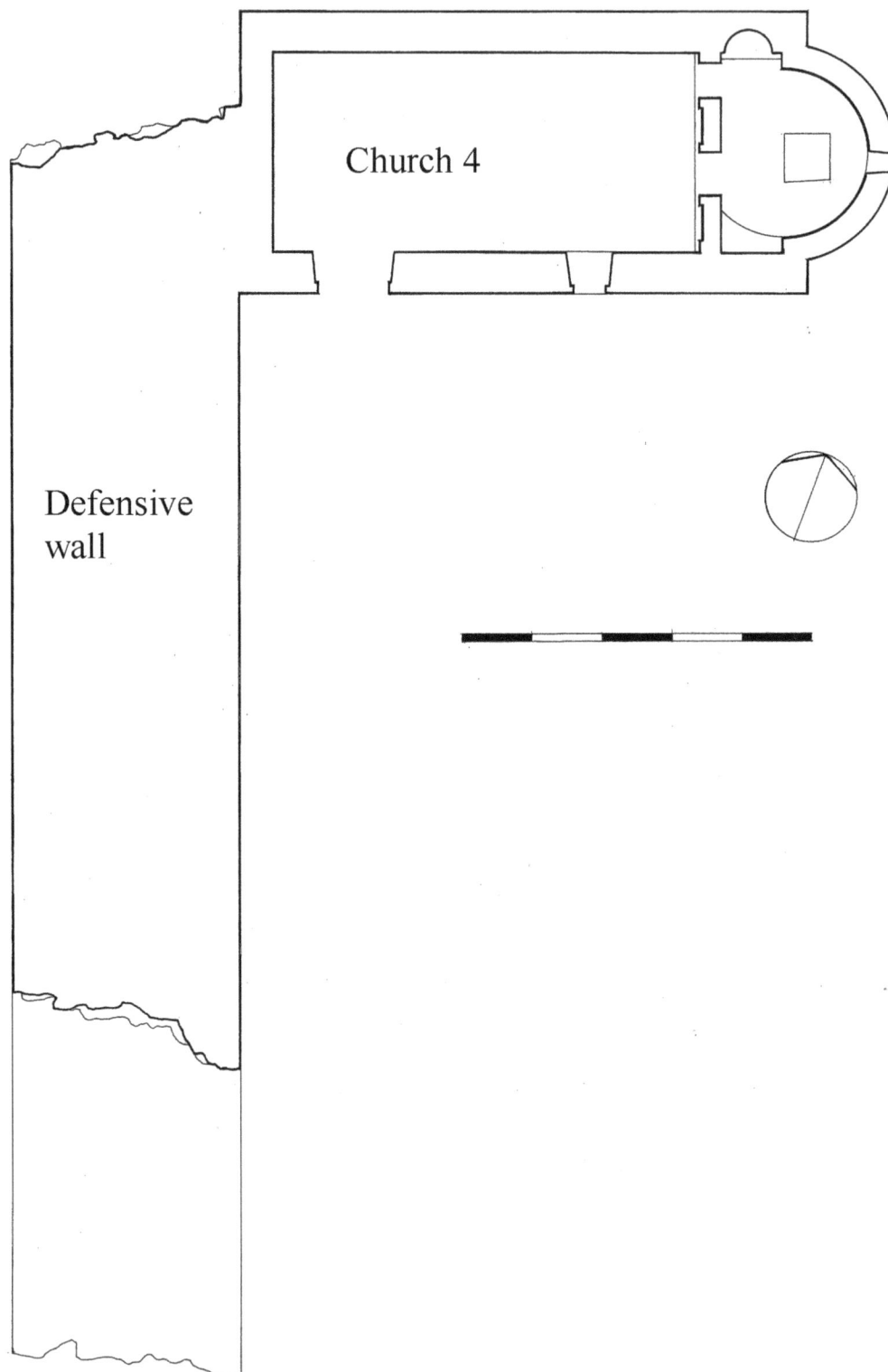

Fig.11 Plan of church 4 (Kyra tou Forou) with attached defensive wall

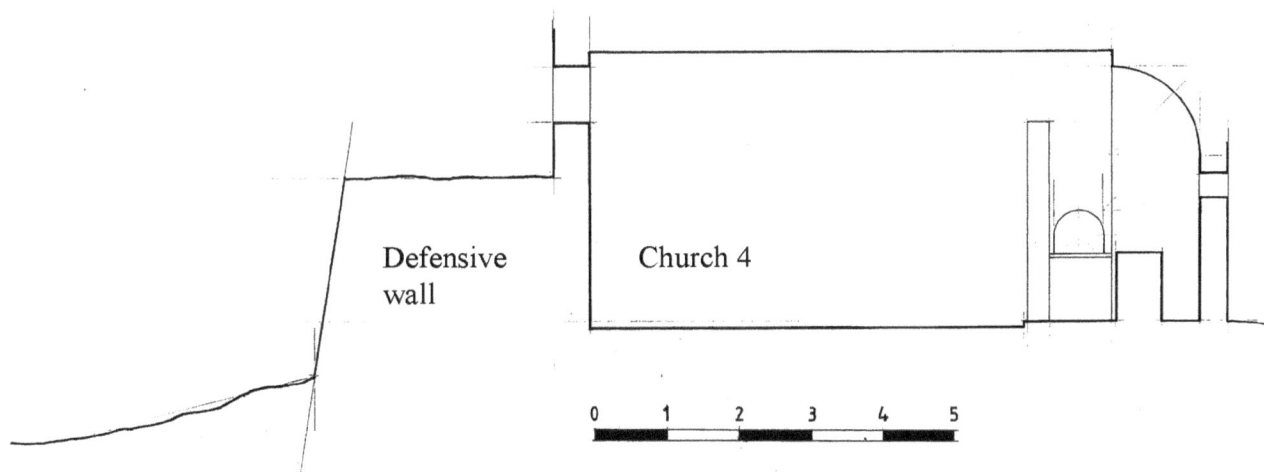

Fig. 12 Section of church 4 (Kyra tou Forou) with attached defensive wall (see figure 59)

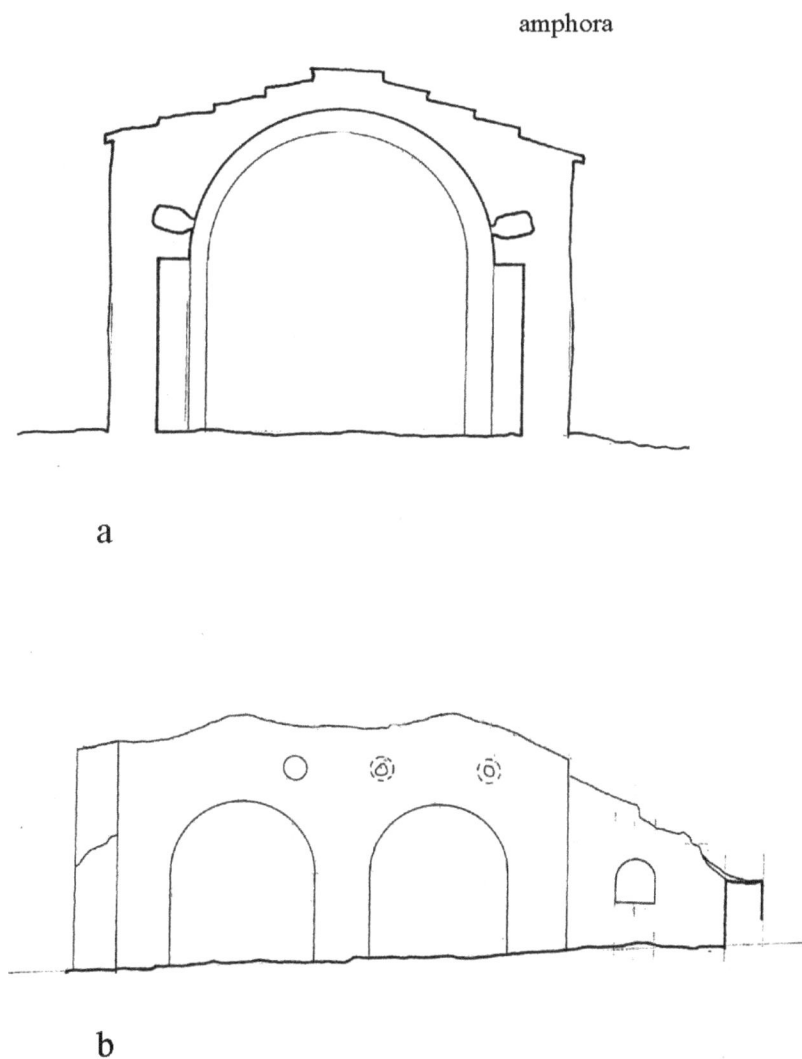

amphora

a

b

Fig. 13 Church 3 sections. a. cross-section reconstruction, showing amphorae set in the thickness of the wall; b. longitudinal section showing the actual state of the church, inclueding positioning of amphorae.

entry

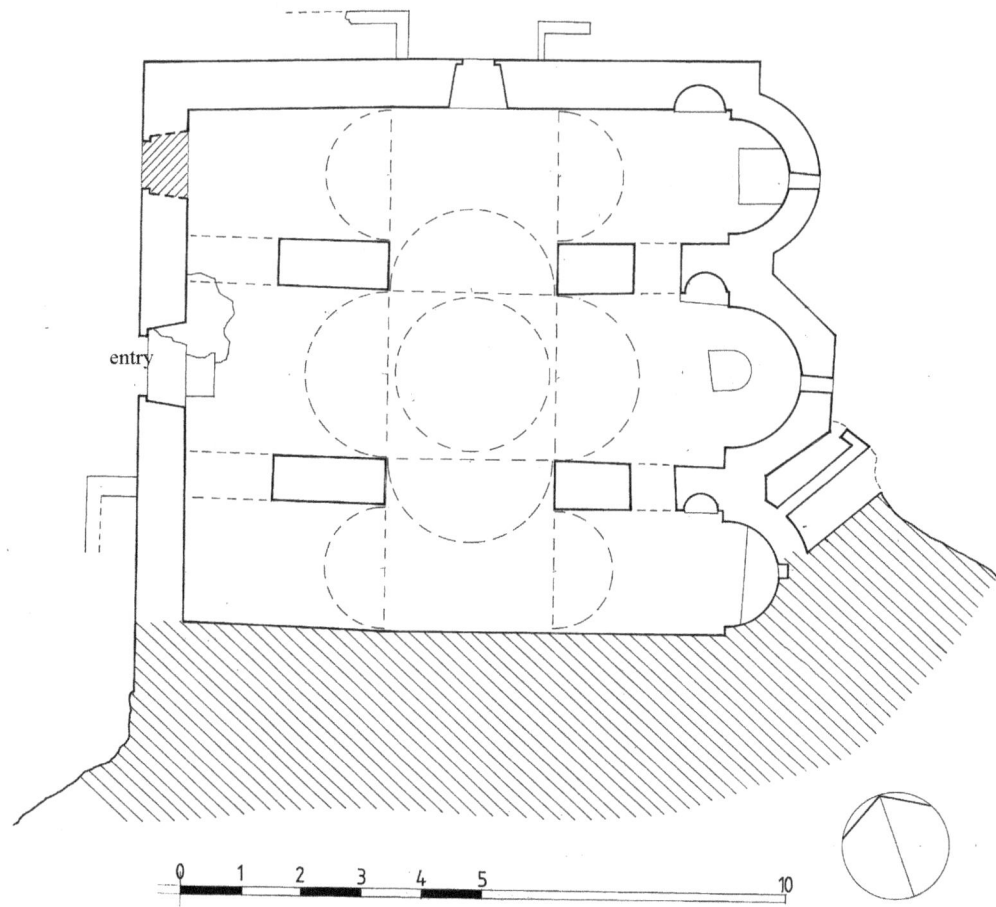

Fig. 14 Plan of church 1 (Agia Barbara)

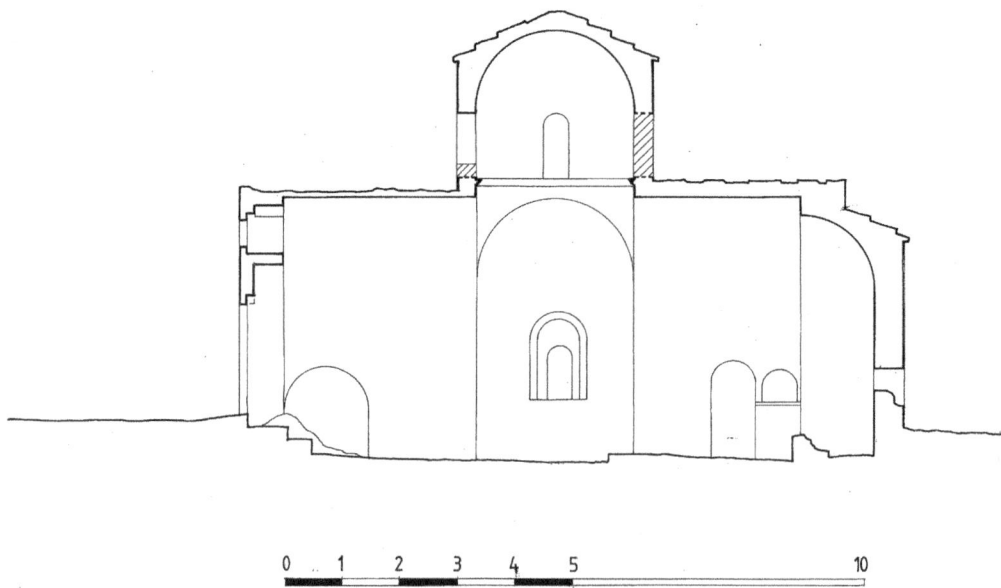

Fig. 15 Section: east-west elevation; north elevation through Church 1 (Agia Barbara)

House

Scale in metres

0   1   2   3   4   5   6

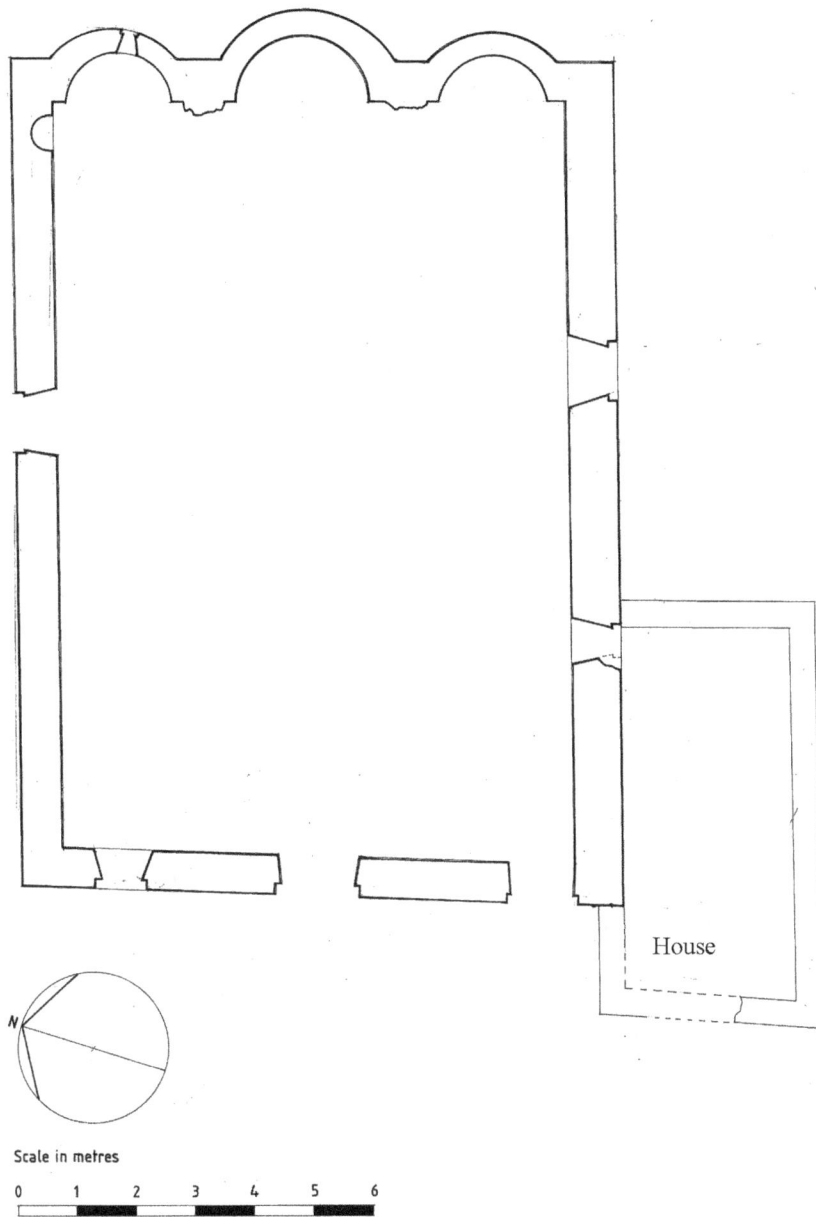

Fig. 16: Church 5 and attached house.

Narthex

Church 16

Church 17

Church 15

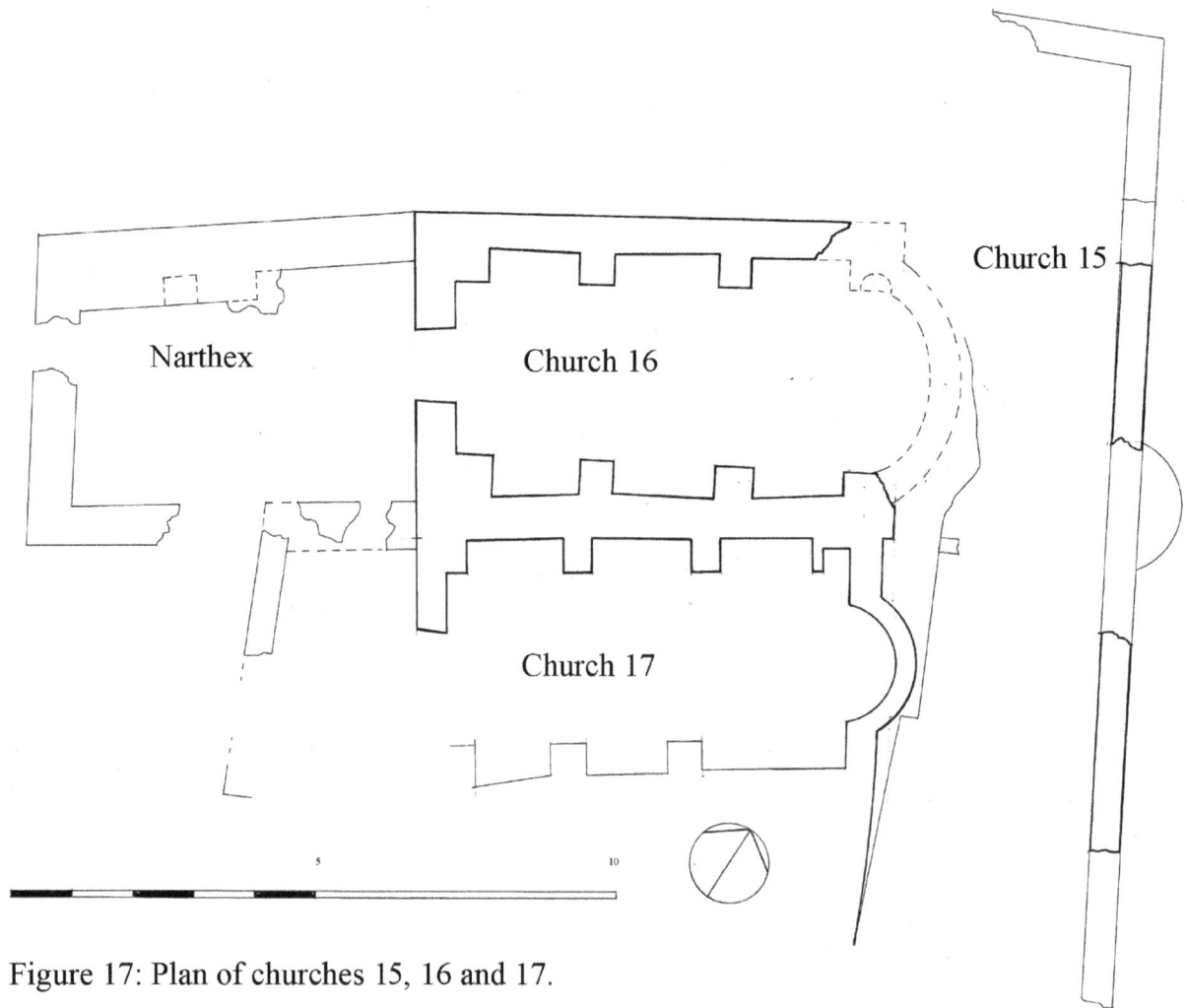

Figure 17: Plan of churches 15, 16 and 17.

Church 17

exterior
of apse

Church 16
(beyond)

Church 15

Blind arcade

0   1   2   3   4   5   10

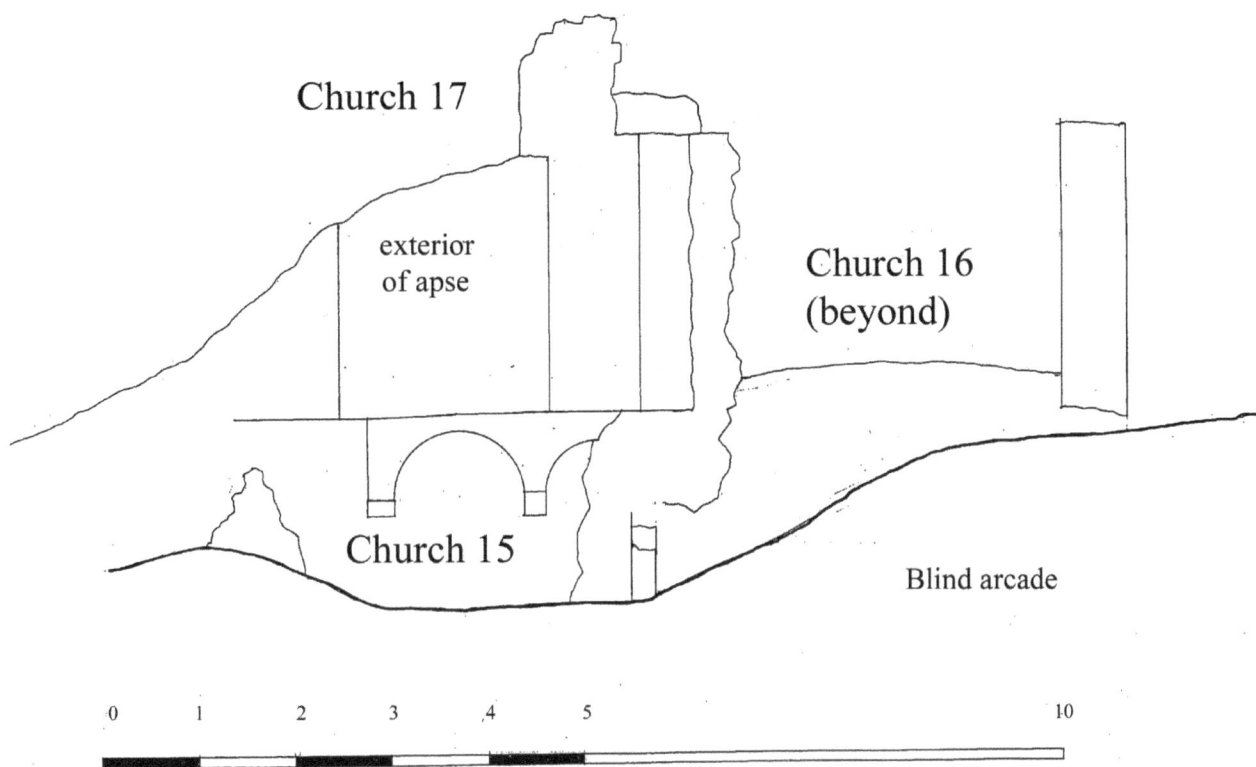

Fig. 18 Section along Church 15, looking east

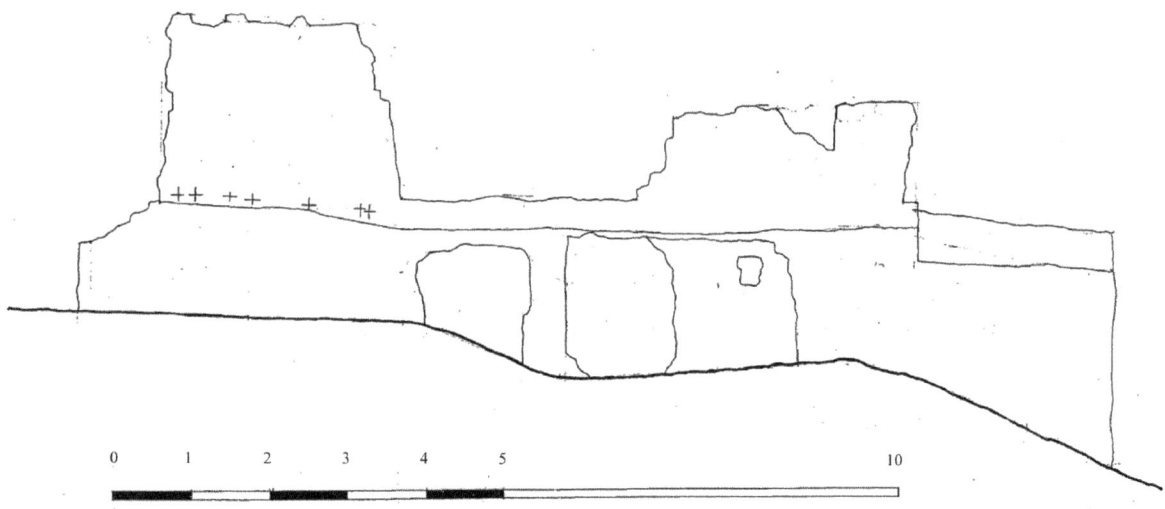

Fig. 19 Plan of church 15

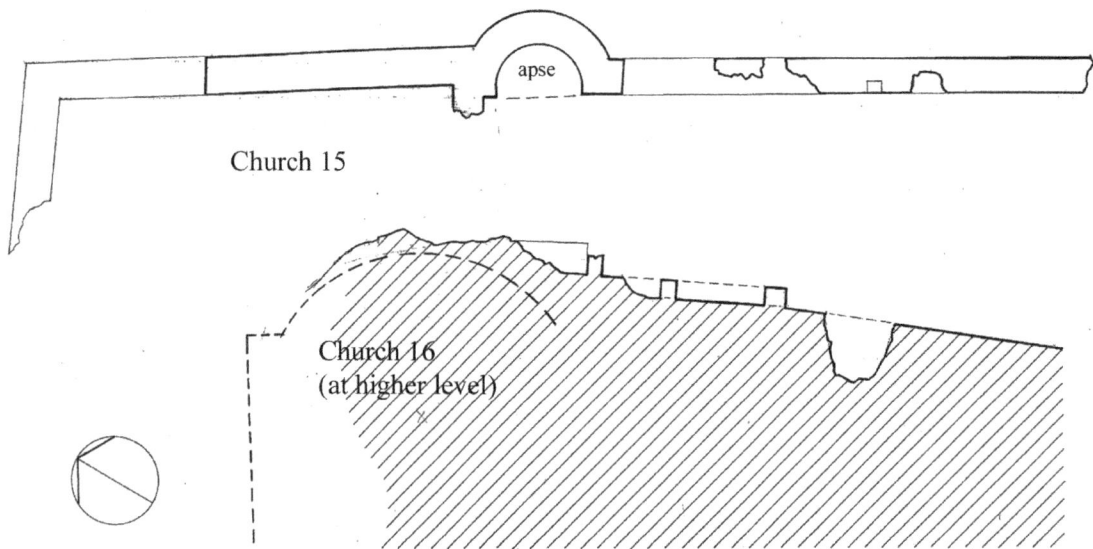

Church 15

apse

Church 16
(at higher level)

Fig. 20. Section along church 15, looking west

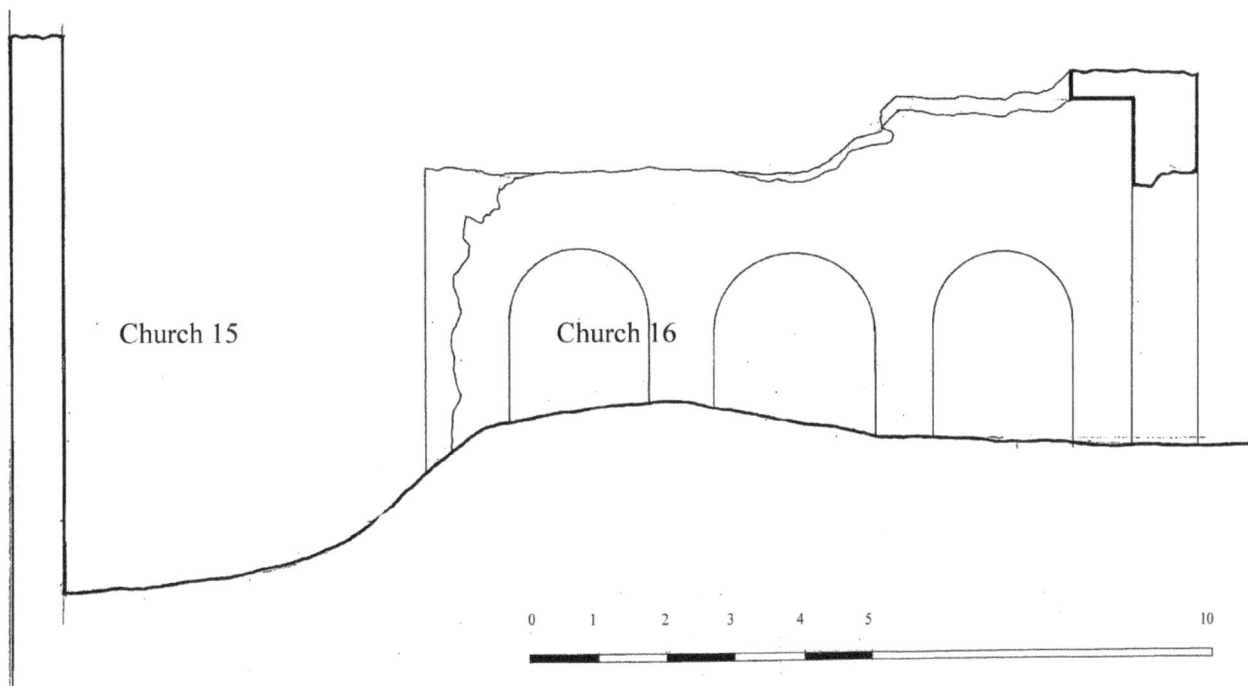

Church 15

Church 16

0   1   2   3   4   5   10

Fig. 21 Section across church 15 and along church 16, looking north

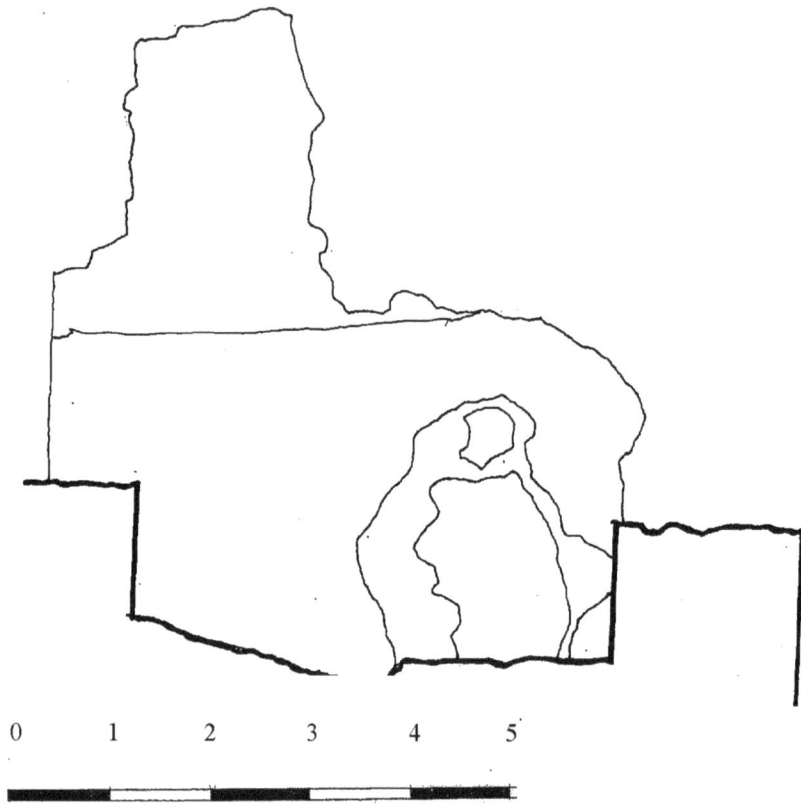

0   1   2   3   4   5

a

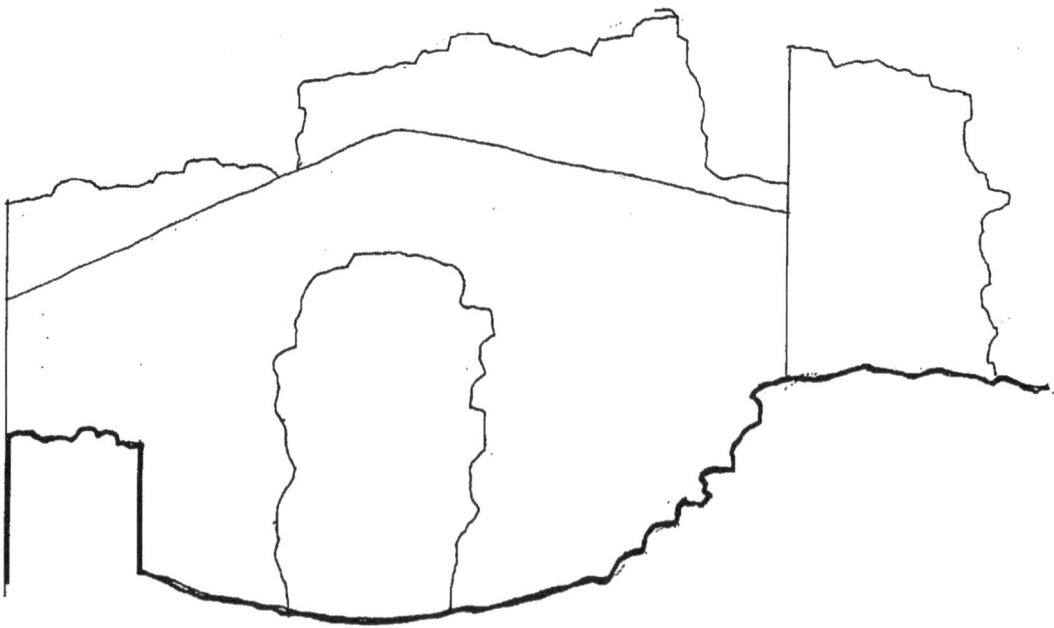

b

Fig. 22 Section across narthex of church 16, a. looking west; b. looking east

Fig. 23 Reconstruction of churches 15, 16 and 17, with dwellings at lower level in the foreground

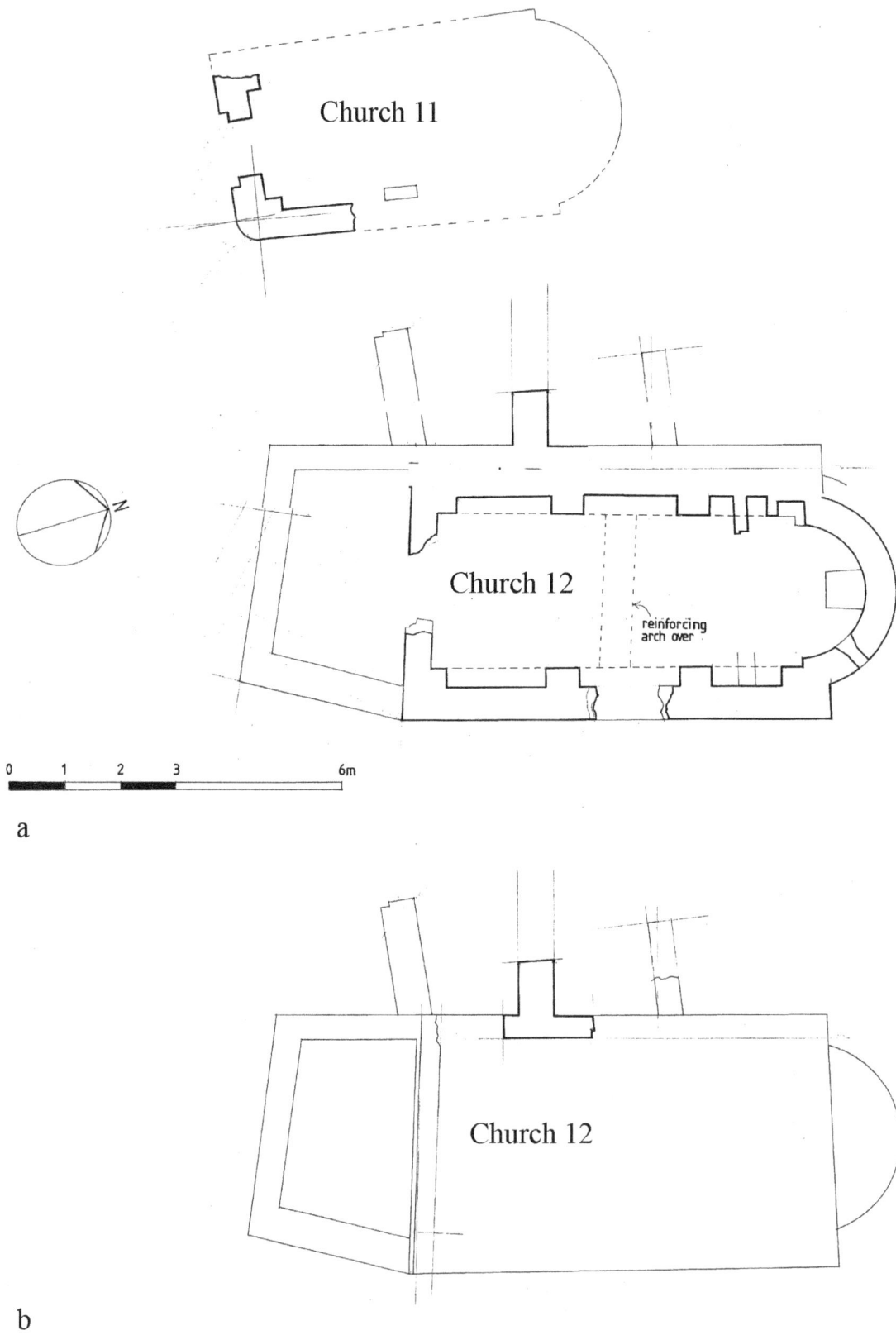

Church 11

Church 12

reinforcing
arch over

N

0 1 2 3   6m

a

Church 12

b

Fig. 24 Plans of churches 11 and 12. a. in relation to each other; b. roof plan of church 12.

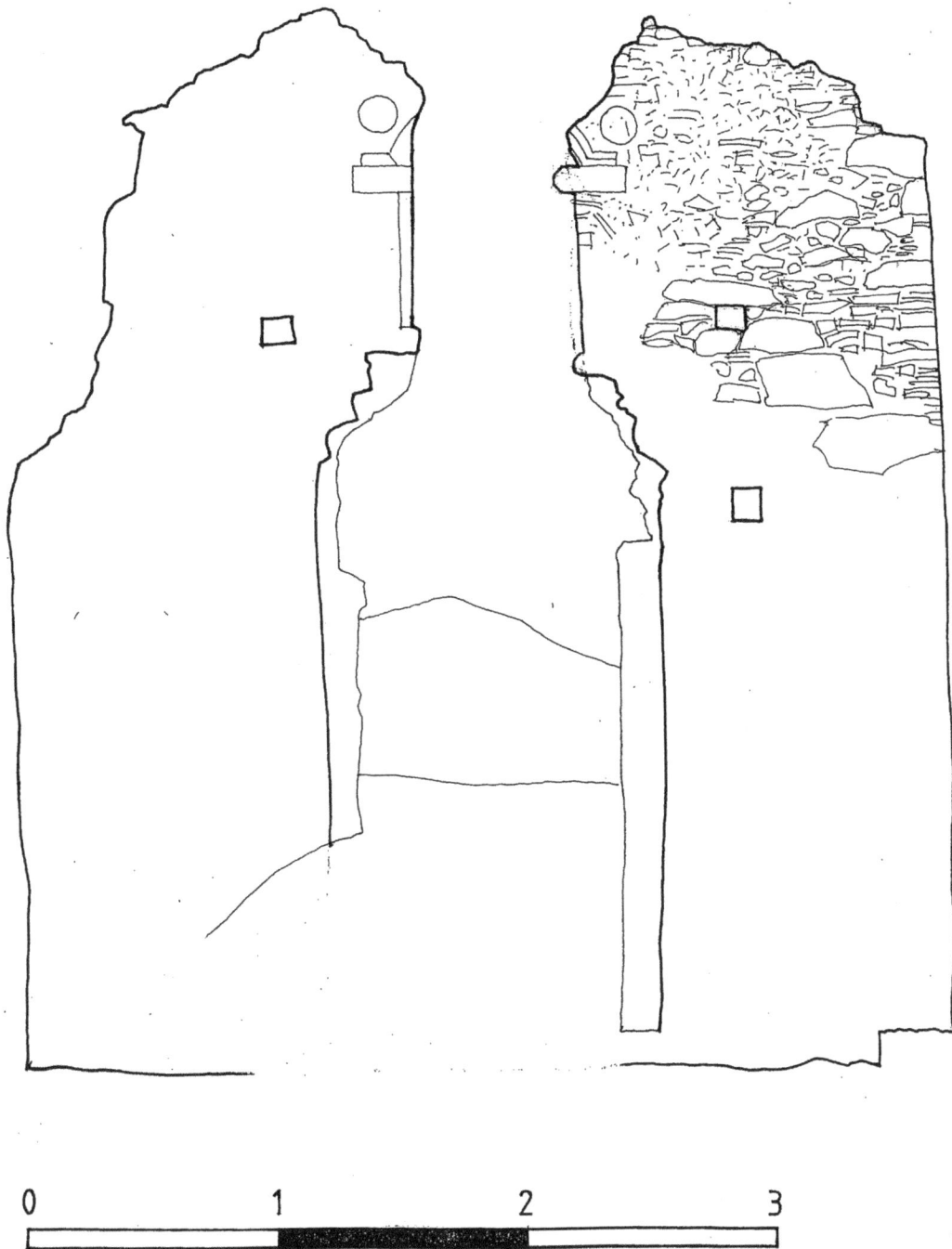

Fig. 25 Elevation of church 11, entrance front

line of masonry at lower level

Church 20

Church 19 (above)

retaining wall with
buttresses (below)

0   1   2   3   4   5   10

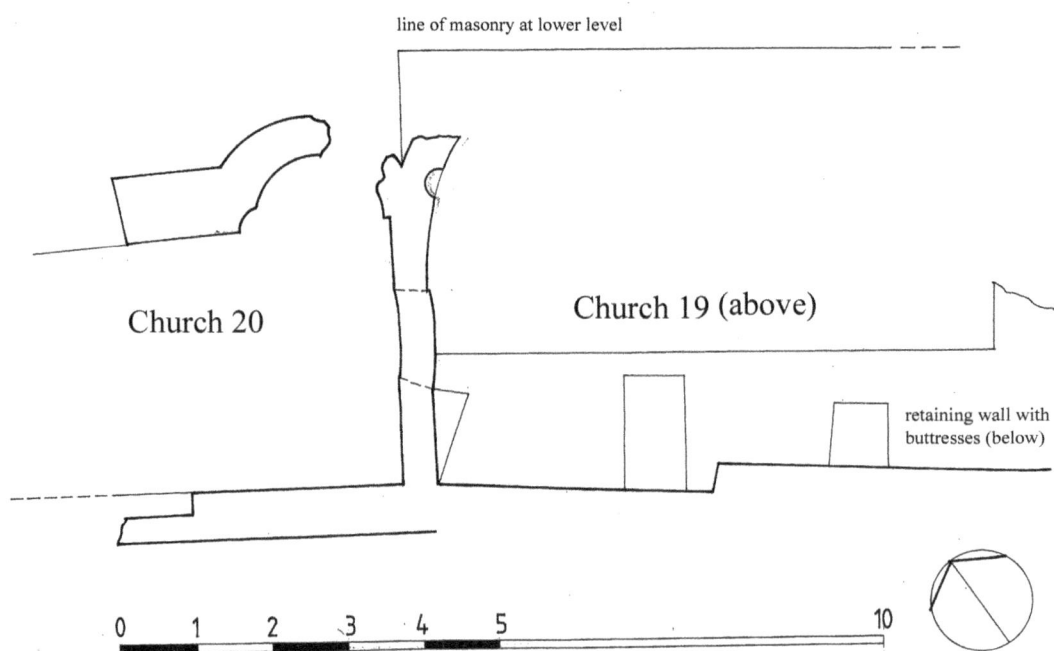

Fig. 26 Plan of churches 19 and 20

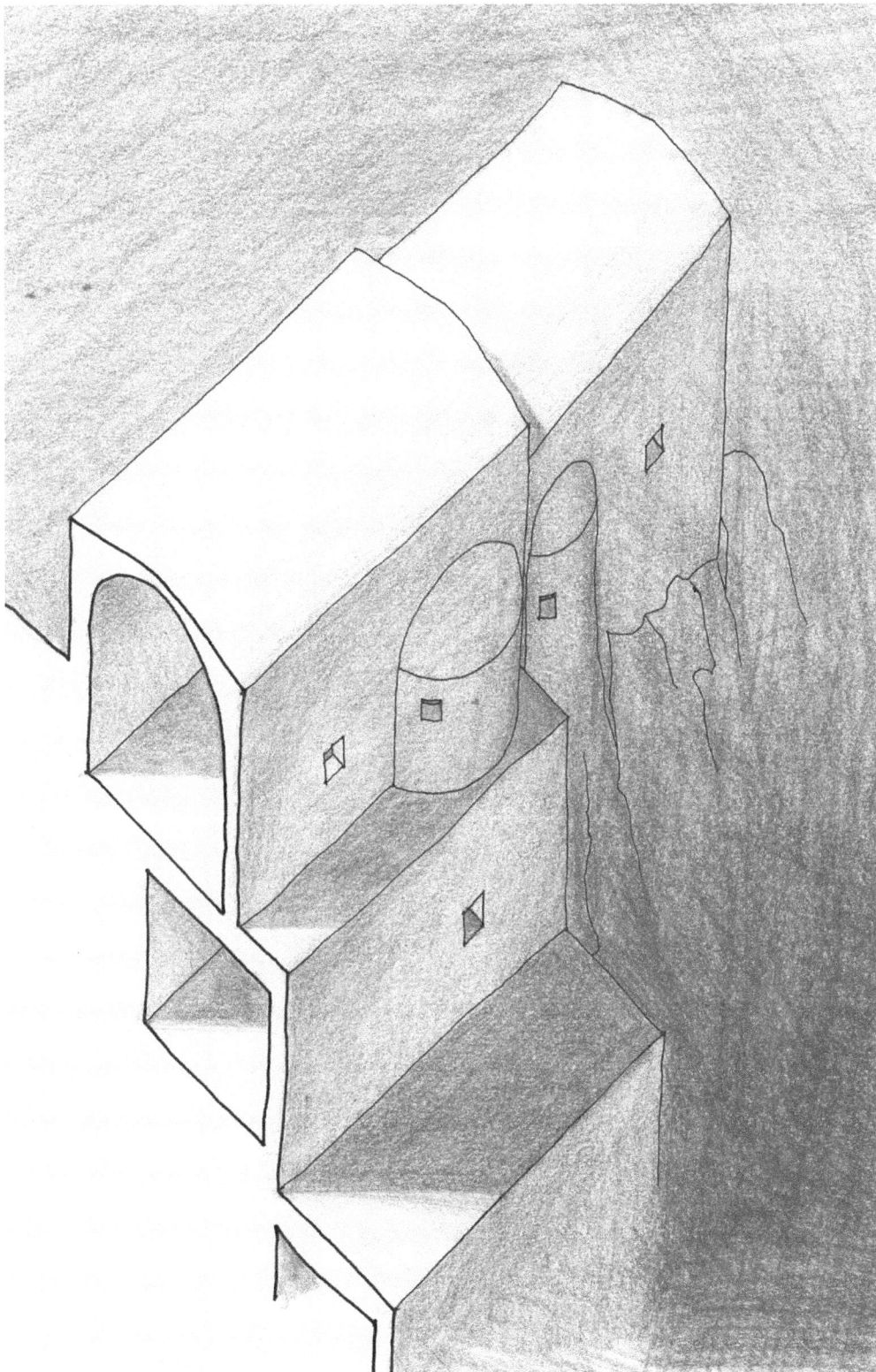

Fig. 27 Reconstruction of churches 19 and 20 and dwellings beneath

a

b

c

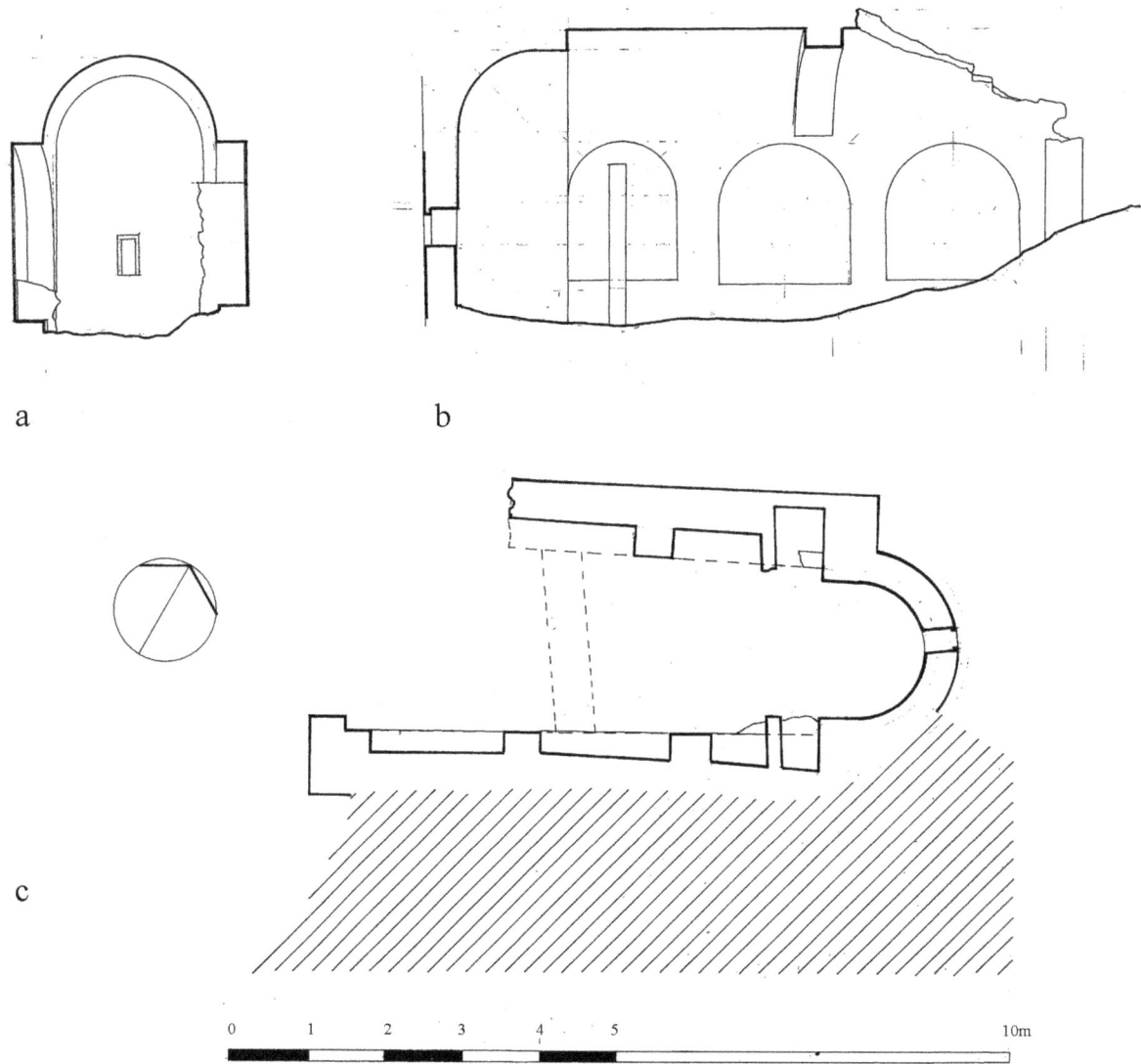

Fig. 28   Church 21. a. section looking east; b. section looking south; c. plan.

Church 22

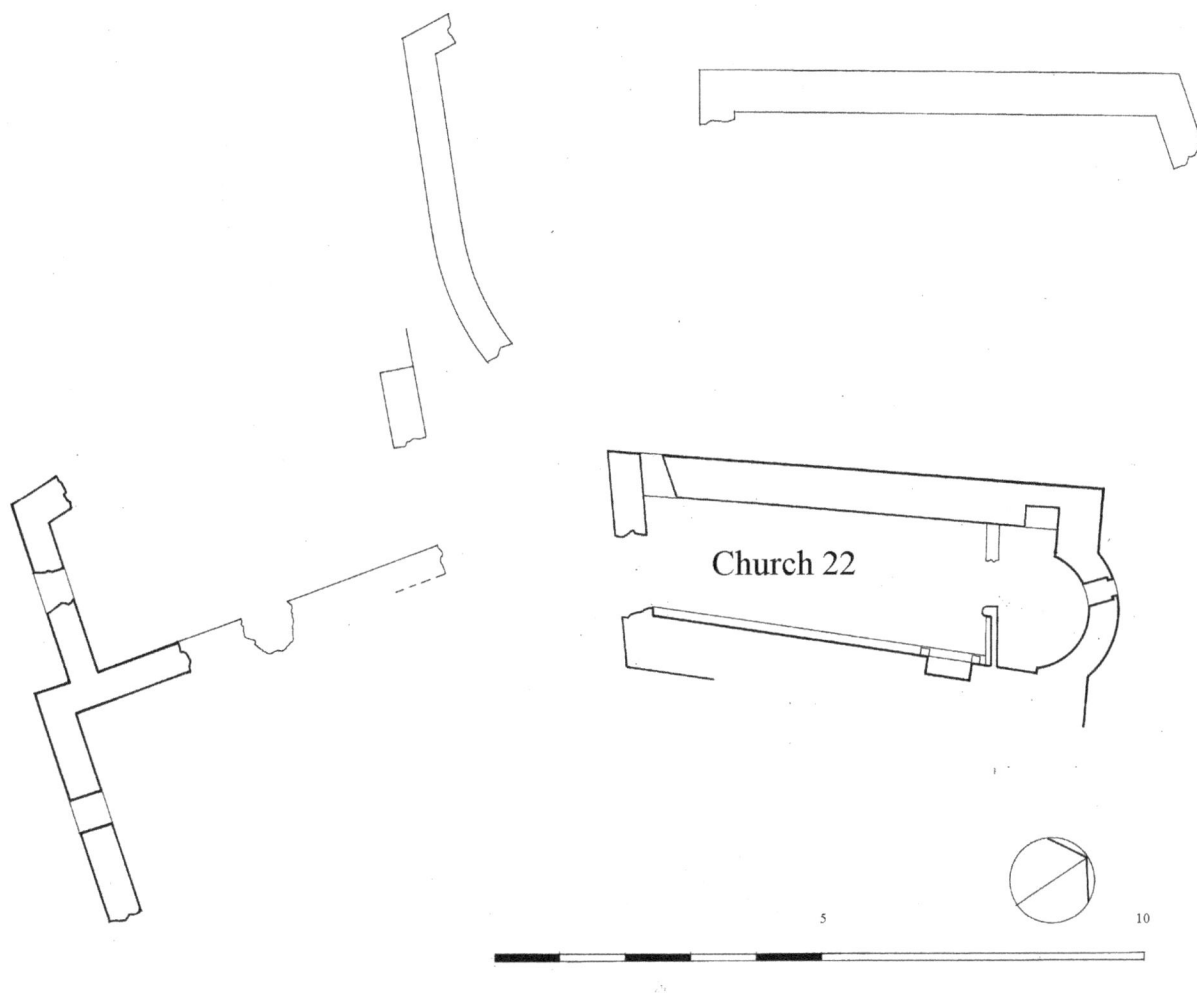

Fig. 29 Plan of church 22 and houses

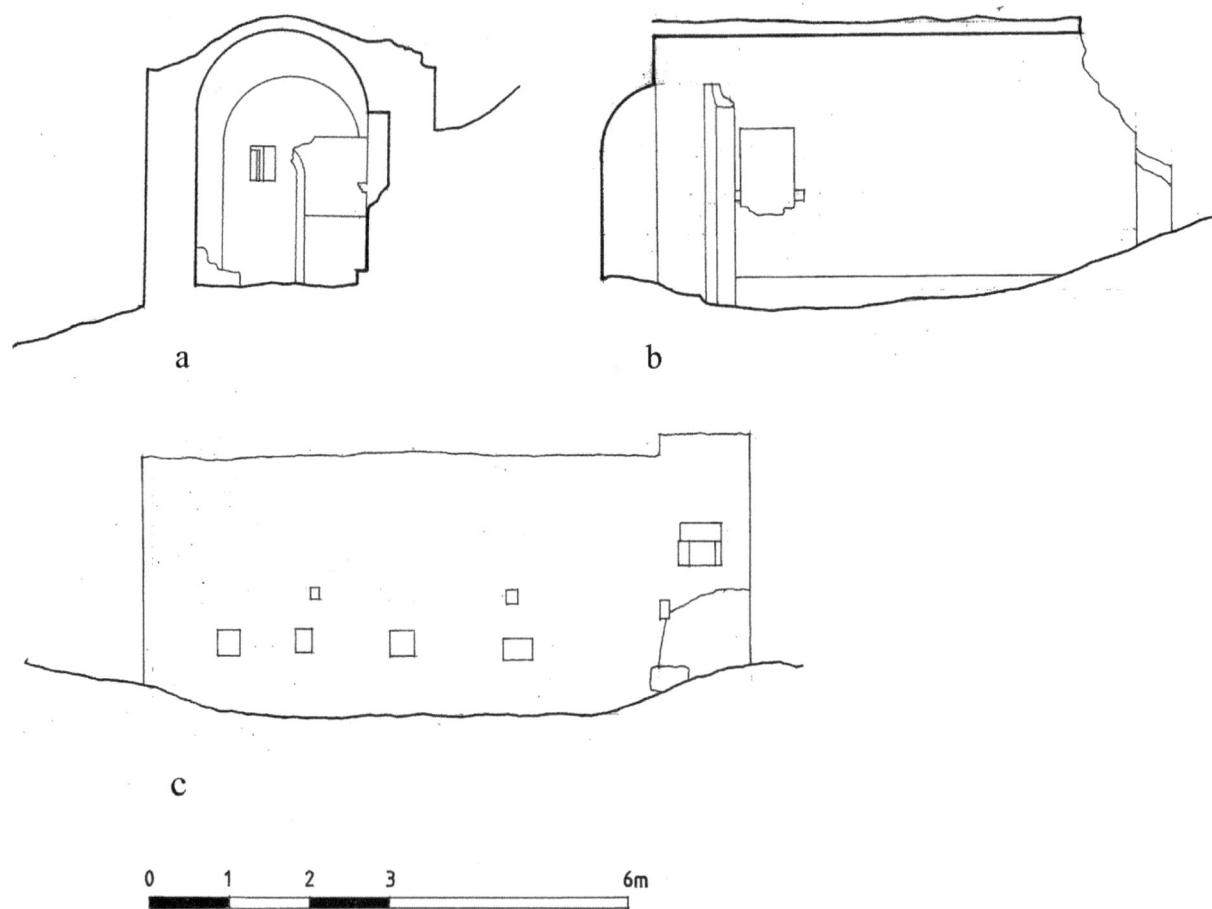

a

b

c

0   1   2   3   6m

Fig. 30 Section through church 22. a. looking west; b. looking south;
c. north elevation showing scaffolding holes and small windiw at west end.

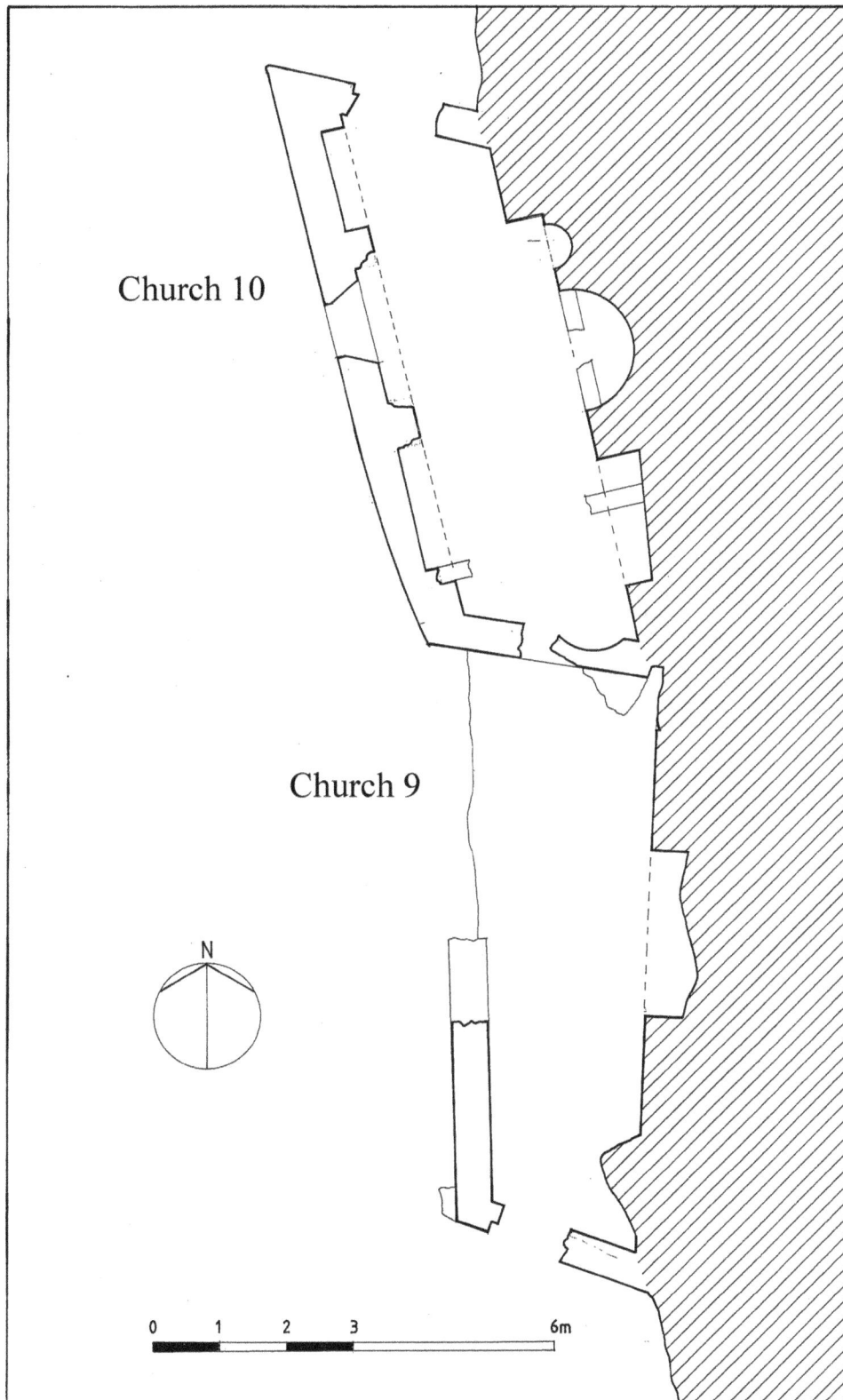

Church 10

Church 9

N

0   1   2   3   6m

Fig. 31 Plan of churches 9 and 10

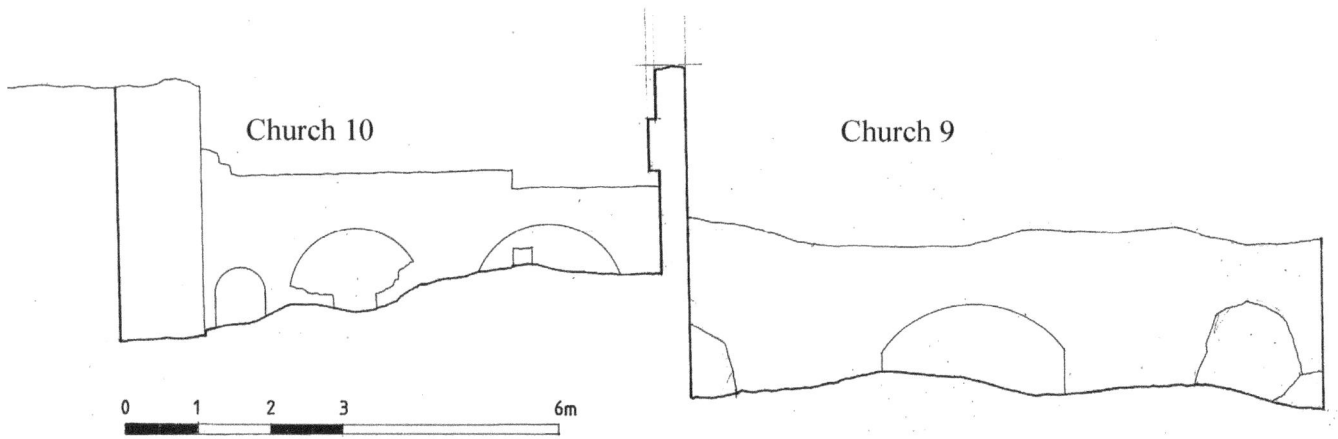

Fig. 32 Section along churches 9 and 10, looking east

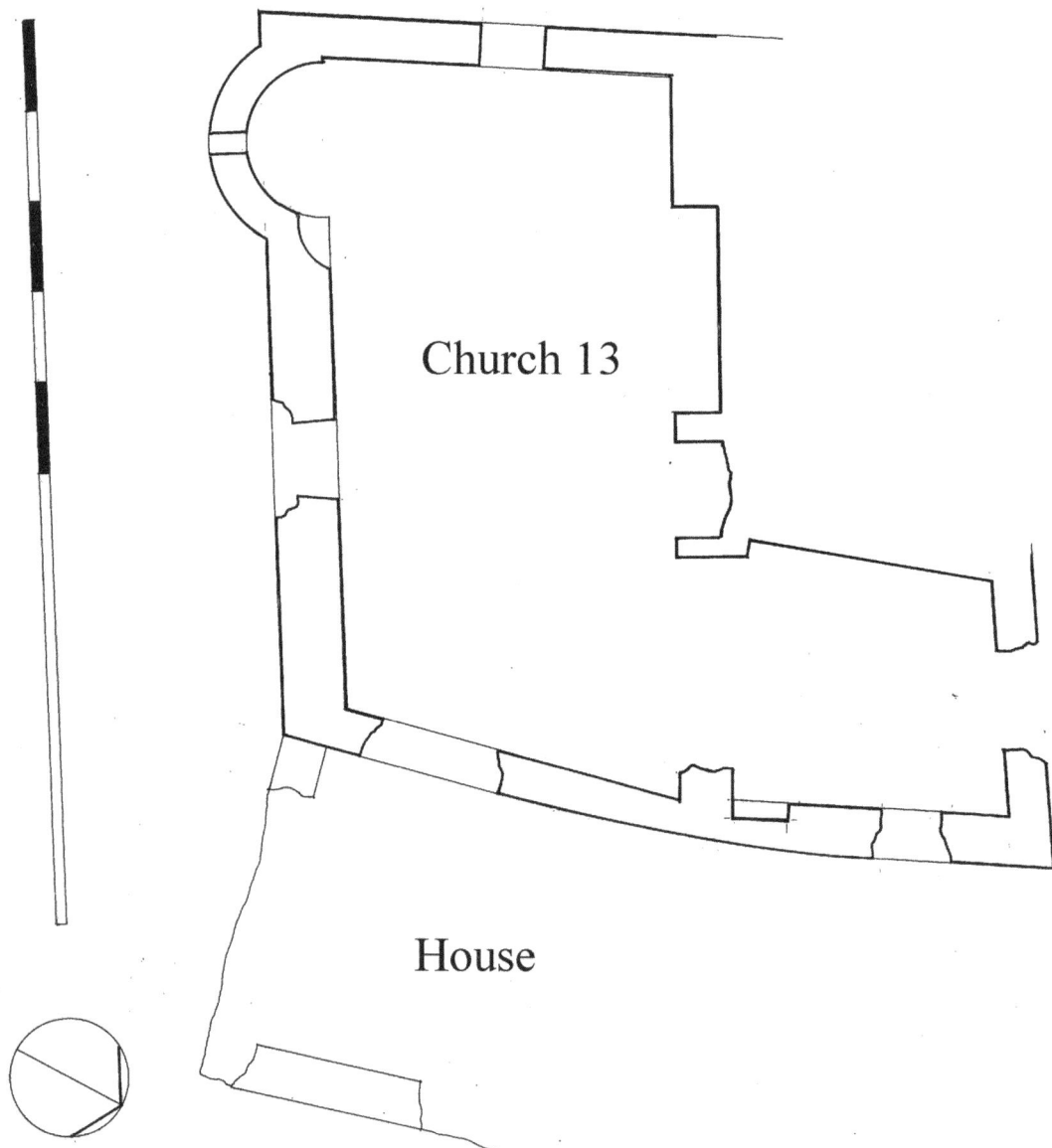

Fig. 33 Plan of church 13 and adjoining house

Church 14

N

0   1   2   3   6m

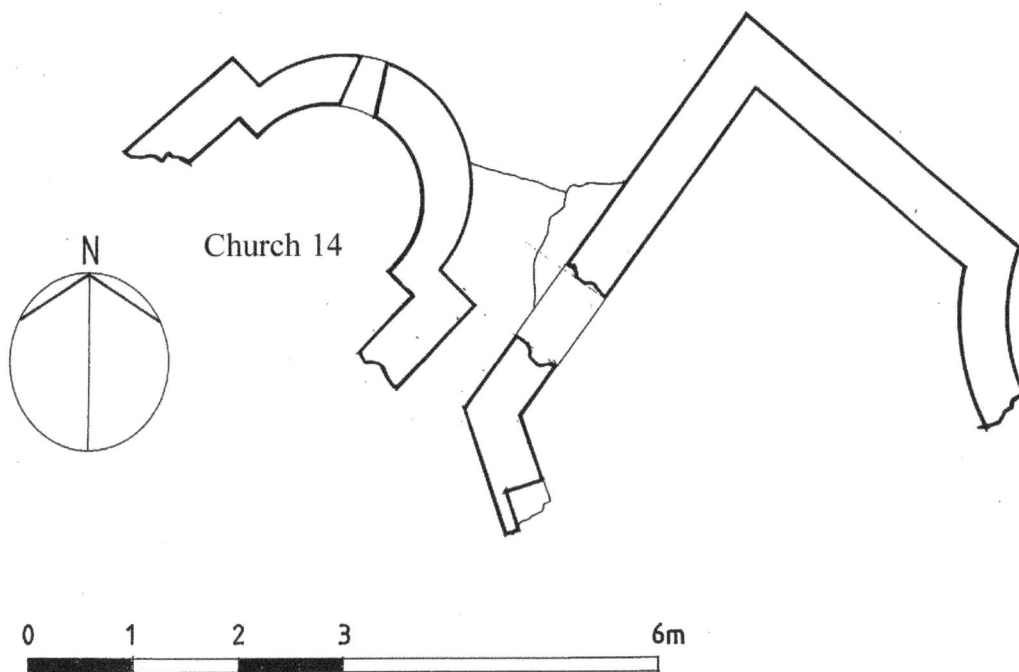

Fig. 34 Plan of church 14 and adjoining house

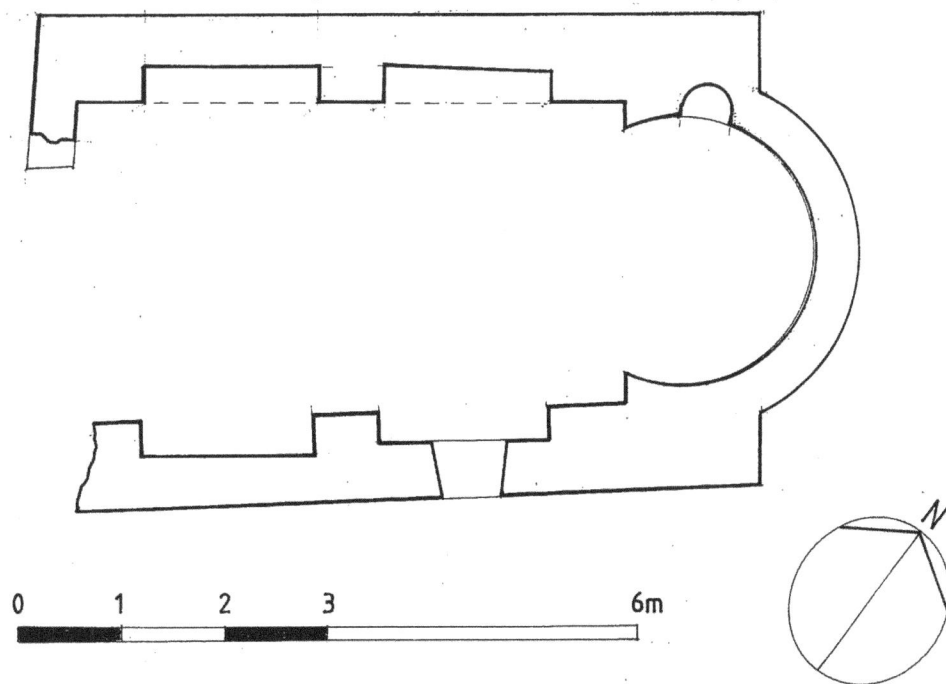

0   1   2   3   6m

N

Fig. 35 Plan of church 8

House D

House E

House F

0 1 2 3 4 5

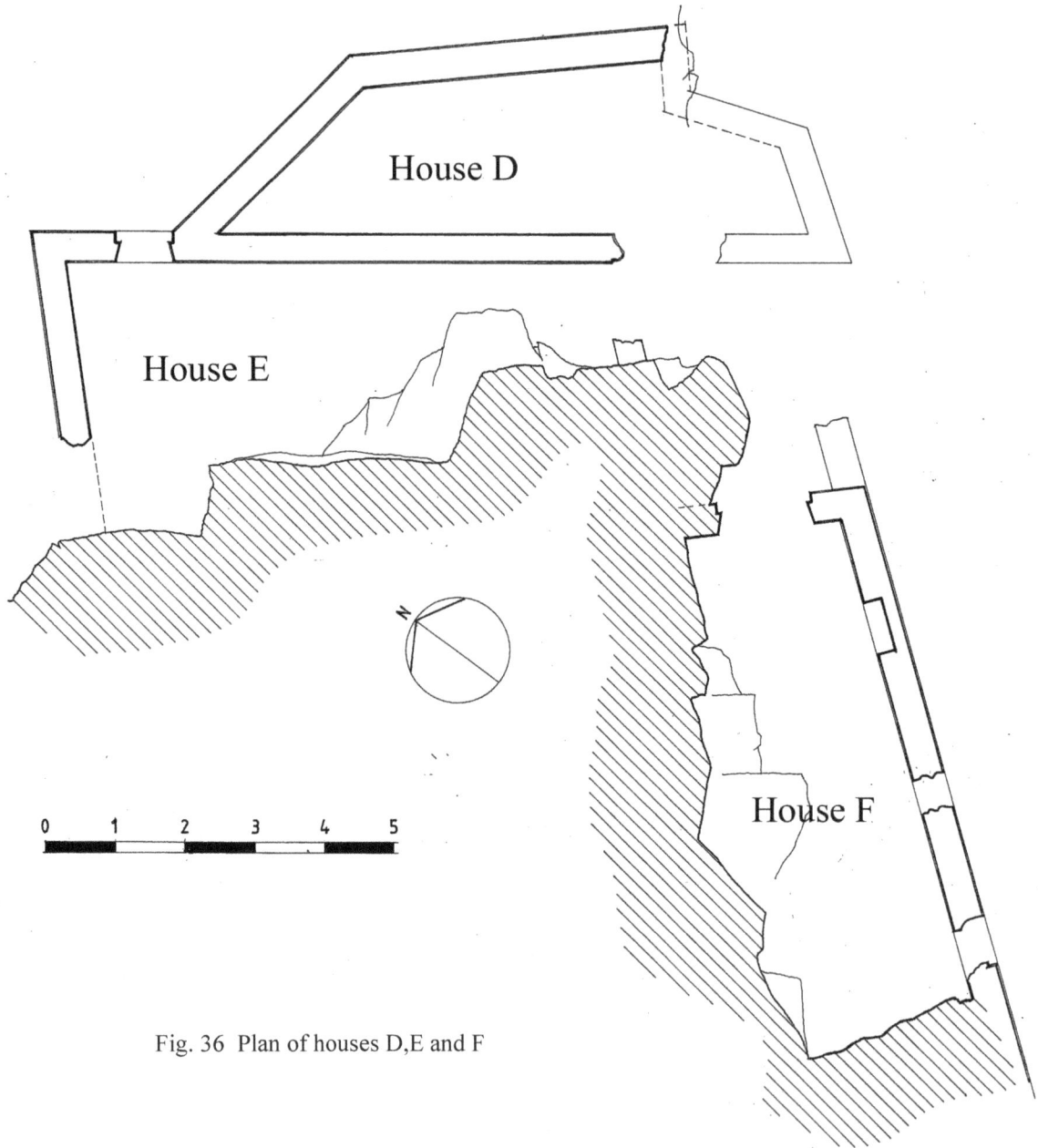

Fig. 36 Plan of houses D,E and F

House N

0   5   10m

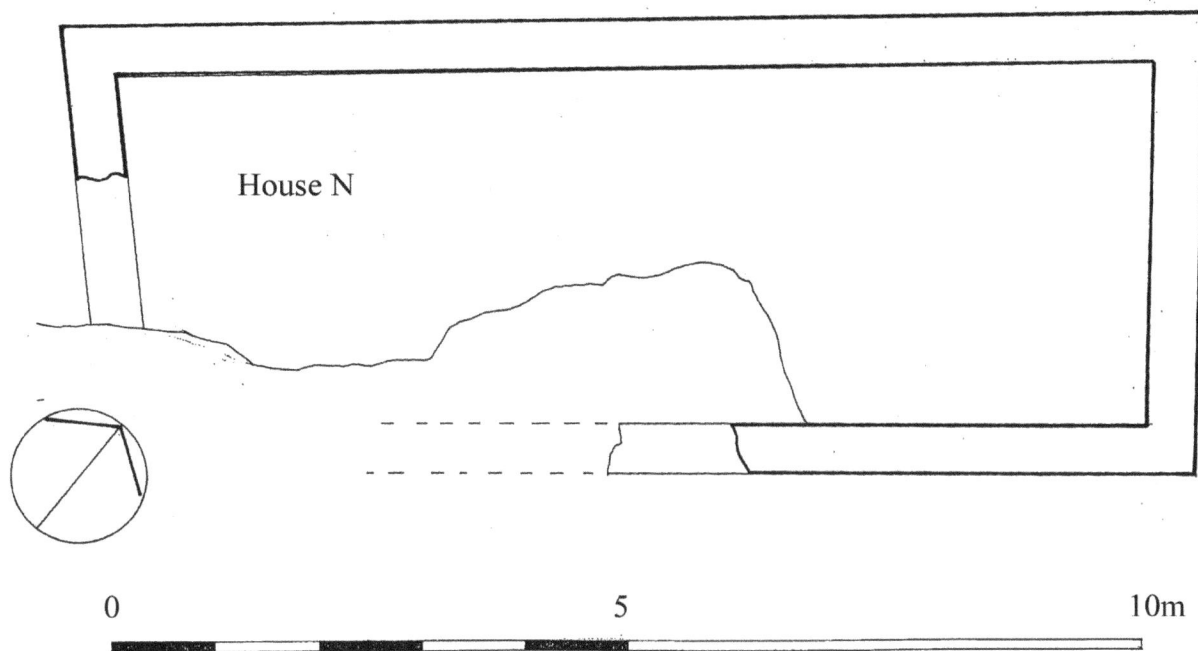

Fig. 37 Plan of house in the north of the settlement (House N)

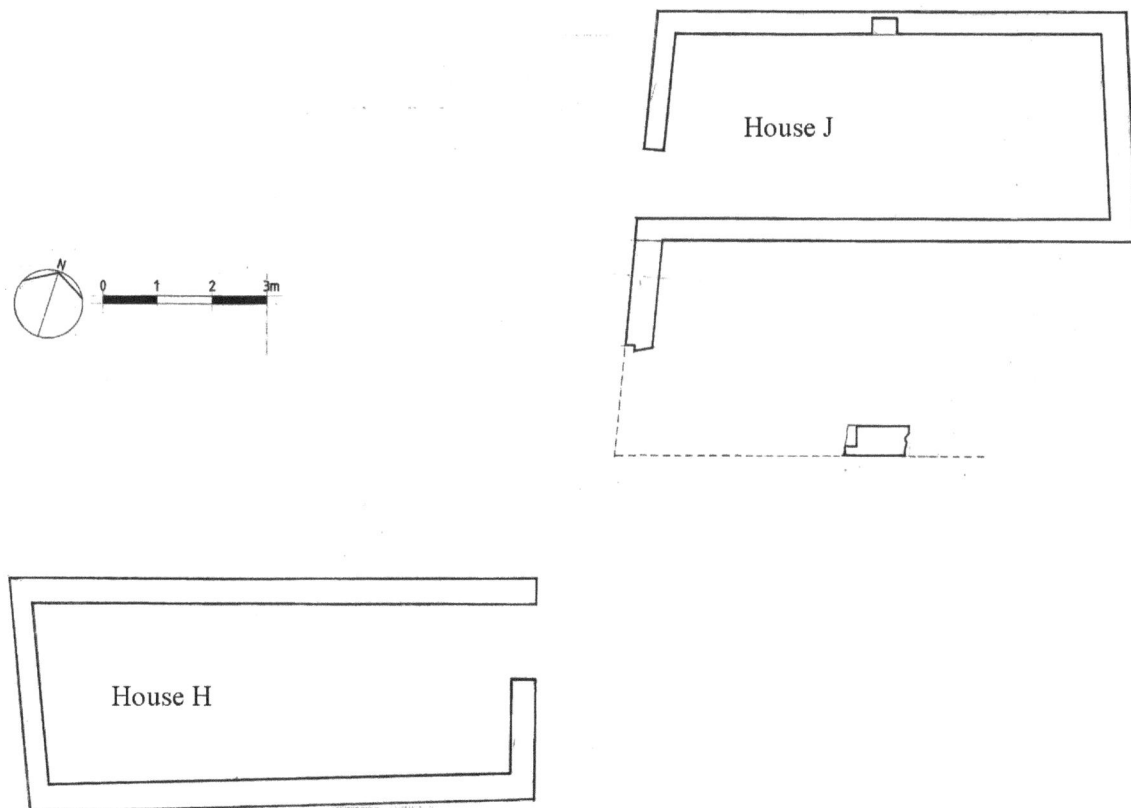

House J

0 1 2 3m

House H

Fig. 38 Plan of group of dwellings (H and J) situated south of the settlement

a

b

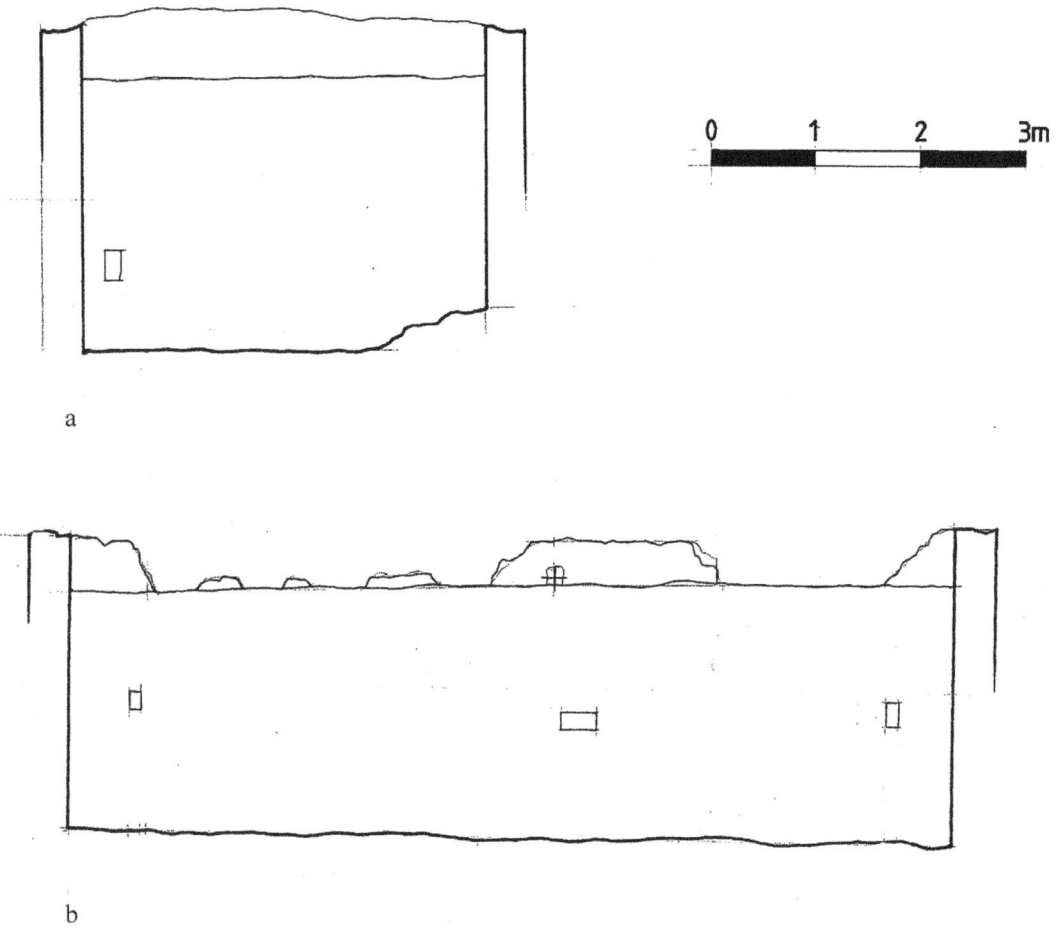

Fig. 39 House H. a. section looking west; b. section looking south.

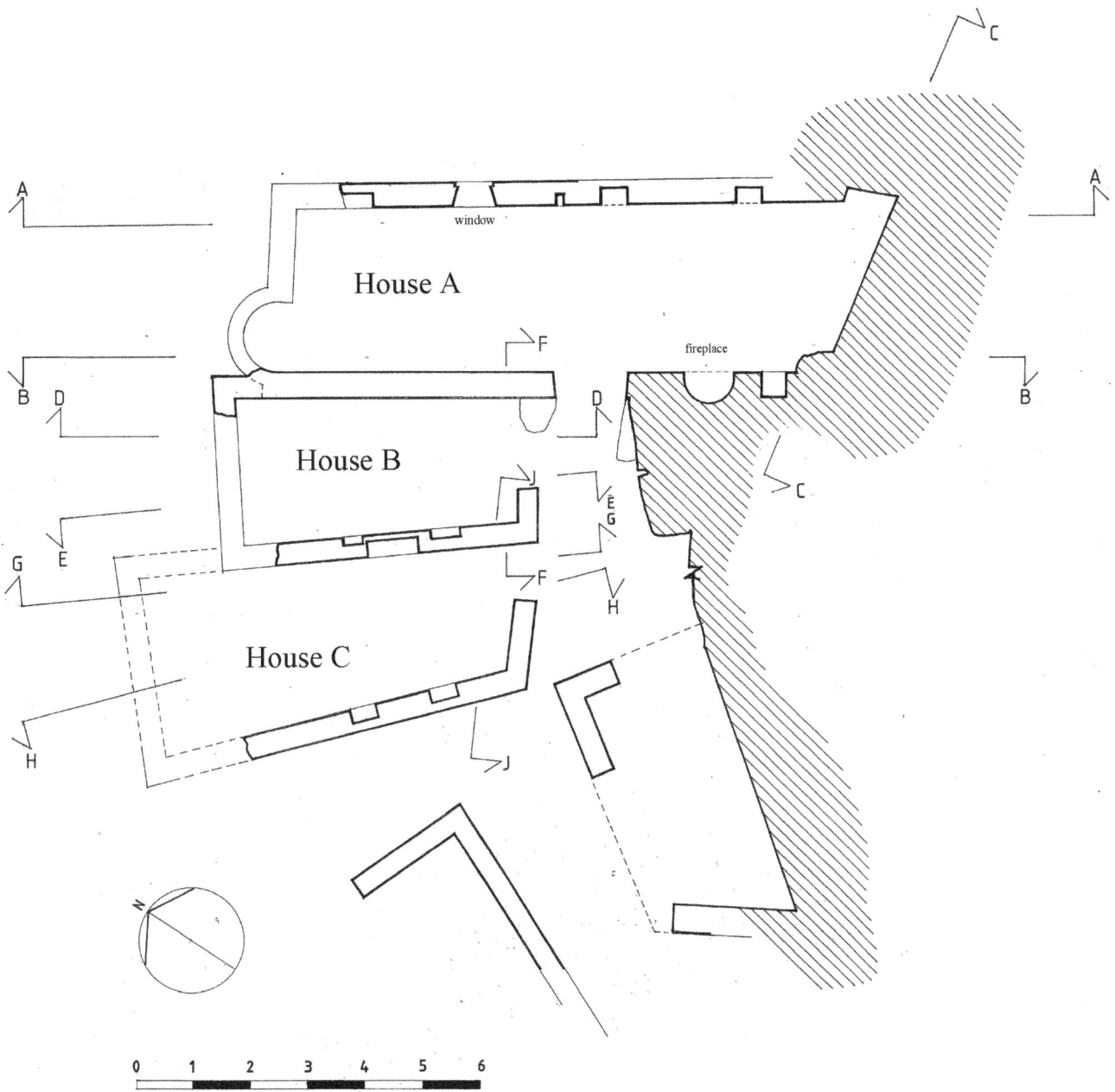

Fig. 40 Plan of Houses A,B and C

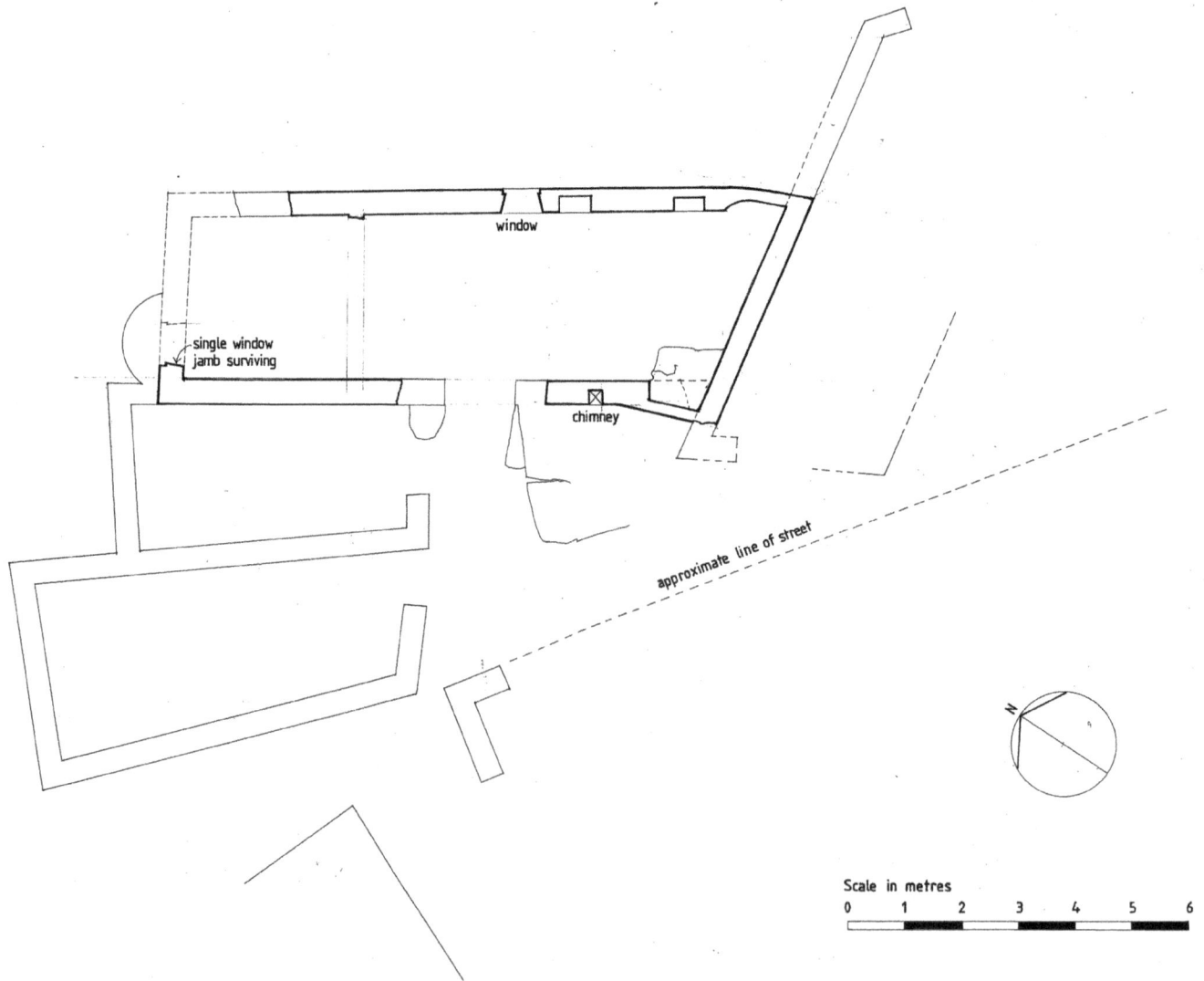

single window
jamb surviving

window

chimney

approximate line of street

N

Scale in metres

0 1 2 3 4 5 6

Fig. 41 Plan of Houses A,B and C showing upper floor

A

C

B

Scale in metres

0 1 2 3 4 5 6

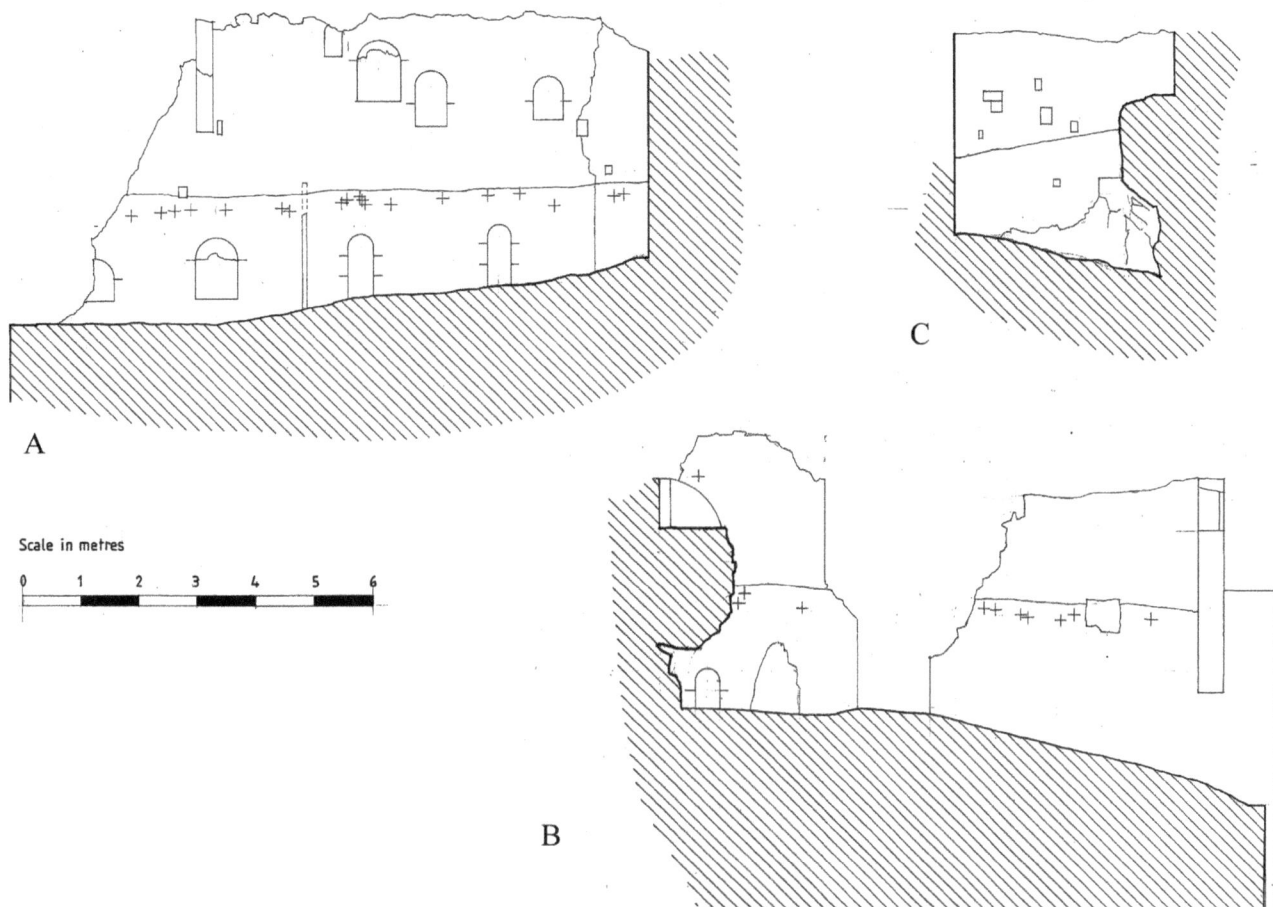

Fig. 42 Sections through House A

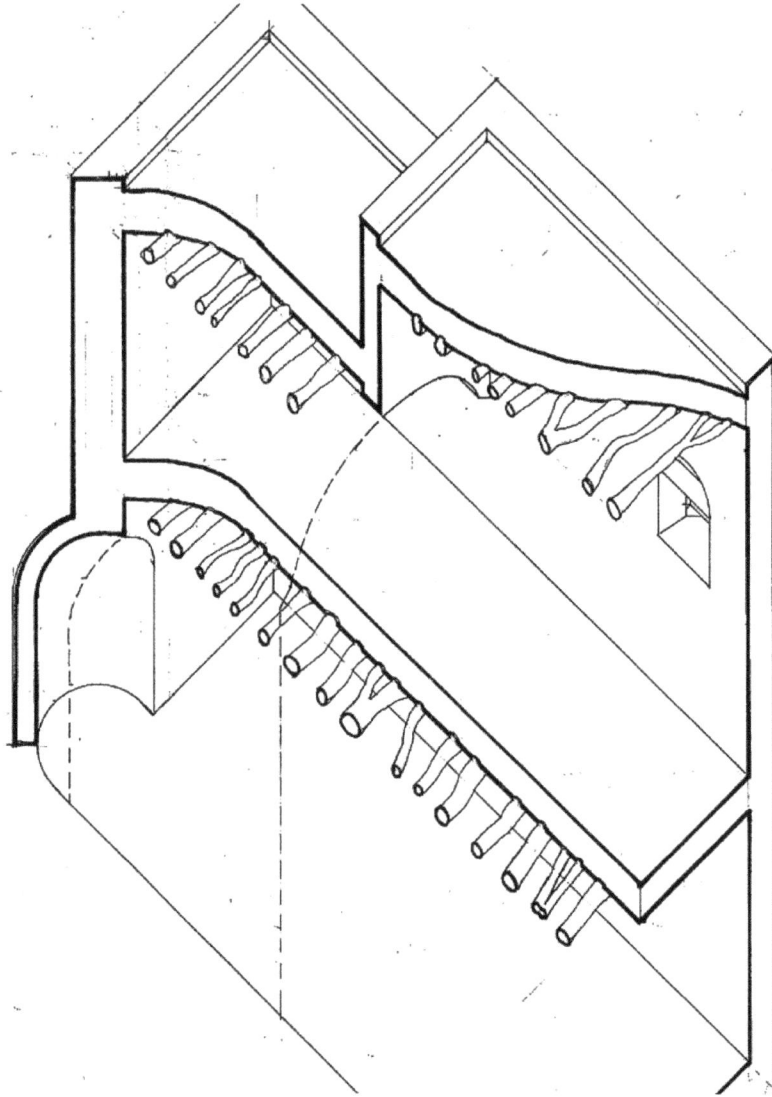

Fig. 43 Reconstruction of sections of House A – construction study

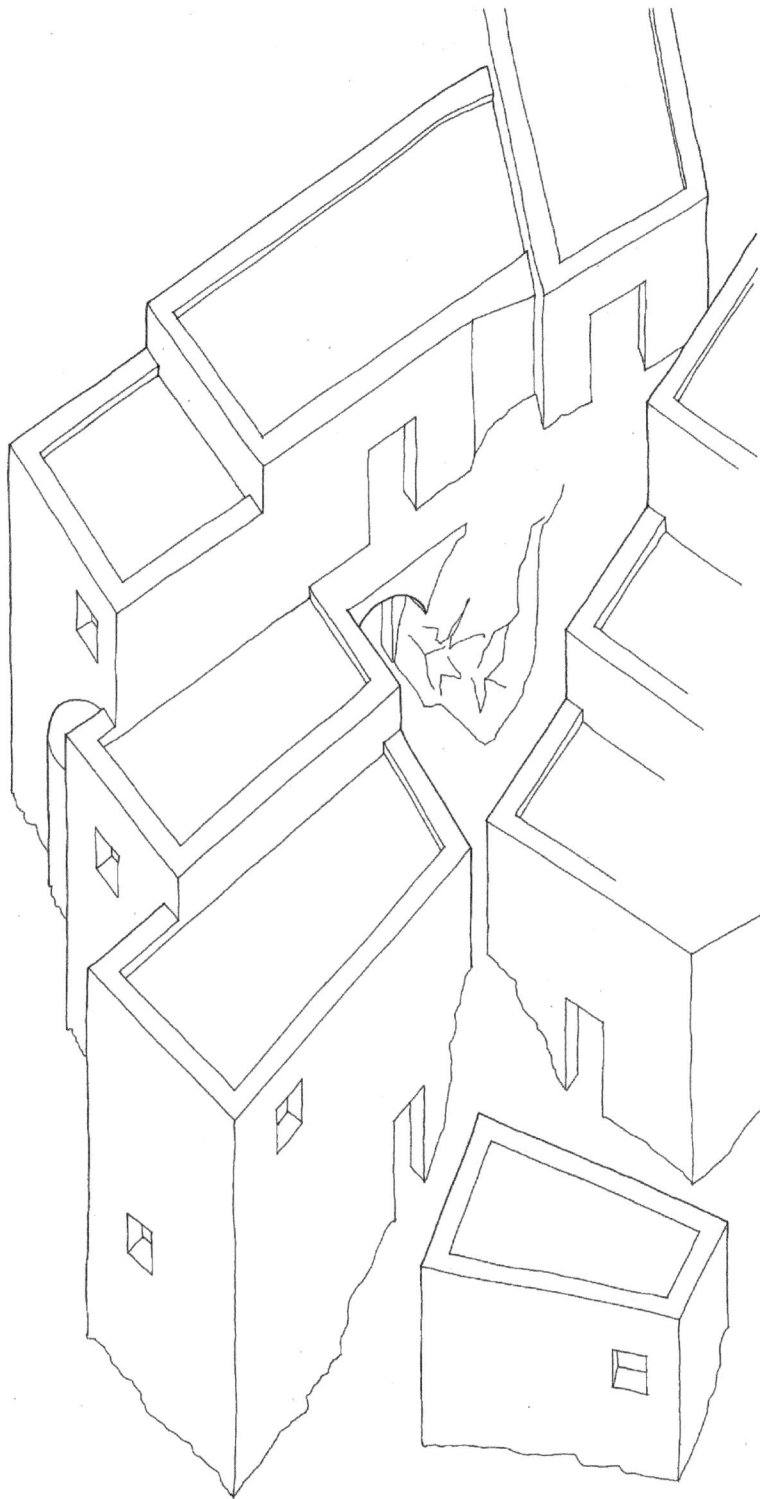

Fig. 44 Reconstruction of Houses A, B and C

a

b

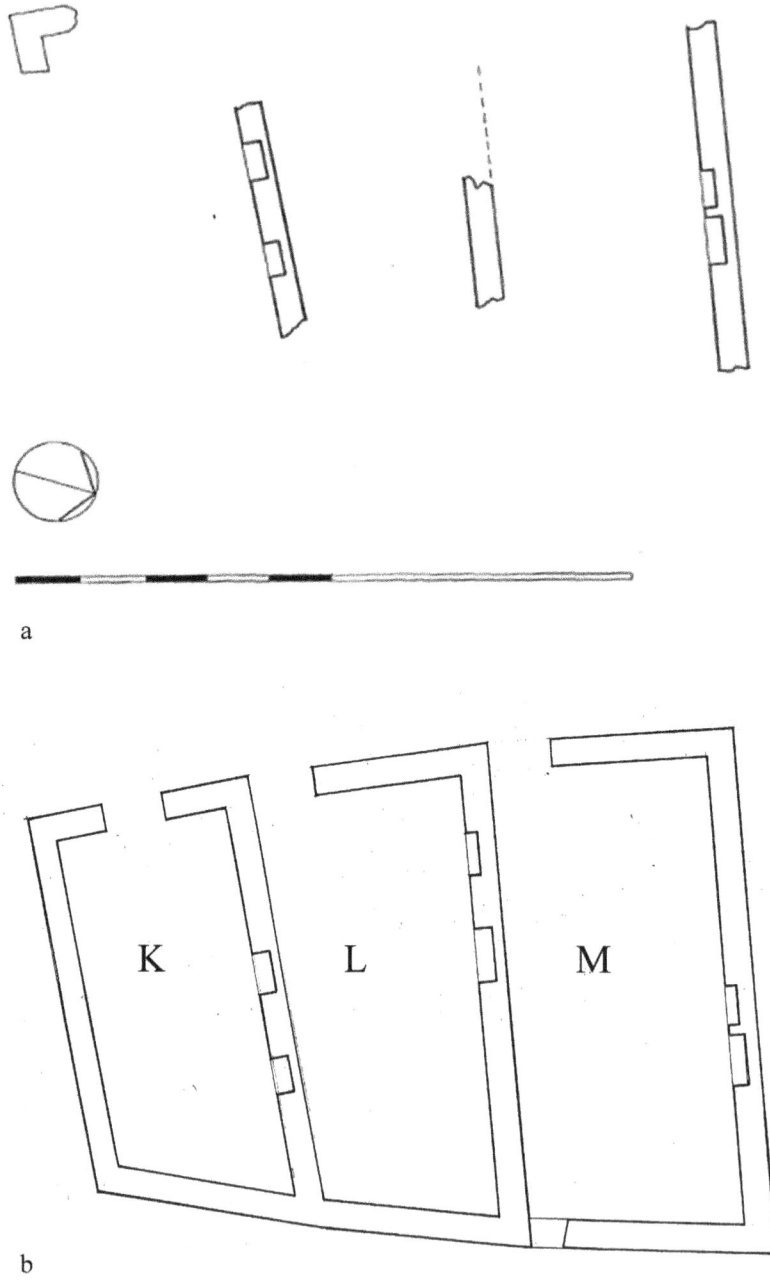

Fig. 45 a. Remains of walls in the north of the settlement;
b. plan and reconstruction of Houses K, L and M, based on a.

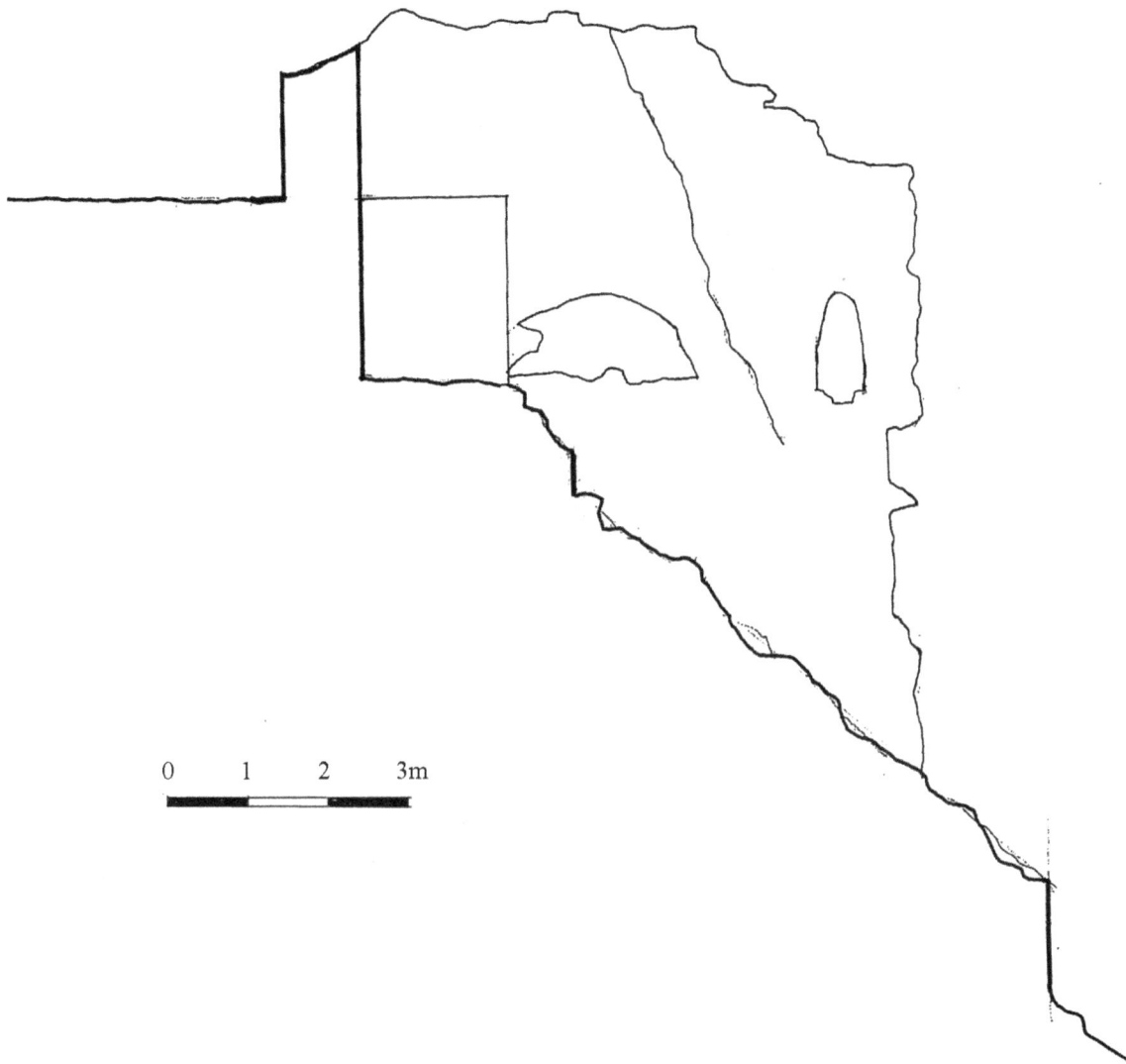

Fig. 46 Section through two-storey house in the north of the settlement (House M)

a

0   1   2   3

b

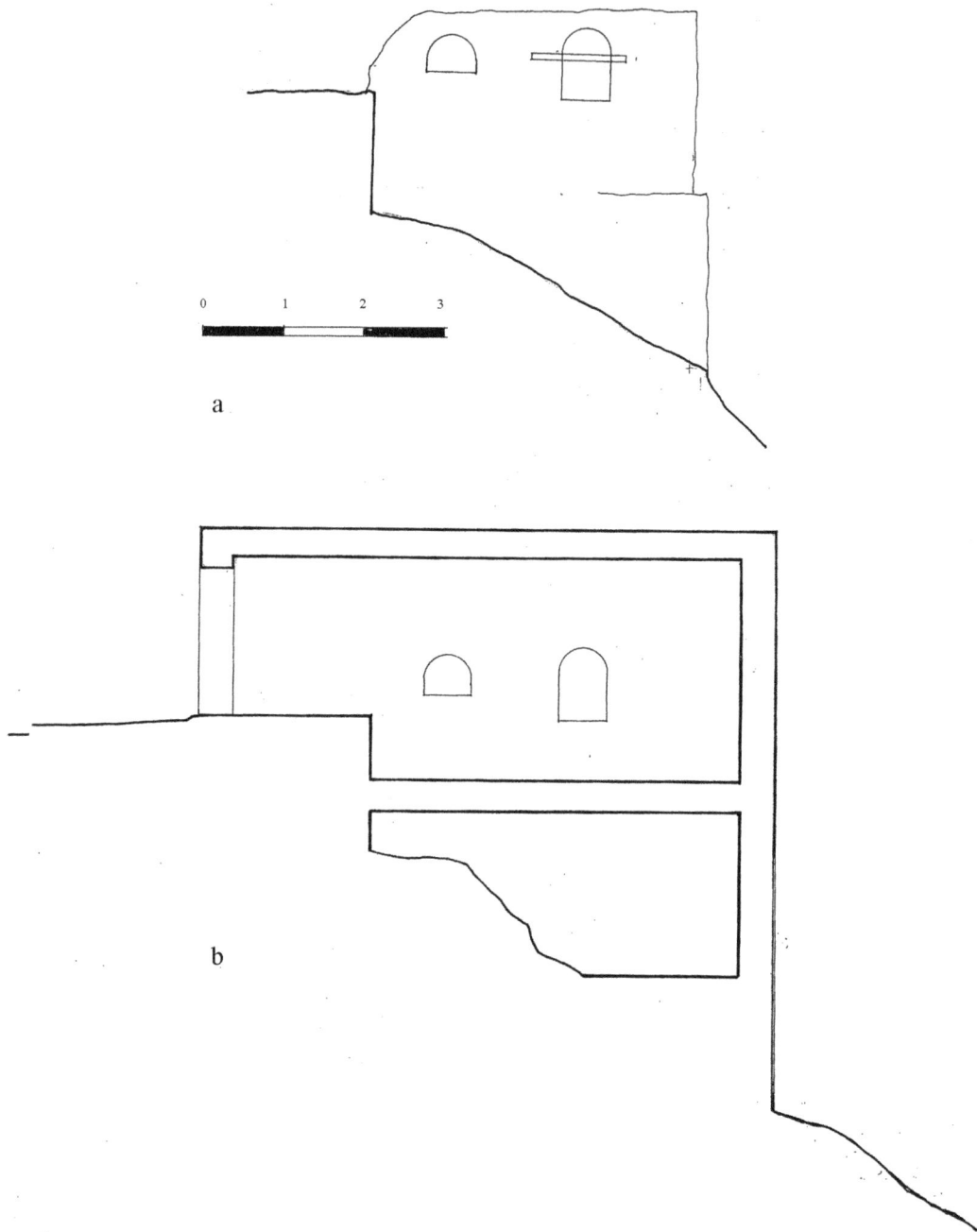

Fig. 47 Section through tw-storey house in the north of the settlement (House K). a. survey; b. reconstruction

Church 9 (at lower level)

Church 10 (at lower level)

Bastion blown away
from this part

N

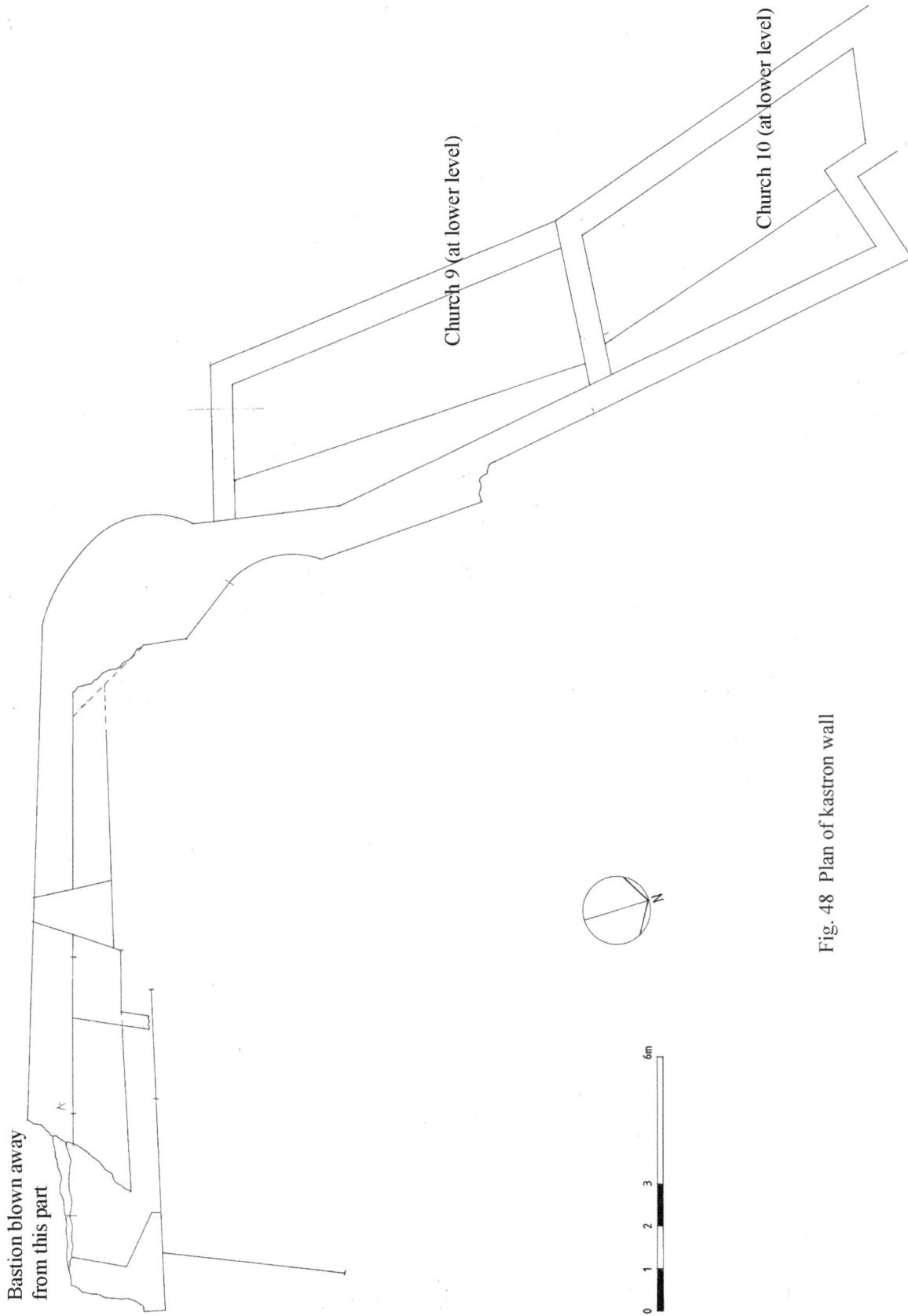

Fig. 48 Plan of kastron wall

0 1 2 3 6m

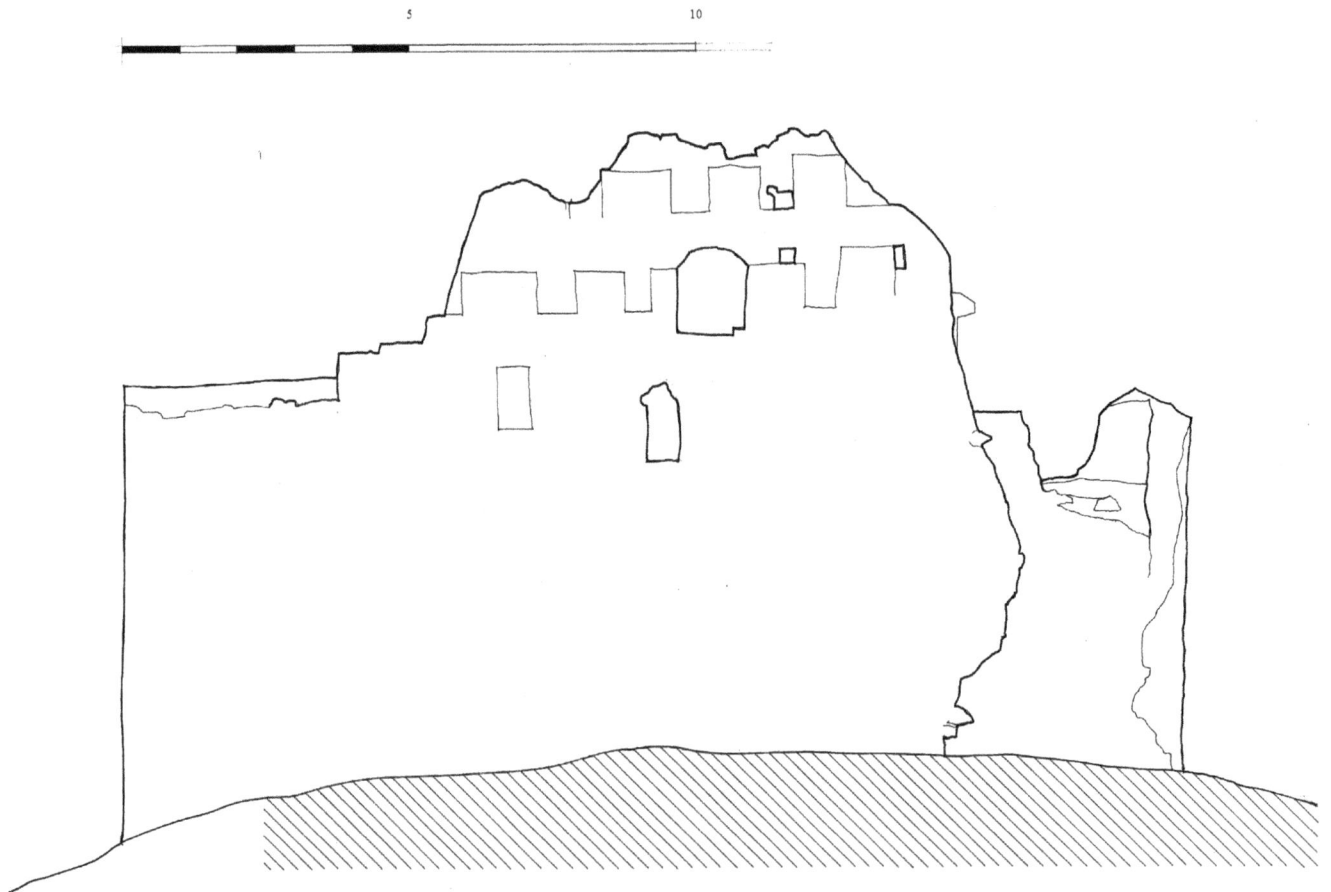

Fig. 49 Exterior elevation of kastron wall

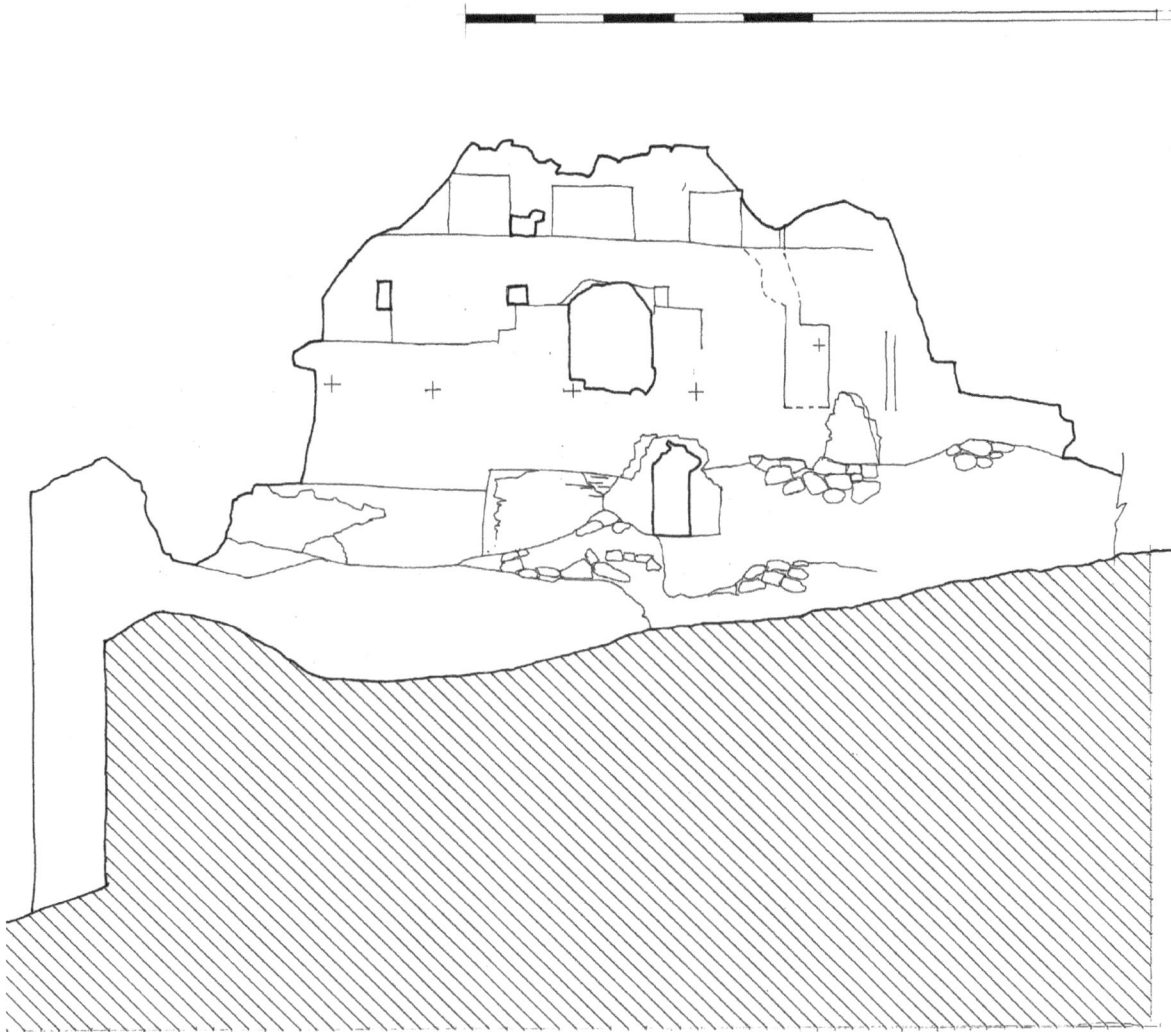

Fig. 50 Interior elevation of kastron wall

Fig. 51 Reconstruction of kastron wall at the point of entry (showing the lowest set of crenellations).

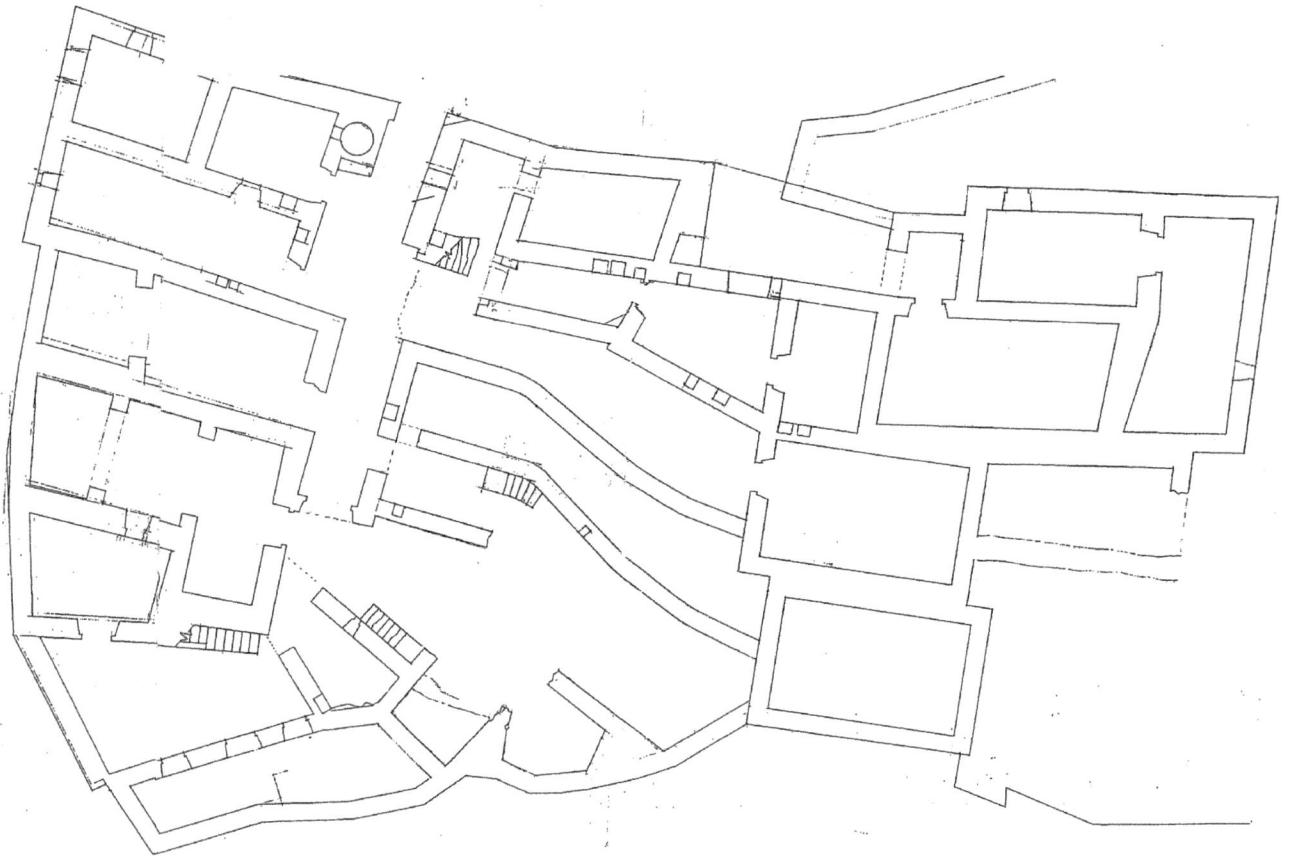

Fig. 52 Plan of Kastrisianika

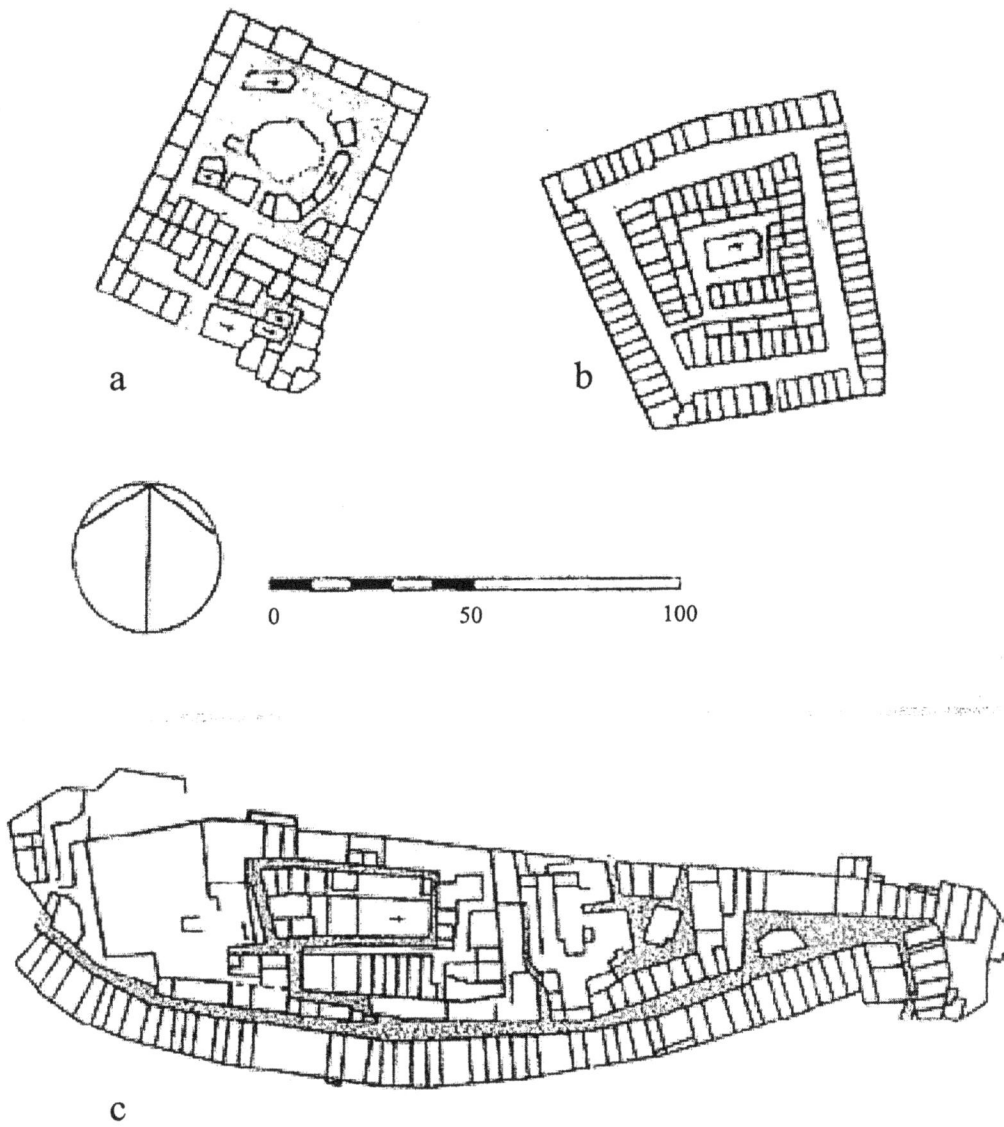

Fig. 53 Sixteenth-century settlements on the Aegean Islands: a. Antiparos; b. Kimolos; c. Sifnos. (Kimolos and Antiparos after Hoepfer and Schmidt, figs. 23 and 4; Sifnos after Philippa-Apostolou, fig. 182)

remains
of fireplace

plastered surface of wall
stops at these points

niche at high level

fireplace

fireplace

niche within chimney

doorway
from street

window at high level
with niche in outside wall above

N

Scale in metres

0   1   2   3   4   5

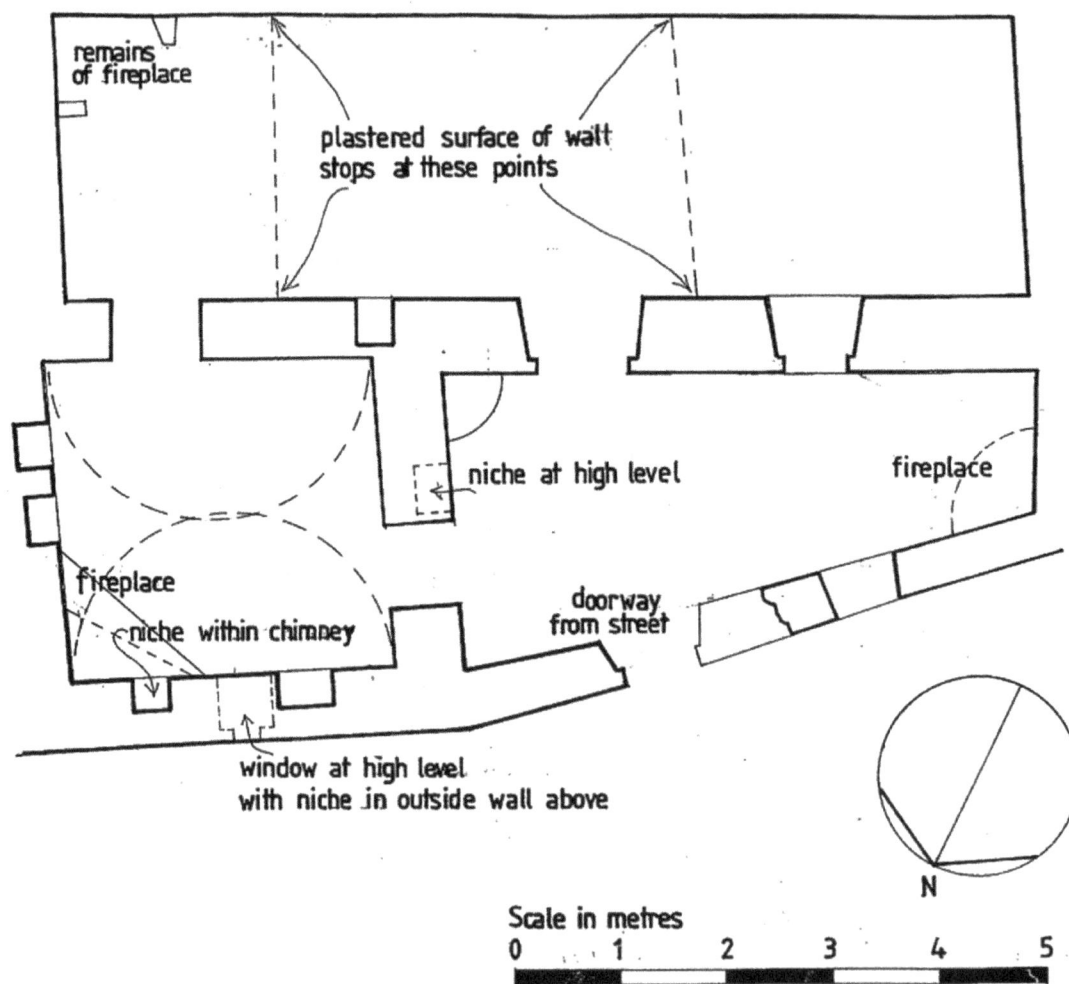

Fig. 54 The House of Antonakes, Katsoulianika, ground floor

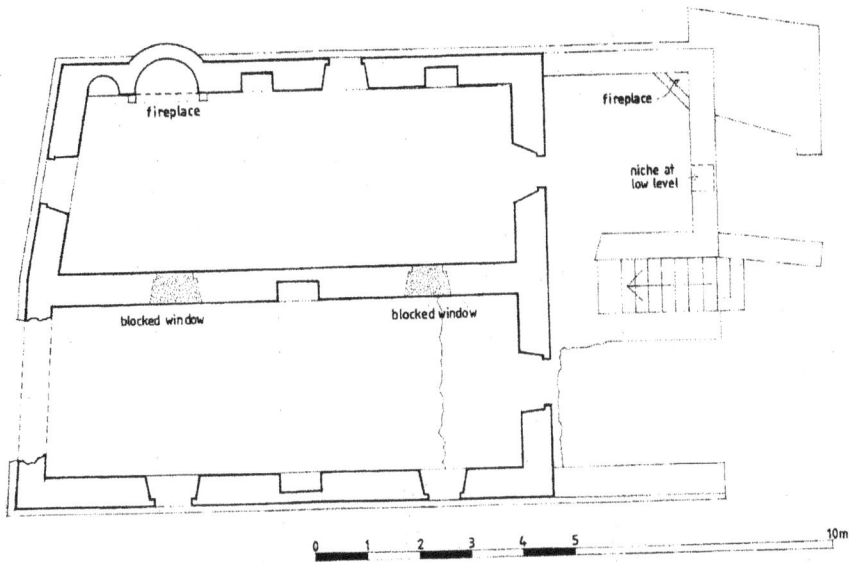

a

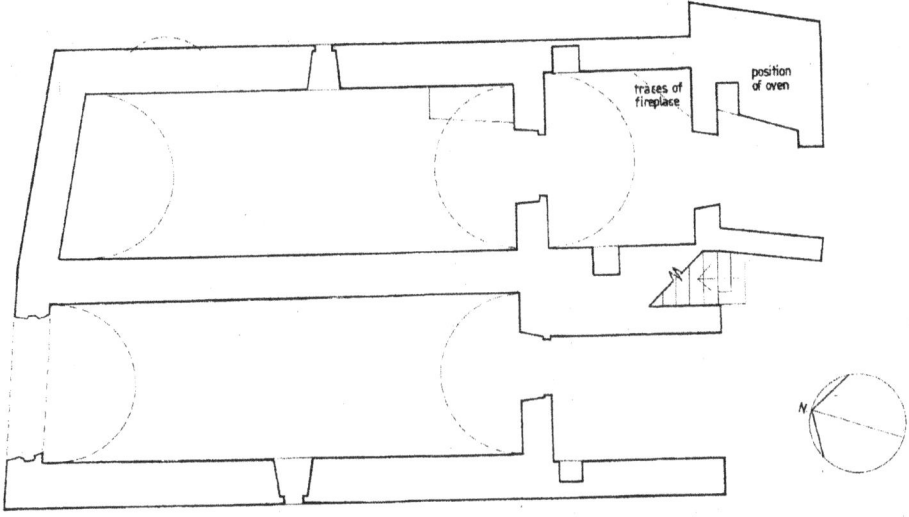

b

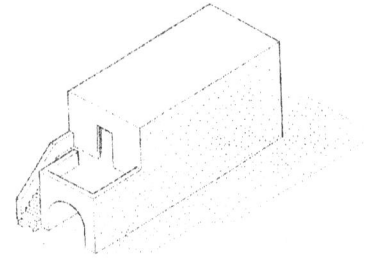

c

Fig. 55 Two-storey house at Katsoulianika a) ground floor b) upper floor c) reconstruction

a

Scale in metres

| 0 | 1 | 2 | 3 | 4 | 5 |

N

arches oven

remains of
partition wall

fireplace

door from
street

b

c

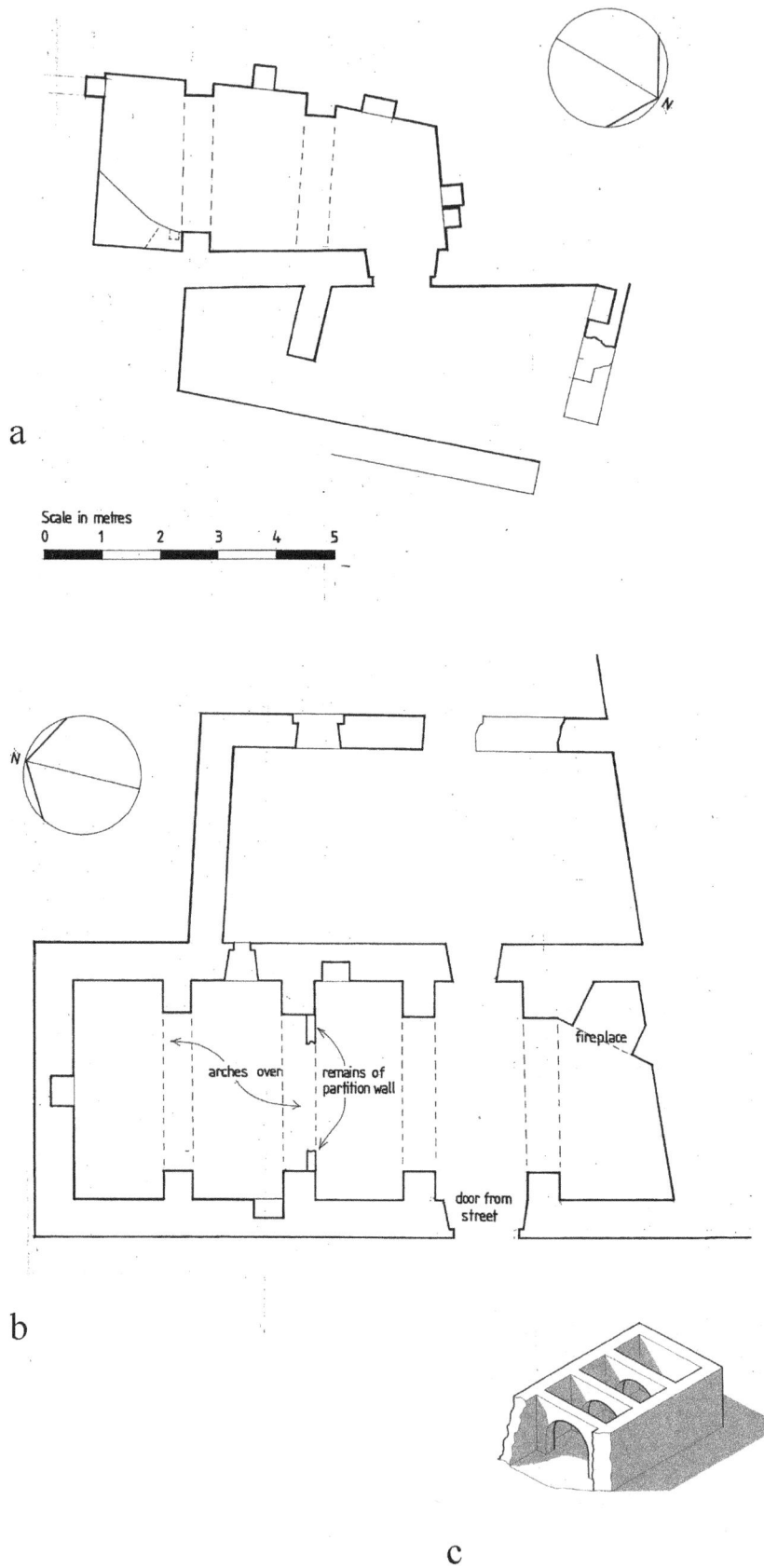

Fig. 56 Single-storey houses at Katsoulianika. a. house of Nikolaos Katsoulis, ground plan;
b. second single-storey house with transverse arches; c. reconstruction of house b.

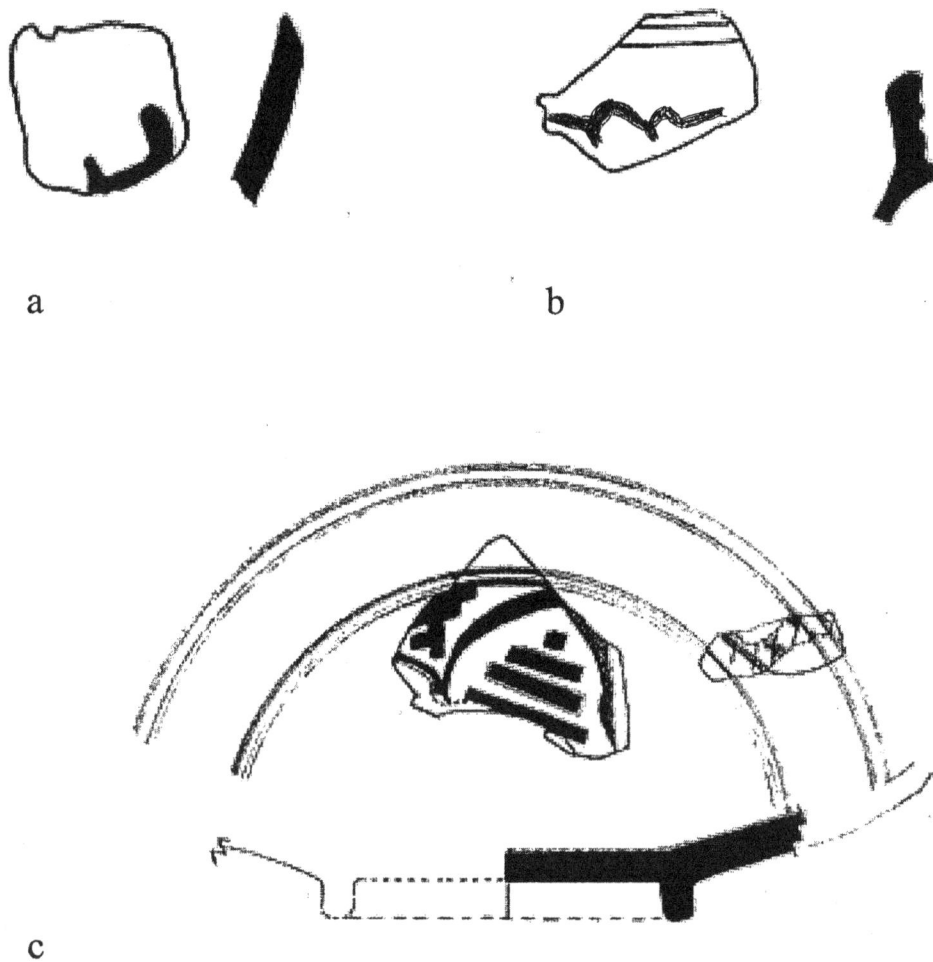

a   b

c

Fig. 57 Green and Brown Painted Ware and Painted Fine Sgraffito Ware

a

b

c

d

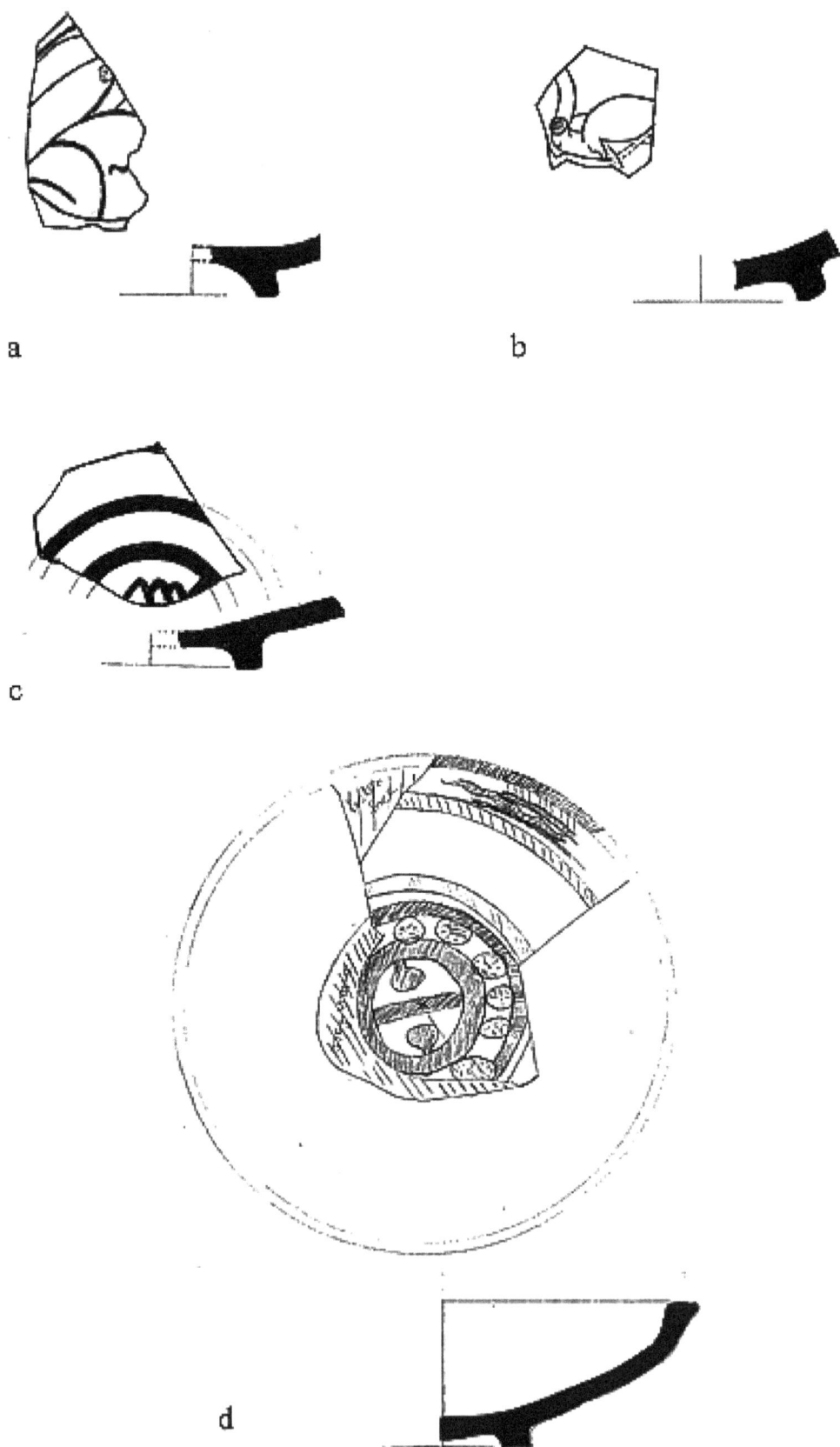

Fig. 58 RMR Ware

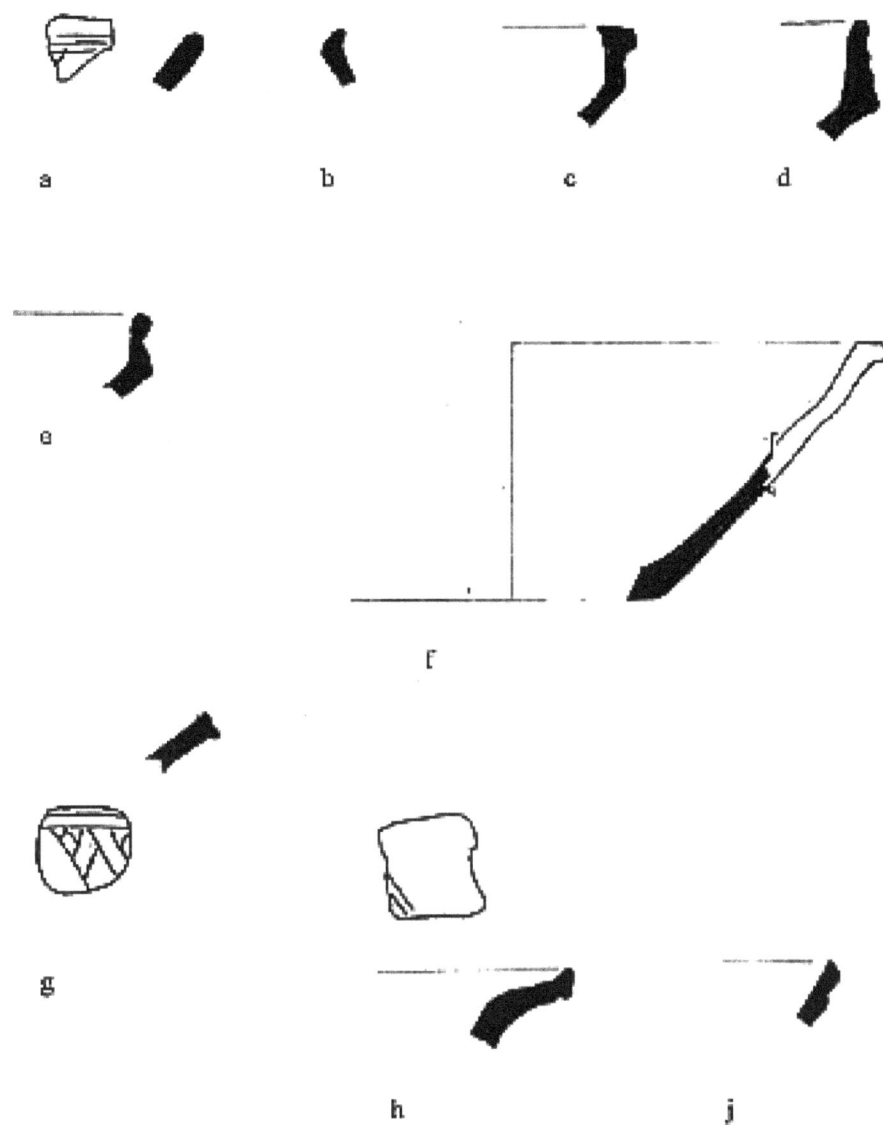

Fig. 59 Monochrome Sgraffito Ware from Italy, a-f; Polychrome Sgraffito Ware from Italy, g, h, j

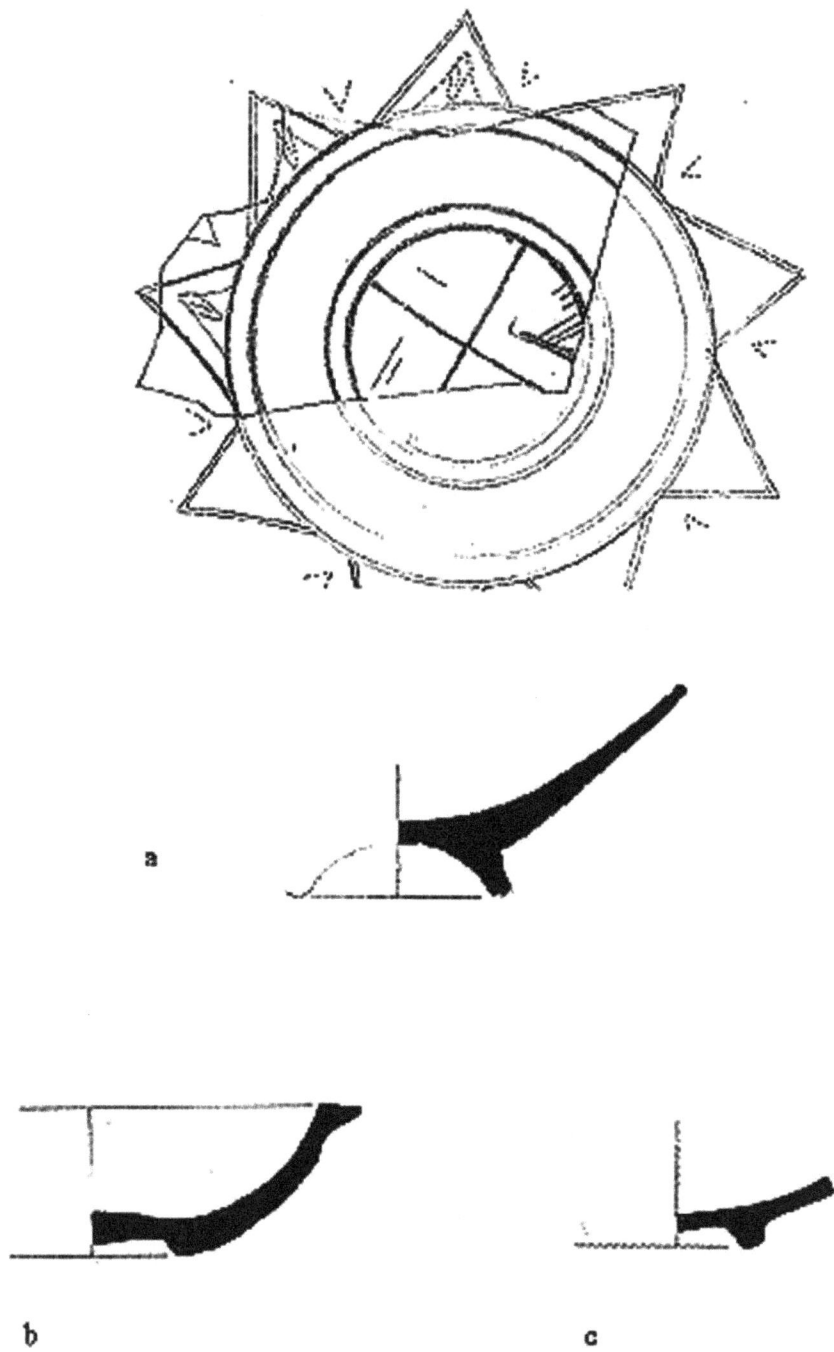

Fig. 60 Bowls immured in church walls. a church 11; b.,c, church 7 (Agios Antonios)

Fig. 61 Glazed jug

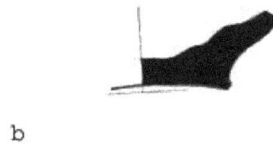

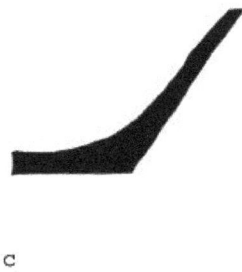

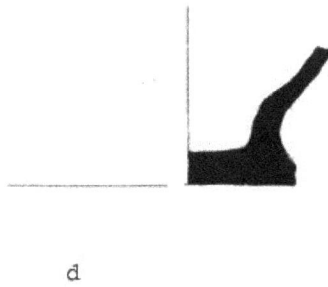

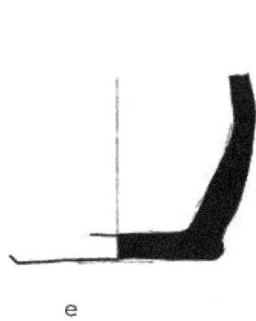

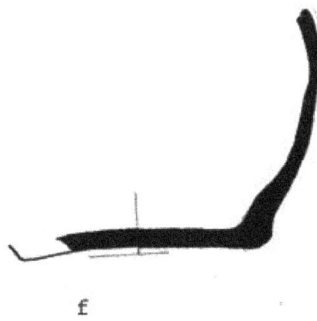

a

b

c

d

e

f

Fig. 62 Amphorae

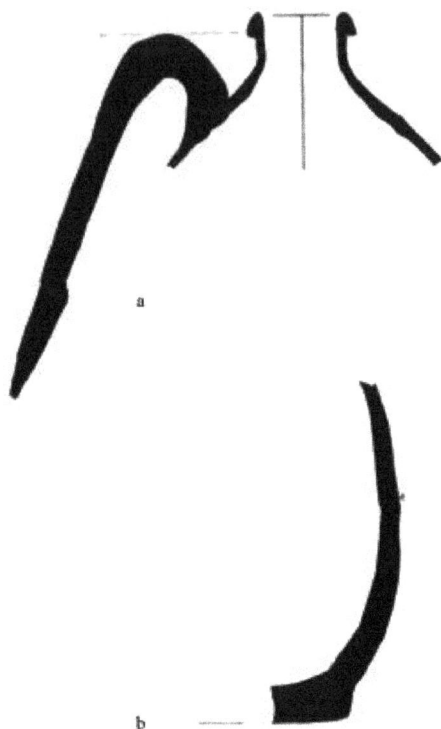

Fig. 63 Amphorae

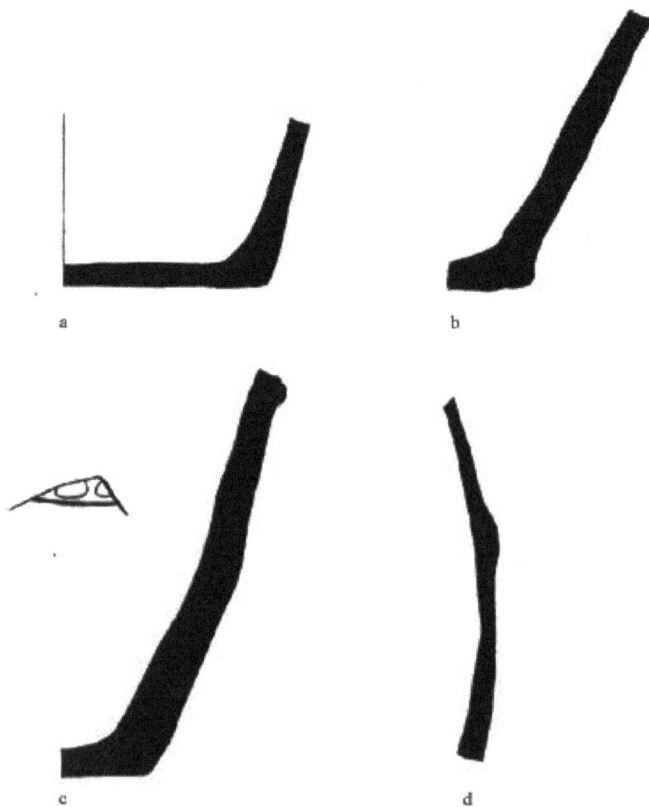

Fig. 64 Pithoi

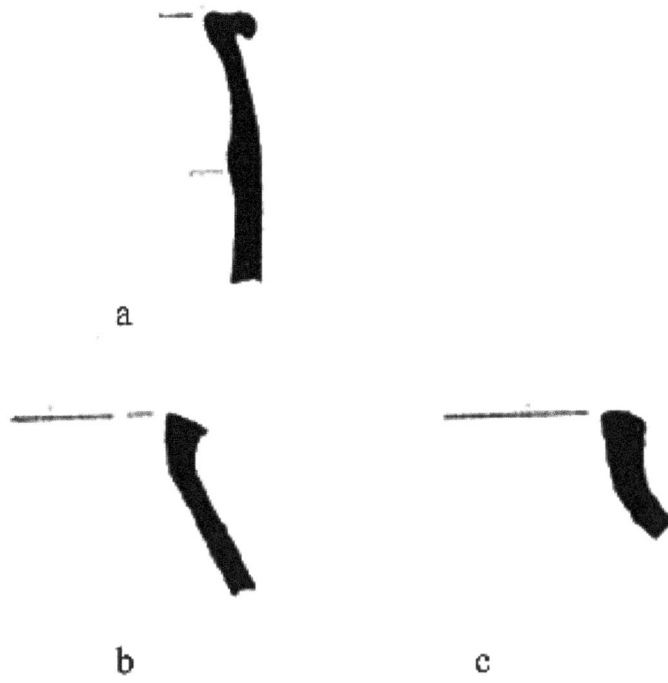

Fig. 65 Cooking pots. a. glazed; b., c. unglazed

Plate 1 above: view of Paliochora from the southwest looking at the southern section of the settlement
below: view of Paliochora from the southwest looking at the western side of the settlement

Plate 2 above: view of kastron wall and houses in the southeastern section
below: Church 4 (Kyra tou Forou) and a section of the small defensive wall

Plate 3 above: Church 3 showing acoustic urns
below: Church 15 looking northwest and showing the point on the wall where the barrel-vault sprung and sections of the second-storey wall.

Plate 4 above: Church 15 with blind arcades along the wall
below: Church 16 (Agios Demetrios) looking southeast towards the narthex.

Plate 5 above: Churches 11 and 12 showing the building attached to Church 12
below: Church 11

Plate 6 above: Church 22
below: houses in the north of the settlement

Plate 7 above: houses in the southeast of the settlement
below: interior of a house in the southeast of the settlement.

Plate 8 above: houses in the southeast of the settlement showing postholes for carrying the roof
below: Houses A, B and C.

Plate 9 above: niche in House A
below: houses in northern section

Plate 10 above: niche in house
below: exterior view of the kastron wall

Plate 11 above: interior view of the kastron wall
below: area of access into the inner enceinte

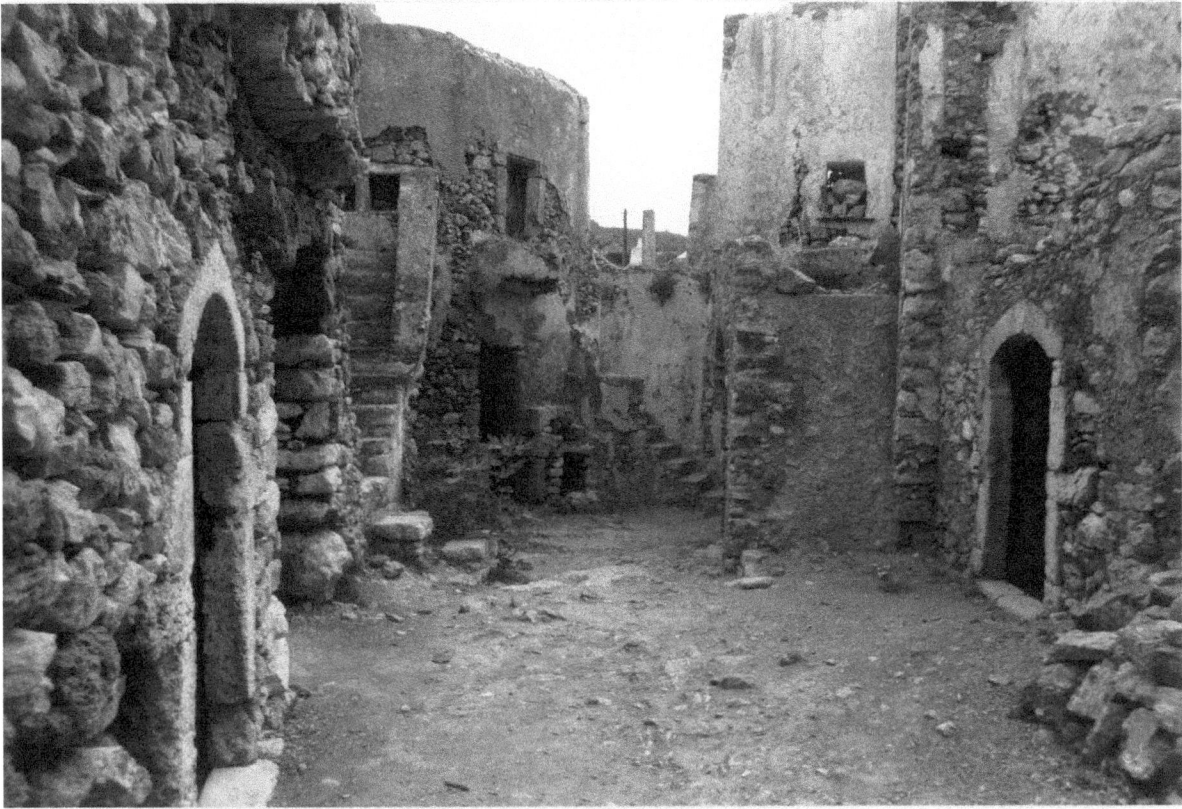

Plate 12   houses at Milopotamos

Plate 13   above: house of Antonakes, Katsoulianika
below: house next to Patrikianas, Katsoulianika

Plate 14 above: Green and Brown Painted Ware, Painted Fine Sgraffito Ware, Monochrome Sgraffito Ware from
Italy, Polychrome Sgraffito Ware from Italy
below: Green and Brown Painted Ware and 'RMR' Ware.

Plate 15 above: Polychrome Sgraffito Ware from Italy and Maiolica from Italy
below: Monochrome Sgraffito Ware from Italy and Polychrome Sgraffito Ware from Italy

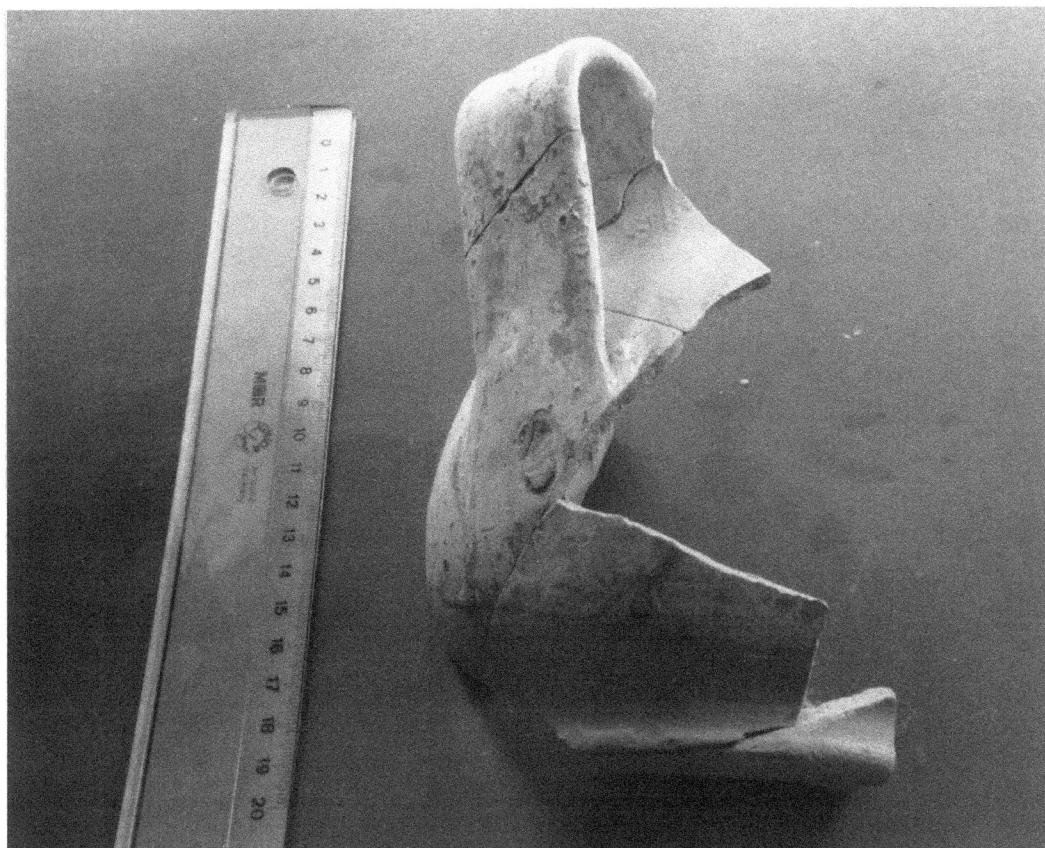

Plate 16 above: Plain glazed jug
below: pithoi

Plate 17 reconstructrion of Paliochora, general view across gorge, looking south

Plate 18 reconstruction of Paliochora, general view from the approach to the settlement, looking north.

www.ingramcontent.com/pod-product-compliance
Lightning Source LLC
Chambersburg PA
CBHW061300270326
41932CB00029B/3414